Joseph Priestley

A Catechism for Children and Young Persons

Joseph Priestley

A Catechism for Children and Young Persons

ISBN/EAN: 9783743441729

Manufactured in Europe, USA, Canada, Australia, Japa

Cover: Foto ©Lupo / pixelio.de

Manufactured and distributed by brebook publishing software (www.brebook.com)

Joseph Priestley

A Catechism for Children and Young Persons

Catechism,

FOR

CHILDREN,

AND

YOUNG PERSONS.

By JOSEPH PRIESTLEY,
LL.D. F.R.S.

The THIRD EDITION.

Train up a Child in the Way he should go, and when he is old, he will not depart from it.
SOLOMON.

LONDON:
Printed for J. JOHNSON, No. 72, St. PAUL'S
CHURCH-YARD.
M.DCC.LXXIX.

[Price THREE-PENCE.

THE
PREFACE.

THE method of communicating inftruction by catechifing is of great antiquity; but this is not my reafon for adopting or recommending it. It feems to be peculiarly adapted to young minds, as it approaches to the eafe and freedom of converfation. And fince queftions refemble thofe inquiries which children themfelves frequently make of their own accord, when they hear or fee any thing that they do not underftand, this method tends to engage the attention of children much more than talking to them in a continued ftrain. Befides, when they are made to repeat a thing themfelves, they will more naturally put queftions to their inftructor, if they do not underftand what they are faying, which will properly introduce the more useful, becaufe the more familiar part of the exercife. For I would propofe, that the queftions in the catechifm ferve only to point out the principal things about which it may be proper to talk with a child, and that they be broken into a greater number of other queftions and anfwers, too particular to be printed at large, but fuch as will naturally fuggeft themfelves in the courfe of catechizing.

It is objected to catechizing, that, in this method of inftruction, we teach children the ufe of words, before we can poffibly give them adequate ideas of their meaning; and therefore, that we only lead them to entertain a confufed and wrong notion of things. But this is, in fact, the cafe with almoft every word a child learns; and there is no remedy for it. Children learn all words mechanically, by imitation; and, from the fame
prin-

The PREFACE.

principle, will even repeat them in connection with other words, long before they have any tolerable idea of their meaning, as may be found by questioning them about the words they use. But by using them themselves, and hearing other persons use them, in a great variety of connections, they learn their true sense by degrees. This, however, is always a work of time.

Besides, an imperfect knowledge of things is often better than no knowledge at all. In this case, if a child do but entertain a very imperfect idea of God, of his duty, and of a future state, he will get such ideas as will be of some use to him at present, but of much more as he grows up: and they will be of the more use then for having been impressed early, when they could be of little use, or even if they should, at that time, be of no use at all. A reverence for religion, for its general dictates, or even for the words and forms belonging to it, without any clear ideas, if it be inculcated early, when the mind is tender, and apt to receive impreffions, will lay a foundation for the principle of confcience; or, however, will come greatly in aid of that principle, and operate as a real reftraint upon vice and immorality as long as a perfon lives. Befides, the ideas that we ourfelves, and even the moft intelligent of mankind, have of God, and of a future ftate are, no doubt, very imperfect; yet who can deny their being ufeful. For my own part, I think I have the greateft reafon to be thankful to God for the happinefs of a religious education, tho' I was taught many things I never underftood, and even many that I do not believe.

This objection to the bufinefs of catechizing, I imagine, took its rife from the ftyle and contents of fome particular catechifms, which were drawn up foon after the reformation from popery, and which were, therefore, neceffarily encumbered

cumbered with the technical terms of a metaphyfical fyftem, that had its rife in times of great darknefs and fuperftition. But if we condemn every thing that has been abufed, we muft deprive ourfelves of every thing that God has made, or that man has ever devifed for our ufe. For there is no good thing we can name, but has, in ignorant or defigning hands, been perverted to fome mifchievous or improper purpofe.

To avoid thefe inconveniences as much as poffible, I have, in imitation of the fimplicity of Dr. WATTS, ftudied to make this catechifm, and efpecially the firft part of it, very plain; and have not introduced into it, the technical terms of any particular fyftem of religion whatever. I think I have inferted nothing but what will be acknowledged to belong to common chriftianity; and I alfo think, that it contains all the truths of chriftianity, that can greatly influence mens practice; for thefe are very few, and fuch as a child may be made to underftand.

The whole bufinefs of practical preaching, copious as the fubject is, ferves only to illuftrate and enforce the few plain principles of the firft part of this fmall catechifm.

In this view, it may be of fome ufe to perfons whofe minds have been bewildered in the labyrinths of theological fyftems; as they may fee, in a fmall compafs, every thing that revelation contains which can influence the hearts and lives of men, all that is of *practical ufe*, and, confequently all that is properly *fundamental* in religion.

However, perfons of all parties muft, I think, agree with me in this, that the firft part of this catechifm contains what is moft neceffary to be known concerning revelation, and therefore may ferve as an introductory catechifm, and may not improperly be taught previous to any other, that may be thought to enter more fully into the doctrines of chriftianity.

I can-

The PREFACE.

I cannot help wishing that ministers in general would draw up their own catechisms, and forms of instruction of all kinds. Had this been the practise for a century past, we should have had something excellent in the kind before this time; and no one particular form, as the *Assembly*'s, would have acquired that degree of superstitious reverence which sets it upon a level with the scriptures. This idea, in a manner, enforces the use of it, and even makes it hazardous for many ministers to attempt to introduce any other; whereby religious knowledge, and all improvements, are kept at a stand; and those ministers who cannot, with a good conscience, make use of that catechism, use no catechism at all, and conceive a dislike to the whole business of catechizing.

The age at which it may be proper to teach the first part of this catechism, I think, will be, in general, about four or five. And I think it will not be improper, in some cases, to teach it to servants as well as to children. But every thing of this nature will depend upon particular circumſtances, concerning which the maſter of a family only can be a judge.

The ſecond part of the catechiſm may either be committed to memory, like the firſt, or not, at the pleaſure of the teacher; or ſome of the anſwers may be committed to memory, and others not. It may be of uſe to young perſons either way. I have endeavoured to make it leſs theoretical, and more practical than any other catechiſm that I have ſeen; and this, I think, is an advantage.

With reſpect to catechizing, and every other method of communicating inſtruction to children, let it be conſidered that it is much more the proper duty of the parent, than of the miniſter. But I would adviſe that miniſters alſo give attention to it, and by hearing the children repeat the catechiſm, either ſtatedly, or occaſionally, encourage both parents and children in the exerciſe. Small rewards, properly diſtributed, may be of uſe to this purpoſe.

I ſhall not, in this place, enlarge upon the motives to a virtuous and religious educa-

The PREFACE.

education of children, to which, I hope, this method of inſtruction by catechizing, will contribute. I ſhall only conclude this preface with obſerving that " This, Pa-
" rents, is the greateſt benefit you can
" confer upon your children. The riches
" and honours of this world are not to be
" compared with the folid advantages of a
" virtuous and religious education. It
" is a debt you owe to fociety ; it is alſo
" an important part of the duty you owe
" to God, the father of our ſpirits; and
" it is, at the fame time, the beſt pro-
" viſion you can make for the peace and
" comfort of your own future lives.
" Children that have received early and
" laſting impreſſions in favour of virtue
" and religon, will be a ſupport to you
" in life, will eafe the pains of death,
" and be your crown of rejoicing in a
" better world heareafter."

N. B. In this third Edition I have thrown into the notes the 8th and 9th queſtions, of the ſecond part of this catechiſm, and part of the 11th, on account of their *length*, and becauſe they are rather *illuſtrations* than neceſſary parts of the ſcheme. But young perſons may ſtill be made to repeat them, if the teacher ſhall think proper.

A CATECHISM, &c.

PART I.

1. Queſtion. *Can you tell me who made you?*
Anſwer. God made me, and all things.

2. Qu. *What did God make you, and all mankind for?*
An. He made us to be good, and happy.

3. Qu. *What is to be good?*
An. To be good is to love and obey our parents, to ſpeak the truth always, and to be juſt and kind to all perſons.

4. Qu. *Can God know whether you are good or not?*

An.

An. Yes: for though we cannot see God, he sees us wherever we are, by night as well as by day.

5. Qu. *What will God do for you if you be good?*
An. If we be good, God will love us, and make us very happy.

6. Qu. *What can you do for God, who is so good to you?*
An. I can only love him, obey him, and be thankful to him. There is nothing that I can do for him.

7. Qu. *Can you speak to God?*
An. Yes. He hath bid us pray to him for every thing that is fit for us, and he is always ready to hear us.

8. Qu. *What will God do if you be not good?*
An. If we be not good, God will be angry with us, and punish us.

9. Qu. *Is God able to punish you, if you be not good?*
An. Yes. God, who made all things, is able to do all things. He can take away all our friends, and every thing that he has given us; and
he

FOR CHILDREN. 15

he can make us die whenever he pleafes.

10. Qu. *When you die, fhall you ever live again?*

An. Yes. God will fome time raife us from the dead, and we fhall die no more.

11. Qu. *Where fhall you live again, if you have been good?*

An. If I have been good, I fhall go to heaven, and be very happy for ever.

12. Qu. *Where fhall you live again, if you have been wicked?*

An. If I have been wicked, I fhall go ~~to hell,~~ where I fhall be very miferable.

13. Qu. *Have you always been very good?*

An. No. I have very often done wrong, and offended God.

14. Qu. *Are you not then afraid of God's anger?*

An. Yes; but he has promifed to forgive us, if we be forry for our fins, and endeavour to fin no more.

15. Qu.

15. Qu. *Who hath told us that God will forgive us, if we repent of our sins, and endeavour to sin no more?*

An. Many persons by whom God spake; and particularly *Jesus Christ*.

16. Qu. *Who was* Jesus Christ? †

An. Jesus Christ was a person whom God sent to teach men their duty, and to persuade and encourage them to practise it.

17. Qu. *What became of* Jesus Christ?

An. He was put to death by wicked men, who would not hearken to him.

18. Qu. *Is* Christ *dead now?*

An. No. God raised him from the dead, and took him up into heaven.

19. Qu. *Where do we learn what we know concerning* Christ, *and what he did, taught, and suffered for the good of men?*

An. In the Bible, which we must diligently read and study, for our improvement in knowledge and goodness, in order to fit us for heaven.

PART

PART II.

1. Queſtion. WHAT is the Bible?

Anſwer. The Bible is a collection of books written by good men, containing an account of what God has done for mankind, what he requires of them, and what they have to expect from him. Theſe books are alſo called *the Scriptures*.

2. Qu. Have the ſcriptures informed us what God himſelf is?

An. We learn in the ſcriptures that God is a being who had no beginning, and will have no end. He is almighty, perfectly wiſe, and infinitely good. He is every where preſent, and never changes in his nature or diſpoſition.

3. Qu.

3. Qu. *In what manner has God made his great power known?*

An. God made this world, together with the sun, moon, and stars. He made all kinds of plants, and trees to grow out of the earth. He made all kinds of animals to live upon it, and he made man the chief and most excellent of them all.

4. Qu. *How is man the chief and most excellent of all the creatures that God has made upon the earth?*

An. God has given us a greater share of reason, whereby we are capable of knowing God, of understanding his works and his will, and of being sensible of our obligations to him. He will, moreover, make men immortal, for he will raise them to life again after they have been dead, and make them live for ever.

5. Qu. *In what does it appear that God is perfectly wise?*

An. In making all things so as that one part shall fit, or correspond to another, throughout the whole frame of nature; in his knowing every thing, even the thoughts of our hearts; in foreseeing all that will ever come to pass, and thereby governing the world by his providence.

6. Qu. *What are the effects of the goodness of God?*

An. He has made all living creatures capable of being happy; having provided for the supply of all their wants, by furnishing them with proper materials for their food, raiment, and every thing they have occasion for; and by giving all of them as much strength and sagacity as are necessary for their preservation and defence.

7. Qu. *In what respects has God been good to man in particular?*

An. Besides the provision he has made for feeding and clothing us, and enabling us to protect ourselves from the inclemencies of the weather, and the various injuries we are exposed to, he has sent good men from time to time to teach us his will, and to persuade men to turn from vice and wickedness, ednefs, and to live good lives; in order to fecure his favour, and obtain immortal happinefs in the world to come.*

[* 8. Qu. *When you faid that God was wife, you aid that he had made one thing to fit or to correfpond to another; give me an inftance or two of this?*

An. Men could not live without feeing, and God has given them eyes to fee, and has alfo made the light, without which our eyes would have been of no ufe to us. We often want to take things, and carry them from place to place, and God has given us hands and fingers, whereby we can lay hold of them, and carry them whither we pleafe. We have occafion to move from one place to another, and he has made us with legs and feet, whereby we can walk, and go where we pleafe. We cannot live without food, and he has both enabled us to get food from the earth, and made us with mouths to take it in, teeth to chew it, and ftomachs to digeft it, and convert it into proper nourifhment. All thefe things are proofs both of the wifdom and goodnefs of God.

9. Qu. *Give me a few inftances of the divine wifdom and Goodnefs in the world in general?*

An. God has provided clouds to give rain, without which corn and plants could not grow: and the fun not only gives light, but alfo heat, to raife the water in vapour, which again forms clouds, and fo produces a perpetual fupply of rain. He has provided different kinds of food, fuited to the natures of the different creatures he has made to live upon the earth; and though other animals have not the reafon of man, God has given them a principle which we call *inftinct*,
whereby

10. Qu. *How doth God govern the World by his providence?*

An. He suffers nothing to come to pass, but what tends to promote his design of making mankind virtuous and happy. His providence also extends to the meanest creatures that he has made, and even a sparrow falls not to the ground without his will.

11. Qu. *If nothing come to pass without the will of God, why doth he suffer storms and tempests, pain and sickness, which occasion such distress and misery to his creatures?*

An. The evils and miseries of which we complain are intended for our good, though we are not always sensible of it. They are the corrections of a wise and affectionate parent.*

whereby birds can build their own nests, and all of them can provide for their subsistence, preservation, and defence; better than we could do for them.]

* Pain urges us to avoid those things which would be hurtful to our bodies, and shame and remorse to abstain from those actions which are sinful and dangerous.

12. Qu. *What doth God require of us, in order to live and die in his favour?*

An. All that God requires of us is comprehended in thefe two precepts, Thou fhalt love the Lord thy God with all thy heart, and thy neighbour as thyfelf.

13. Qu. *In what manner muſt we expreſs our love to God?*

An. By a grateful fenfe of his goodnefs to us, by a conftant care to do his will, and by an intire and chearful fubmiffion to all the difpenfations of his providence.

14. Qu. *How muſt we expreſs our love to our fellow creatures?*

An. By doing, to others as we fhould think it right for them to do to us, in the fame circumftances.

gerous. The more we difcover concerning thofe things which are commonly called evil, the more good do we fee attend them, or to follow them; fo that we have reafon to believe, there is the fame kind intention in all thofe evils that we do not yet underſtand.

15. Qu. *By what method must we cherish our love to God, and increase our confidence in him?*

An. We must frequently consider the benefits he confers upon us. We must also address ourselves to him in prayer, thanking him for the mercies he bestows upon us, confessing our sins before him, and asking of him whatever he knows to be needful and good for us.

16. Qu. *How shall we bring ourselves into the best disposition for performing our duty to God and man?*

An. By a proper government of our passions, according to the dictates of reason and conscience; by living in temperance and chastity, and never indulging a proud, malicious or selfish temper.

17. Qu. *What must we do when persons affront and injure us?*

An. We must not return evil for evil; and if they repent, we must forgive them, as we hope that God will forgive us our offences against him.

18. Qu.

A CATECHISM FOR

18. Qu. *Hath the Divine Being any where delivered diſtinct directions concerning the ſeveral branches of our duty to him and to our fellow creatures?*

An. Yes, in the ten commandments, which he delivered to the children of Iſrael from mount Sinai.

19. Qu. *What is the firſt of theſe commandments?*

An. Thou ſhalt worſhip no God but one.

33. Qu. *What is the ſecond?*

An. Thou ſhalt not worſhip God by images, as if he had any particular form or ſhape.

21. Qu. *What is the third?*

An. Thou ſhalt not take the name of God in vain, by calling him to witneſs a falſehood, or by profane curſing and ſwearing.

22. Qu. *What is the fourth?*

An. Thou ſhalt reſt one day in ſeven from all worldly buſineſs.

23. Qu. *What is the fifth?*

An.

An. Thou ſhalt honour and obey thy parents.

24. Qu. *What is the ſixth?*
An. Thou ſhalt not commit murder.

25. Qu. *What is the ſeventh?*
An. Thou ſhalt not commit adultery.

26. Qu. *What is the eighth?*
An. Thou ſhalt not ſteal.

27. Qu. *What is the ninth?*
An. Thou ſhalt not bear falſe witneſs.

28. Qu. *What is the tenth?*
An. Thou ſhalt not covet any thing that belongs to another perſon.

29. Qu. *What are thoſe principles which will moſt effectually lead to the obſervance of theſe, and all other of God's commandments?*
An. A high reverence for God, and a ſincere good will towards our fellow creatures, joined with a juſt regard to our own real intereſt.

30. Qu. *What is the beſt method we can take to guard ourſelves from all vice and wickedneſs?*   *An.*

An. By being careful not to indulge sinful thoughts, and by correcting every thing that is amiss in the beginning, before we have become accustomed to it, and have gotten a habit, which cannot easily be broken; particularly, by avoiding the company of wicked persons, who would soon make us like themselves; and by being, in a more especial manner, upon our guard against those vices to which our situation and circumstances make us peculiarly prone.

31. Qu. *What is the best method to guard ourselves against being seduced by wicked company?*

An. To chuse virtuous and good persons for our favourite companions; and to propose to ourselves the imitation of good men whom we read of in the Scriptures; especially, the imitation of Christ, who was a perfect pattern of all the most excellent christian virtues.

32. Qu.

32. Qu. *What are the vices and follies to which young perſons are moſt expoſed?*

An. Young Perſons are moſt in danger of vanity, peeviſhneſs, diſobedience to parents, an exceſſive love of pleaſure, and extravagance; all ariſing from ſtrong and ungoverned paſſions.

33. Qu. *What are the vices that poor people are liable to?*

An. The poor are moſt in danger of being induced to ſteal, and of envying and undermining their ſuperiors.

34. Qu. *What vices are the rich moſt in danger of?*

An. The rich are moſt in danger of being proud, of living in idleneſs and luxury, of oppreſſing the poor, and of forgetting God.

35. Qu. *In what virtues, then, muſt the poor and the rich endeavour to excel?*

An. The poor ſhould be content with their low ſituation in life, and by frugality and induſtry endeavour to make their circumſtances as eaſy as they can. And the rich ſhould be humble, and thankful to God for all they enjoy, and endeavour to do as much good to others as poſſible.

36. Qu. *Is any man able to fulfil all the commands of God, ſo as to live intirely without ſin?*

An. No. Our merciful God and father knows that we are not able to do this, and therefore doth not expect it of us. He only requires that we rèpent of the ſins we commit, and endeavour to live better lives for the future.

37. Qu. *What ſhould a ſenſe of our frailty and proneneſs to ſin teach us?*

An. It ſhould teach us humility and watchfulneſs, make us earneſt in our prayers to God, to enable us to reſiſt temptation, and to ſtrengthen and confirm our good diſpoſitions.

38. Qu. *In what manner will God reward our faithful, though imperfect obedience to his will?*

An.

An. He will fo order all the events of this life, profperous and adverfe, as that they fhall be the beft for us, whether we can fee them to be fo or not; and he will make us completely happy in another and a better world.

39. Qu. *In what manner muſt all men ſpend the greateſt part of their time in this world?*

An In a diligent application to that kind of honeft labour or employment, which is neceffary for procuring fuitable fupplies of the good things of this life for ourfelves, and thofe who immediately depend upon us, and by which we can at the fame time, be of the moft ufe to our fellow creatures in general.

40. Qu. *Will not an application to worldly buſineſs interfere with the duties of religion?*

An. No, provided it be not i.; ·· derate. On the contrary, idle ,·.. the greateft inlet to vice and wi   · nefs of all kinds. Befides, we ple · God the moft, by doing that wh. n   ·

makes

makes ourselves and others the most happy.

41. Qu. *Whom do the scriptures inform us that God sent into the world, in order to reclaim men from wickedness, and to perſuade and encourage them to return to virtue and goodneſs?*

An. Beſide the notices which mankind in general had of his will, God was pleaſed to favour the Jews with a particular revelation. To them he sent Moſes, who gave them laws, aſſured them of the favour of God in caſe of obedience, and threatened them with his diſpleaſure in caſe of diſobedience.

42. Qu. *In what character did the Divine Being repreſent himſelf to the Iſraelites by Moſes?*

An. Speaking to Moſes from mount Sinai, he proclaimed himſelf, The Lord, the Lord God, merciful and gracious, long ſuffering, and abundant in goodneſs and truth, keeping mercy for thouſands, forgiving iniquity,

quity, transgression, and sin. *Ex.* xxxiv. 6.

43. Qu. *Who succeeded Moses as messengers from God to the people of Israel?*

An. Samuel, Isaiah, Jeremiah, and many others, who are called prophets; and who succeeded one another almost without intermission, for the space of several hundred years.

44. Qu. *What was the general strain of their preaching and exhortation?*

An. Turn ye, turn ye from your evil ways; why will ye die, oh house of Israel. As I live, says God, I will not the death of a sinner, but had rather that he would return and live.

45. Qu. *Did the Divine Being enjoin the people of Israel nothing besides the practice of moral virtue?*

An. He enjoined them the performance of various ceremonies, to keep up the remembrance of certain remarkable facts, to prevent them from mixing with idolatrous nations, and to teach them many important moral truths in a symbolical manner, suited to their low apprehensions.

46. Qu. *What proof did Moses and the prophets give, that they were sent of God?*

An. They performed many miracles, which could not have been done without the power of God being with them. Under Moses the people of Israel walked on dry land through the red sea, and were fed with manna from heaven for forty years. The strong walls of Jericho fell down before them; the nation was often delivered from their enemies by the immediate hand of God; and most of the prophets foretold some great event which came to pass in their own time.

47. Qu. *By whom did God speak not only to the Jews, but to the whole world of mankind?*

An. By Jesus Christ, who brought the most complete and extensive revelation of the will of God to man.

48. Qu. *What was the proper design and end of* Christ's *coming into the world?*

An. He came to make men happy in turning them from their iniquities, and to purify unto himself a peculiar people, zealous of good works.

49. Qu. *In what respects was* Christ *superior to the prophets who went before him?*

An. In the perfection of his example, the purity of his precepts, and the importance of the motives by which he enforced them; more especially, as he gave us more distinct information concerning a future state of rewards and punishments. He also put an end to the ceremonial law of Moses, sent his disciples to teach all nations the knowledge of God, and abolished the distinction between the Jews and the rest of the world.

50. Qu. *Who put* Christ *to death, and by what death did he die?*

An. At the instigation of the Jews, the Romans, (under whose dominion
they

they then were) caused him to be put to death by crucifixion? which is a very painful and lingering death, and that to which only slaves and the vilest malefactors were exposed.

51. Qu. *What was the chief strain of* Christ's *preaching?*

An. He reformed many abuses, by which the Jewish teachers had corrupted the law of God. He taught men to worship God not by external services, but in spirit and truth. He frequently inculcated the duties of loving another, of forgiving our enemies, and of doing to others as we would they should do to us. And he enforced a regard to these virtues by the doctrines of resurrection, and of a judgment to come.

52. Qu. *What proof did* Christ *give of his divine mission?*

An. He healed multitudes of sick persons by a word speaking. He gave sight to the blind, raised persons from the dead, and rose himself from the

the grave, after he had been dead three days, as he had foretold.

53. Qu. *Did* Chrift *appoint no outward ordinances, as a means of promoting his religion?*

An. He commanded his difciples to go and baptize all nations, upon their converfion to chriftianity; and he alfo appointed them to eat bread and drink wine in remembrance of him. This rite is called the *Lord's Supper.*

54. Qu. *What is the meaning of baptifm?*

An. The wafhing of water in baptifm, probably reprefents the purity of heart and life required of all who become the difciples of Chrift.

55. Qu. *What is the nature and ufe of the Lord's fupper?*

An. By eating bread and drinking wine in remembrance of Chrift, we keep alive the memory of his death and refurrection; we acknowledge ourfelves to be chriftians; we cherifh a grateful fenfe of the bleffings of the gofpel

gofpel of Chrift, and ftrengthen our refolution to live as becomes his difciples.

56. Qu. *What provifion did* Chrift *make for propagating his religion after his death?*

An. He appointed twelve perfons, called apoftles, to be witneffes of his life and doctrine. Thefe he fent into all the nations of the world, giving them the power of working miracles in his name. From this time the knowledge of chriftianity was fpread over a great part of the world; and in all chriftian countries there are mi-- nifters of the gofpel, whofe office it is to inftruct men in it, and to perfuade and encourage them to practife the duties of it.

57. Qu. *Had* Chrift *no particular reward for what he did and fuffered on the behalf of men?*

An. Becaufe he humbled himfelf into death, God has highly exalted him, and made him head over all things

things to his church; and at the end of the world, he will come to judge the quick and the dead. For this hope that was set before him, he endured the cross, and despised the shame of that ignominious death.

58. Qu. *What do the scriptures say concerning the day of judgment?*

An. That Christ shall come in the clouds of heaven with power and great glory, when every eye shall see him; that he will separate the wicked from the good; that he will send the wicked into a place of punishment, and take the righteous into a place of happiness, where they shall live for ever with himself.

59. Qu. *Do the scriptures inform us of any other intelligent beings besides men?*

An. We read of angels, who have some times made their appearance in human forms, and who have been sent by God upon messages of importance to men.

60. Qu. *What was the state of the world before revelation?*

An. The greatest part of mankind, when they were without a revelation, worshipped a great number of false and imaginary gods, bowing down to images of wood and stone, the work of their own hands. They were abandoned to wickedness, and even practised very abominable customs, as methods of serving and pleasing their Gods; and they had no clear notion of a future state, for the reward of virtue and the punishment of vice.

61. Qu. *Has the religion of* Christ *always remained pure, as it came from the hands of its author?*

An. No. It soon began to be corrupted; and, about the end of a thousand five hundred years, it was (among the Papists) such as almost intirely defeated the original design of it, to promote virtue and piety in the world. In many cases it was made to serve as a cover for vice and wickedness.

nefs. But at length it pleafed God to bring about a reformation, which is going on, and, we hope, will go on, till our religion be, in all refpects, as pure, and as efficacious to promote real goodnefs of heart and life, as it was at the firft.

A PRAYER

A PRAYER for a CHILD.

Almighty God and heavenly father, I thank thee for all thy goodnefs to me, and thy daily care over me, in preferving me from the many dangers to which I am continually expofed. Forgive, I pray thee, whatever I have done that is difpleafing to thee, and teach me to offend thee no more, but to love and obey thee better as long as I live. Grant unto me, and to all my relations and friends,* whatever thou feeft to be good for us in this world, and bring us to heaven and happinefs hereafter, according to thy gracious promife, to all thy faithful fervants, by Jefus Chrift. Amen.

A PRAYER

---

*˙ *Here the child may be taught to name his father, mother, brothers, fifters, or any other near relation or friend.*

A Prayer for a Young Person.

Almighty God and moſt merciful father! I adore thee as my maker and preſerver, and the giver of every good thing that I enjoy. I thank thee for the gift of reaſon, whereby I am capable of knowing thee, and of learning and doing thy will; but more eſpecially I thank thee for thy promiſe of the forgiveneſs of ſins, to all ſincere penitents, and of eternal life to all who carefully obey thee, delivered to the world by thy ſon Chriſt Jeſus. Do thou, out of thy abundant goodneſs, forgive all my ſins, and ſtrengthen my reſolution to keep thy holy commandments for the time to come. Enable me to be, in a more eſpecial manner, upon my guard againſt thoſe vices and follies to which my youth is peculiarly prone. Particularly, teach me to avoid the ſnares
of

of bad company, and to continue in the practife of my duty, notwithftanding all the temptations to which I am expofed. Make me refigned to thy will in all the events of life, and to grow wifer and better by all the difpenfations of thy providence. May I love all mankind as my brethren, and forgive thofe that have offended me, as I myfelf hope to be forgiven. And, after a faithful and chearful difcharge of my duty on earth, may I be received into thy kingdom of glory, and into the company of all good men, and of Jefus Chrift for ever. Amen.

The Lord's Prayer.

OUR Father, who art in heaven, hallowed be thy name. Thy kingdom come. Thy will be done on earth, as it is in heaven. Give us this day our daily bread. Forgive us our trefpaffes, as we forgive them that

that trespass against us; and lead us not into temptation, but deliver us from evil: for thine is the kingdom, and the power, and the glory, for ever and ever. Amen.

A CATALOGUE of BOOKS,

WRITTEN BY

JOSEPH PRIESTLEY, LL. D. F. R. S.

AND PRINTED FOR

J. JOHNSON, BOOKSELLER, at No. 72,

St. Paul's Church-Yard, London.

1. THE HISTORY and PRESENT STATE of ELECTRICITY, with original Experiments, illustrated with Copper-plates, 4th Edition, corrected and enlarged, 4to. 1l. 1s. Another Edition, 8vo. 12s.

2. A Familiar INTRODUCTION to the STUDY of ELECTRICITY, 3d Edition 8vo. 2s. 6d.

3. The HISTORY and PRESENT STATE of DISCOVERIES relating to VISION, LIGHT, and Colours, 2 vols. 4to. illustrated with a great Number of Copper-plates, 1l. 11s. 6d. in Boards.

4. A Familiar INTRODUCTION to the Theory and Practice of PERSPECTIVE, with Copper-plates, 5s. in Boards.

5. Experiments and Observations on different Kinds of Air, with Copper-plates, 3 vols. 18s. in Boards.

6. PHILOSOPHICAL EMPIRICISM: Containing Remarks on a Charge of Plagiarism respecting Dr. H———s, interspersed with various Observations relating to different Kinds of Air, 1s. 6d.

7. Direc-

BOOKS *written by* JOSEPH PRIESTLEY, LL. D.

7. Directions for impregnating Water with FIXED AIR, in order to communicate to it the peculiar Spirit and Virtues of PYRMONT WATER, and other Mineral Waters of a similar Nature, 1s.

N. B. The two preceding Pamphlets are included in No. 5.

8. A New CHART of HISTORY, containing a View of the principal Revolutions of Empire that have taken Place in the World; with a Book describing it, containing an Epitome of Universal History, 4th Edition, 10s. 6d.

9. A CHART of BIOGRAPHY, with a Book, containing an Explanation of it, and a Catalogue of all the Names inserted in it, 6th Edition, very much improved, 10s. 6d.

10. The RUDIMENTS of ENGLISH GRAMMAR, adapted to the Use of Schools, 1s. 6d.

11. The above GRAMMAR, with Notes and Observations, for the Use of those who have made some Proficiency in the Language, 4th Edition, 3s.

12. OBSERVATIONS relating to EDUCATION : more especially as it respects the MIND. To which is added, an Essay on a Course of liberal Education for Civil and Active Life, with Plans of Lectures on, 1. The Study of History and General Policy. 2. The History of England. 3. The Constitution and Laws of England, 4s. sewed.

13. A COURSE of LECTURES on ORATORY and CRITICISM, 4to. 10s. 6d.

14. An ESSAY on the FIRST PRINCIPLES of GOVERNMENT, and on the Nature of POLITICAL, CIVIL, and RELIGIOUS LIBERTY, 2d Edition, much enlarged, 4s. sewed.

15. An EXAMINATION of Dr. REID's Inquiry into the Human Mind on the Principles of Common Sense, Dr. BEATTIES's Essay on the Nature and Immutability of Truth, and Dr. OSWALD's Appeal to Common Sense in Behalf of Religion, 2d Edition, 5s. sewed.

16. HART-

BOOKS *written by* JOSEPH PRIESTLEY, LL. D.

6. Atonement for Sin by the Death of Chrift, 5th Edit. 1d.

34. A Familiar Illuftration of certain Paffages of Scripture relating to the fame Subject, 4d, or 3s. 6d per Dozen.

35. The TRIUMPH of TRUTH; being an Account of the Trial of Mr. Elwall for Herefy and Blafphemy, at Stafford Affizes, before Judge Denton, 2d Edition, 1d.

36. CONSIDERATIONS for the Ufe of YOUNG MEN, and the Parents of YOUNG MEN, 2d Edition, 2d.

Alfo, publifhed under the Direction of Dr. PRIESTLEY.
THE THEOLOGICAL REPOSITORY:
Confifting of Original Effays, Hints, Queries, &c. calculated to promote religious Knowledge, in Three Volumes, 8vo. Price 18s. in Boards.

In the Firft Volume which is now reprinted, feveral Articles are added, particularly Two Letters from Dr. THOMAS SHAW to Dr. BENSON, relating to the Paffage of the Ifraelites through the Red Sea.

37. *history of the corruptions of Christianity*.

A

SCRIPTURE CATECHISM,

CONSISTING OF

A Series of QUESTIONS, with References to the *Scriptures* inftead of ANSWERS.

By JOSEPH PRIESTLEY,
LL.D. F.R.S.

From a Child thou haſt known the Holy Scriptures.
PAUL.

L O N D O N:
Printed for J. JOHNSON, No. 72, St. Paul's
Church-Yard.
M. DCC. LXXII.

[Price THREE-PENCE.]

THE
PREFACE.

ST. Paul mentions it as a great advantage to Timothy, and a subject of great commendation to his parents, that *from a child he had known the holy scriptures; which*, he says, *were able to make him wise unto salvation.* 2 Tim. iii. 15. By the scriptures the apostle must have meant the books of the *Old Testament*; but the collection is now rendered much more valuable by the addition of those of the *New.* Since these inestimable writings are *profitable for doctrine, for reproof, for correction, and for instruction in righteousness*, and are calculated to make men *perfect, thoroughly furnished unto all good works.* ver. 16, 17, it must be a matter of the greatest

im-

importance that young persons be instructed in the knowledge of them; and this course of instruction, in order to be effectual, cannot be begun too early.

The sooner the mind is impressed with just maxims of conduct, with a sense of the divine authority, the hope of his favour, and the fear of his displeasure; the sooner a person is made sensible of the charms of good example, and filled with abhorrence by a view of what is odious and contemptible in human characters (and for all these purposes the books of scripture are most excellent) the more probable it is that the effect will be lasting and happy. This course of instruction, I know by experience, may be begun, and carried on with success, as soon as a child is capable of any kind of oral instruction whatever; and none but those who have made the trial can imagine, with how much pleasure children will listen to the most instructive scripture histories, and how soon they

they will enter into the meaning and spirit of them.

But the following catechism is not designed for the use of young children. These muſt be taught without book, by the parent telling them the ſtories in the moſt familiar manner, ſelecting the moſt important and engaging circumſtances, and making them tell the particulars in their own way after him. But as ſoon as perſons are capable of reading the bible with underſtanding, I think it may be ſufficient to propoſe to them ſuch queſtions as I have here drawn up, and to refer them to the ſcriptures themſelves for the anſwers. I do not, indeed, think that it can be reaſonably expected that a perſon ſhould be able to prepare tolerably judicious anſwers to *ſome* of the queſtions in this catechiſm, under ſixteen or eighteen years of age; but there are others which will not be too difficult for thoſe who are but nine or ten years old; ſo that, with a little judgment in the uſe of it, this collection of queſtions may be uſeful in the inſtruction of young perſons of any age. Upon the whole, however, I would adviſe, that this catechiſm be taught to a claſs of perſons not quite ſo young as thoſe for whoſe uſe my other catechiſm, and eſpecially the firſt part of it, was particularly calculated.

The queſtions in this catechiſm are chiefly *hiſtorical*, becauſe this part of the bible may be moſt conveniently taught in this manner; and that young perſons may have a clearer idea of the order of events, I have collected the hiſtory of the kings of Judea and Iſrael from the *Prophets*, as well as the books of *Kings* and *Chronicles*; reſerving only a few miſcellaneous prophecies for a ſeparate ſection. I have alſo reduced the four evangeliſts into a harmony, and have referred to all the different accounts of the ſame ſtory. Thoſe who have made a greater proficiency in the knowledge of the ſcriptures may be required to compare them, and note the variations.

The PREFACE.

On the books of Proverbs, Pfalms, Ecclefiaftes, and other books, and parts of books, which are not hiftorical, I have made but few queftions. Thefe books can only be recommended in general to the attention and ftudy of young perfons; or particular parts of them may be committed to memory. Other books of fcripture, efpecially the prophetical, and fome of the apoftolical epiftles, can hardly be well underftood, except by perfons of riper years. For this reafon I have been very fparing of the queftions which refer to them.

In many cafes, I am aware, that it will be neceffary to divide thefe queftions into various others, and alfo to diverfify the form of expreffion, in order to lead thofe who are lefs experienced to the proper anfwers; but a very fmall degree of judgment and addrefs will be fufficient for this purpofe.

It will be a confiderable advantage attending this method of inftruction, that

that by it young perfons will be introduced to an acquaintance with *the scriptures themfelves*, which will give them the trueft idea of their contents and value. No anfwers framed to their hands could poffibly effect this great and good purpofe. If the anfwers to catechifms be given in the very words of fcripture, yet the connection in which fuch fentences are introduced, and confequently much of the peculiar propriety and force of them, is neceffarily loft. Befides, catechifms, upon this plan, cannot well comprife more than the *moral maxims* of fcripture, fo that the *hiftorical*, which is, in fact, the moft ufeful part to young perfons, muft be omitted.

I hope alfo that thofe parents who have the true wifdom to fee it to be a duty incumbent upon themfelves to fuperintend the religious inftruction of their children, and who will not refufe to take fome pains for fo valuable a purpofe, will not be difpleafed with the opportunity which this fcheme
of

of a catechism will afford them, of renewing and perfecting their own acquaintance with the history of the bible. Indeed it cannot be supposed that the most knowing in the scriptures should be able to make use of such a catechism as this, in the instruction of his children, without some previous preparation; so that no person need to be ashamed, if it appear that he himself has something to learn in this business, as well as his child. But I hope that few of those who will make any inquiry after this catechism, will object to it, because it is calculated to give themselves, as well as their children, a more perfect knowldege of important facts and truths.

A SCRIP-

A

SCRIPTURE CATECHISM.

Genesis.

IN how many days did God create the heavens and the earth? i.

What was the work of each of the six days? i.

What was the reason of the inftitution of the fabbath? ii. 2, 3. Ex. xx. 11.

On what account were Adam and Eve caft out of the garden of Eden? iii.

Recite

Recite the hiſtory of Cain and Abel? iv.

What was the cauſe of the general deluge, and who ſurvived it? vi, vii, viii.

What token did God give that the earth ſhould be no more deſtroyed by a flood? ix. 12.

What ſin was Noah guilty of? ix. 21.

What occaſioned the diſperſion of mankind over the face of the earth? xi. 1—9.

Of what country was Abraham a native; and on what account did he leave it, to dwell in the land of Canaan? xi. 31. xii. 1—10.

What promiſe did God make to Abraham when he firſt called him, and which he repeated afterwards? xii. 23. xviii. 18. xxii. 17. 18.

What ſervice did Abraham render to Lot? xiv.

Recite the hiſtory of the birth of Iſhmael? xvi.

On what account, and in what manner were Sodom and Gomorrha deſtroyed? xviii. xix.

What

CATECHISM.

What was there extraordinary in the birth of Isaac? xvii. 16—22. xxi. 1—8.

What became of Ishmael after the birth of Isaac? xxi. 9—21.

How did God try the obedience of Abraham, with respect to his son Isaac? xxii. 1—19.

How did Abraham procure a wife for his son Isaac? xxiv.

What children had Isaac, and what were their different characters? xxv. 19—28.

In what manner did Jacob deprive Esau of his birthright? xxv. 29—34. xxvii. 1—40.

Whither did Jacob flee from the anger of his brother Esau? xxvii. 41. xxviii. 14.

What wives and children had Jacob? xxvii. 15. xxx. 25.

On what account did Jacob leave Laban? xxxi.

How was Jacob received by his brother Esau? xxxii. xxxiii.

Of what crime were Simeon and Levi guilty, with respect to the Shechemites? xxxiv.

How came Joseph to go into Egypt? xxxvii.

On what account was he cast into prison? xxxix.

On what occasion was he introduced to Pharaoh? xl. xli. 1—49.

What brought Jacob and his other sons into Egypt? xlii—xlvi.

Exodus.

HOW were the children of Israel treated in Egypt, after the death of Joseph? i.

Relate the history of the birth of Moses, and of his flight from Egypt. ii.

How came Moses to undertake to deliver the Israelites from their bondage in Egypt? iii.

What miracle did Moses work, in order to prove that God sent him, and what effect had it on Pharaoh? vii. 1—13.

What were the plagues with which God afflicted Egypt, and especially that which induced Pharaoh to per-

CATECHISM. 15

mit the Israelites to go out of his country? vii. 14. viii.—xii.

What was the original and meaning of the passover? xii. 1—31.

What great calamity befel the Egyptians, at the time that the Israelites left their country? xiv.

What miracle was performed at Marah? xv. 23, to the end.

What was the chief food of the Israelites, in their travelling through the wilderness? xvi.

How were they supplied with water at Mount Horeb? xvii. 1—7.

By what means did the Israelites prevail over the Amalekites? xvii. 8, to the end.

What advice did Jethro give to Moses? xviii.

What extraordinary appearances were there at Mount Sinai? xix.

Repeat the ten commandments, which God spake from thence. xx. 1—17.

Of what crime were the Israelites guilty in the absence of Moses, and what were the consequences of it? xxxii.

Leviticus.

WHAT was the crime and punishment of Nadab and Abihu? x. 1—12.

What was done to the person who cursed and blasphemed God? xxiv. 10, to the end.

Numbers.

HOW were the children of Israel directed in their march through the wilderness? ix. 15, to the end.

What was the consequence of the Israelites loathing manna, and longing for flesh meat? xi.

What was the offence of Aaron and Miriam, and the consequence of it? xii.

What happened upon sending the spies to discover the land of Canaan? xiii. xiv.

What was the offence and the punishment of Corah, Dathan and Abiram? xvi. xvii.

Recite the history of the fiery serpents. xxi. 4—9.

Who

Who were the firſt kings that the Iſraelites conquered? xxi. 21, to the end.

Recite the hiſtory of Balak and Balaam. xxii—xxiv.

Into what wickedneſs did the Moabites tempt the children of Iſrael, and what was the iſſue of it? xxv.

What was the fate of the Midianites? xxxi. 1—20.

Deuteronomy.

IN what manner were the children of Iſrael to treat the idolatrous inhabitants of Canaan? vii. 1—3.

For what reaſon were they ordered to exterminate them? vii. 4—11.

In what were the Iſraelites to be particularly careful to inſtruct their children? xi. 18—21.

In what manner were the Iſraelites to treat other nations, with whom they might be at war, beſides the inhabitants of Canaan? xx. 10—15.

Who ſucceeded Moſes in the conduct of the Iſraelites? xxxi. 3.

Joshua.

RECITE the hiftory of the fpies, whom Jofhua fent to examine the condition of Jericho. ii.

In what manner did the Ifraelites crofs the river Jordan? iii. iv.

In what manner did they get poffeffion of Jericho? v.

How did they take Ai, and what followed upon it? vii. viii.

How did the Gibeonites deceive the Ifraelites? ix.

In what manner were the five kings that warred againft Gibeon defeated? x. 1—28.

How many kings did Jofhua take after the Ifraelites had croffed the river Jordan? xii.

Did the Ifraelites under Jofhua conquer all the land of Canaan? xiii. 1—13. xv. 16. xvi. 10.

In what part of the land of Canaan was the tabernacle fet up? xviii. 1.

In what place, and at what time, was Jofeph buried? xxiv. 32.

Judges.

JUDGES.

HOW was Adonibezec requited? i. 5—7.

What was the confequence of the Ifraelites having a communication with the idolatrous nations that were not conquered? iii. 5—7.

In what manner did God punifh their idolatry? iii. 8.

Who delivered them from the king of Mefopotamia? iii. 9—11.

What were the circumftances which attended their deliverance from the power of Eglon king of Moab, when they had relapfed into idolatry? iii. 12—30.

Recite the hiftory of Deborah and Barak. iv.

Recite the hiftory of Gideon and the Midianites. vi. vii. viii.

What was the hiftory and fate of Abimelech? ix.

What rafh vow did Jephthah make, and into what difficulties did he bring himfelf in confequence of it? xi. 29, to the end.

Relate

Relate the hiſtory of the birth of Sampſon. xiii.

What was Sampſon's riddle, and what were the occaſion and iſſue of it? xiv.

In what manner did Sampſon revenge himſelf on the Philiſtines, for taking his wife from him? xv.

What exploits did Sampſon perform at Gaza? xvi. 1—3.

Who betrayed Sampſon into the hands of the Philiſtines, and what were the circumſtances which attended his death? xvi.

Relate the hiſtory of the great deſtruction of the Benjamites. xix—xxi.

Ruth.

WHO was Ruth, and how did ſhe come to reſide at Bethlehem? i.

To whom was Ruth married, and what remarkable perſon deſcended from her? iv.

1 Samuel.

RELATE the hiſtory of the birth of Samuel. i. What

CATECHISM. 21

What judgment was inflicted upon the houſe of Eli, and what was the reaſon of it? ii. iii.

What calamitous events preceded the death of Eli? iv.

How did the Philiſtines difpoſe of the ark, and what induced them to ſend it back again? v. vi.

For what reaſon did the Iſraelites defire to be governed by a king? viii.

In what manner was Saul choſen king? ix.

What offence was Saul guilty of when he went to fight againſt the Philiſtines? xiii.

What great exploit did Jonathan perform in this war, and what danger was he brought into by the imprudence of his Father? xiv.

What offence was Saul guilty of, with reſpect to the Amalekites? xv.

In what manner was David choſen king? xvi.

Recite the hiſtory of David and Goliah. xvii.

What was the cauſe of the hatred that Saul bore to David, and what were the effects of it? xviii.

What

What friendship did Jonathan and Michal shew to David? xix. xx.

Whither did David flee from Saul? xxi. 10, to the end.

What did Saul do to the priests, when he suspected them to be in the interest of David? xxii.

How did David spare Saul in the cave of Engedi? xxiv.

Recite the history of David and Abigail. xxv.

How did David spare Saul a second time at Hachilah? xxvi.

Recite the history of the death of Saul and Jonathan. xxviii. xxxi.

2 SAMUEL.

HOW did David receive the news of the death of Saul and Jonathan? i.

Who succeeded Saul in opposition to David? ii. 8.

What was the fate of Abner, the general of Saul and Ishbosheth? iii.

What became of Ishbosheth? iii.

What place did David conquer, and fix upon for his residence? v. 6—11. 1 Chron. xi. 4—10.

What

What nations did David conquer? viii. 1 Chron. xviii.

How did David behave towards Mephibosheth? ix.

What crime was David guilty of on account of Bathsheba? xi.

In what manner did Nathan reprove David for his sin? xii.

What was the crime, and the fate of Amnon? xiii.

Recite the history of Absalom. xv—xvii.

What was the consequence of David's numbering Israel? xxiv. 1 Chro. xxi.

1 KINGS.

WHO succeeded David in the kingdom of Israel? i.

What choice did Solomon make? iii. 1—16. 2 Chro. i. 7—13.

How did Solomon decide between the two harlots? iii. 16, to the end.

What things distinguished Solomon and his reign? iv. 2 Chro. i. 13 .to the end.

What great undertaking did Solomon

lomon execute, which had been intended by his father? v. vi.

What was the purport of Solomon's prayer at the dedication of the temple? viii. 2 Chro. vi.

By what circumftance did it appear that God approved of Solomon's building the temple? 2 Chro. v. 11, to the end.

Who came to vifit Solomon, on account of his great wifdom? x. 2 Chro. ix. 1—13.

Into what fins did Solomon fall in his old age? xi.

What occafioned the revolt of the ten tribes from Rehoboam, the fon of Solomon? xii. 2 Chron. x.

What was the event of the war between Abijah and Jeroboam? 2 Chro. xiii.

Relate the hiftory of the old prophet, who prophefied againft the altar at Bethel. xiii.

What calamity befel the kingdom of Judah in the reign of Rehoboam? xiv. 25, to the end. 2 Chron. xii.

What was the character of Afa's reign? xv. 8—25.

By

CATECHISM. 25

By what favourable events was the reign of Afa diftinguifhed? 2 Chron. xiv. xv.

What connection had Jehofaphat with Ahab, and what were the confequences of it? 2 Chro. xviii.

What fuccefs had Jehofaphat in his wars with the Moabites and Ammonites? 2 Chro. xx.

What was the character of the reign of Ahab? xvi. 27—34.

How was Elijah maintained, when he fled from Ahab? xvii. 1—8.

What did Elijah do for the poor widow, who entertained him in the time of the famine? xvii. 8. to the end.

What was the confequence of Ahab's attempt to take Elijah? xviii. 17. to the end.

Relate the hiftory of the fiege of Samaria by Benhadad king of Syria. xx.

What injuftice. was Ahab guilty of, with refpect to Naboth? xxi.

What were the circumftances of the death of Ahab? xxii. 1—37.

What was the character of Jehofaphat's reign? xxii. 41—50. 2 Chro. xvii.

C 2 KINGS.

2 KINGS.

HOW was Elijah defended againſt thoſe perſons whom Ahaziah ſent to apprehend him? i.

How was Elijah diſtinguiſhed at the cloſe of his life? ii. 1—12.

In what manner were the young perſons that mocked Eliſha puniſhed? ii. 23. to the end.

What bleſſing did God beſtow upon the widow who applied to Eliſha? iv. 1—8.

How did God bleſs the Shunamite who received Eliſha? iv. 8—38.

Recite the hiſtory of Naaman the Syrian and Gehazi. v.

Relate the particulars of the ſiege of Samaria in the time of Eliſha. vi. 8. to the end. vii.

What was the hiſtory of Hazael king of Syria? viii. 7—16.

What was the fate of Jezebel? ix. 30. to the end.

How did Jehu deſtroy the prieſts of Baal? x. 18—29.

How was Jehoaſh ſaved from his grandmother Athaliah? xi. 2 Chro. xxii. 23.

What

CATECHISM.

What did Elisha prophesy to Jehoash, at the time of his death? xiii. 14—20.

What miracle was performed by the bones of Elisha? xiii. 20—22.

What was the offence of king Uzziah? 2 Chro. xxvi. 16—22.

What was the character and history of the reign of Ahaz? xvi. 2 Chro. xxviii.

What was the conclusion of the kingdom of Israel? xvii.

What was the character, and what were the events of the reign of Hezekiah? xviii—xx. 2 Chro. xxix.

What was the event of Senacherib's invasion of Judah? 2 Chro. xxxii. Isa. xxxvi. xxxvii.

What was there remarkable in the sickness and recovery of Hezekiah? xxxviii.

How did Hezekiah behave to the ambassadors of the king of Babylon, and what followed upon it? Isa. xxxix.

What was the character and fate of Manasseh? xxi. 1—23. 2 Chro. xxxiii. 1—20.

What was the character of Josiah? xxii. 1—8. 2 Chro. xxxiv.

What happened with refpect to the book of the law in his reign? xxii. 8. to the end. 2 Chro. xxxiv. 14. to the end.

In what manner did Jofiah come to his death? xxiii. 1—31. 2 Chro. xxxv.

What calamity befel the kingdom of Judah in the reign of Jehoiakim? xxiv. 1—6. 2 Chro. xxxvi. 6—11.

How did king Jehoiakim behave with refpect to the written prophecies of Jeremiah? xxxvi.

What did Jeremiah prophefy concerning the iffue of the fiege of Jerufalem in the reign of Zedekiah? xxxvii.

What did Jeremiah prophefy concerning the return of the Jews from the Babylonifh captivity, and alfo concerning the kingdom of Chrift? xxiii. 1--8.

What was the fate of Zedekiah, and the end of the kindom of Judah? xxiv. 17. to the end. xxv. 2 Chro. xxxvi. 11. to the end. Jer. xxxix. lii.

How long did Jeremiah prophefy that the Babylonifh captivity would continue? xxv. 8—15. xxix. 10.

What evil befel Jeremiah for his perfevering to prophefy concerning the Babylonifh captivity? xxxvii. xxxviii.

What

What became of Jeremiah after the taking of Jerufalem? xl.

What was the fate of Gedaliah, who was appointed governor of thofe Jews who were not carried captive? xl. xli. 1—11.

What part did Johanan act after the death of Gedaliah, and what advice did Jeremiah give him? xlii.

How did Johanan act, and what became of Jeremiah? xliii. 1—7.

DANIEL.

HOW did Daniel come into favour at the court of Babylon? i.

Recite the hiftory of Nebuchadnezzar's firft dream. ii.

What was the confequence of Nebuchadnezzar's fetting up a golden image to be worfhipped? iii.

What was the occafion, and the circumftances of Nebuchadnezzar's being driven from the fociety of men, and from his kingdom? iv.

Relate the hiftory of Belfhazzar. v.

How came Daniel to be caft into the den of lions? vi.

Ezra.

WHAT King of Perfia permitted the Jews to return from captivity and rebuild their temple? i.

What obftructions did the Jews meet with in that building? iv. v.

What favour did Darius fhew the Jews? vi.

What did Artaxerxes do in favour of the Jews? vii.

What difficulty did Ezra and Nehemiah meet with, in reforming the Jewifh ftate? ix. x. Neh. xiii.

Nehemiah.

What favour did Artaxerxes fhew the Jews by Nehemiah? ii.

What difficulties did Nehemiah meet with in building the wall of Jerufalem? iv. vi.

What great folemnity did the Jews keep on their fettlement in their own country? viii. ix.

Esther.

CATECHISM.

ESTHER.

WHAT occasioned the rise of Esther and Mordecai in the court of Ahasuerus? i. ii.

Into what danger did Haman bring the Jews? iii. iv. v.

What was the fate of Haman? vi. vii.

THE PROPHETS.

WHAT was prophesied by Isaiah concerning Babylon, when it was the capital of a rising and splendid kingdom? xiii.

What was prophesied concerning Cyrus? Isa. xlv. 1—8.

Repeat some of the prophecies of Isaiah concerning the humiliation of Christ, and the success of his gospel. lii. 13. to the end. lxi. 1—3.

Repeat one of the exhortations of the prophet Isaiah against hypocrisy, and his promises to those who were sincere. i. 10—20. lviii.

What did Jeremiah prophesy concerning Egypt? xliii. 8, to the end. xlvi. 11.   What

What did Jeremiah prophefy againſt Babylon? l. li.

What did Ezekiel prophefy concerning Egypt, and the king of Babylon? xvii. 11—22. xxix—xxxii.

How did God explain his threatnings and his promiſes by the prophet Ezekiel? xxxiii. 11—20.

What did Ezekiel prophefy concerning Tyre? xxvi—xxviii.

What did Amos prophefy concerning the kingdom of Iſrael? vii. 7. to the end.

What was the confequence of Jonah's fleeing from the command of God? i. ii.

What was the event of his preaching to the Ninevites? iii.

What ſin was Jonah guilty of after the repentance of the Ninevites? iv.

What did Nahum prophefy concerning Nineveh? ii. iii.

What was Daniel's viſion of the four beaſts? vii.

Give an account of Daniel's prophecy of ſeventy weeks. ix. 22. to the end.

What did Haggai prophefy concerning the glory of the ſecond temple? ii. 1—10.

Who

Who was to make his appearance before the coming of Chrift, according to the prophet Malachi? iv.

MORAL and DEVOTIONAL WRITINGS.

RELATE the hiftory of the afflictions of Job. i. ii.

What was his profperity afterwards? xlii.

Repeat the following Pfalms. i. xv. xix. xxiii. xxxiii. xxxix. l. xc. xcvii. c. ciii. cxlv.

What cautions does Solomon give concerning bad company? Prov. i.

What defcription does Solomon give of the artifices of an harlot? vii.

Repeat the following chapters and paffages in the book of Proverbs. iv. viii. xxx. 7—9.

What does Solomon fay of a virtuous woman? xxxi. 10. to the end.

Repeat fome of the advice which Solomon gives to young perfons, in the book of Ecclefiaftes. xi. 9, 10. xii. 1. 13, 14.

The

The FOUR GOSPELS.

GIVE an account of the birth of John the Baptift. Luke i. 1—57.

What circumftances attended the naming of John the Baptift? Luke i. 58—80.

Recite the hiftory of the birth of Jefus. Matt. i. 18—25. Luke ii. 1—20.

What circumftances attended the circumcifion of Jefus? Luke ii. 21—40.

What did Jefus do at Jerufalem, when he went thither at twelve years of age? Luke ii. 41—52.

What was the fubject of the preaching of John the Baptift? Matt. iii. 1--12. Mark i. 1--8. Luke iii. 3--18.

What circumftances attended the baptifm of Jefus? Matt. iii. 13—17. Mark i. 9—11. Luke iii. 21, 22.

Recite the hiftory of Chrift's temptation. Matt. iv. 1—11. Luke iv. 1—13.

What was the teftimony of John concerning Jefus? John i. 19—34.

How came the apoftle Peter and his brothers acquainted with Jefus? John i. 35—44. How

How was Nathaniel introduced to Jesus? John i. 45—51.

What happened at a marriage feast in Cana of Galilee? John ii. 1—12.

Which of the rulers of the Jews came to Jesus by night? John iii. 1.

What conversation had Jesus with the woman of Samaria, and what was the issue of it? John iv. 1—42.

In what manner did Jesus cure the son of a nobleman at Capernaum? John iv. 43—54.

What miracle attended the call of Peter? Luke v. 3—11.

What cure did Jesus perform in the synagogue at Capernaum? Mark i. 21—28. Luke iv. 14—37.

What other cure did Jesus perform in Capernaum? Mark i. 29—38. Luke iv. 38—44. Matt. viii. 14—17.

Repeat the blessings which our Saviour pronounced at the beginning of his sermon upon the mount. Matt. v. 1—13.

To what did our Saviour compare his disciples? ver. 13—16.

In what respects did Christ condemn murder and hatred more than the scribes and Pharisees? ver. 21—26.

What did our Saviour enjoin with refpect to oaths? ver. 33—37.

What precepts did Chrift give refpecting the moft perfect humanity and mercy? ver. 38—48.

What advice did Chrift give refpecting alms and prayer? vi. 1—8.

Repeat the Lord's prayer. ver. 8--13.

What advice did Chrift give refpecting earthly treafures and covetoufnefs? ver. 19—34.

What caution did he give with refpect to rafh judgment? vii. 1—5.

In what manner did Chrift encourage perfons to pray? ver. 7—11.

What general rule did Chrift lay down, comprehending all focial virtues? ver. 12.

In what manner did our Lord exprefs the great importance of a practical regard to his precepts? ver. 15—29.

What cure did Jefus perform as he came down from the mountain? Matt. viii. 1—4. Mark i. 39—44. Luke v. 12—16.

What miracle did Jefus perform in favour of a Centurion at Capernaum? Matt. viii. 5—13. Luke vii. 1—10.

Whom

CATECHISM. 37

Whom did Jesus raise from the dead at Nain? Luke vij. 11—17.

What circumstances attended the cure of the demoniacs at Gadara? Matt. viii. 18—34. Mark iv. 35. to the end. v. 1—21. Luke viii. 22—40.

How did Jesus cure a person sick of the palsy at Capernaum? Matt. ix. 1—8. Mark ii. 1—12. Luke v. 17—26.

In what manner did Christ call the apostle Matthew, and what conversation had he with the Pharisees at his house? Matt. ix. 9—17. Mark ii. 14—22. Luke v. 27—39.

What method did a woman, who had a bloody issue, take, in order to be cured by Jesus, as he was going to the house of Jairus; and what great miracle did he perform in favour of Jairus? Mark v. 22—43. Matt. ix. 18—26. Luke viii. 41—56.

What discourse had Jesus with the Pharisees on occasion of his disciples plucking some ears of corn, and his healing the man who had a withered hand? Matt. xii. 1—13. Mark ii. 23. to the end. iii. 1—6. Luke vi. 1—11.

Relate the parable of Christ concerning the sower, and his explanation of
D   it.

it. Matt. xiii. 1—51. Mark iv. 1—29. Luke viii. 4—18.

In what manner was Jefus received at Nazareth? Matt. xiii. 53—58. Mark vi. 1—6. Luke iv. 16—30.

What inftructions did Chrift give to the twelve apoftles when he fent them forth to preach? Matt. x. 1—43. Mark vi. 7—11. Luke ix. 1—12.

What happened when Jefus dined with Simon the Pharifee? Luke vii. 36—50.

In what manner was John the Baptift put to death? Matt. xiv. 1—13. Mark vi. 14—29.

What miracle did Jefus perform when the multitude flocked to him in the wildernefs? Matt. xiv. 14—21. Mark vii. 33—44. Luke ix. 10—17. John vii. 5—14.

What miracle did Jefus perform on the fea of Galilee? Matt. xiv. 22—36. Mark vii. 45—56. John vii. 15—21.

What was the cure of the impotent man at the pool of Bethefda, and the confequence of it? John v. 1—47.

What did Jefus do in favour of a woman of Canaan? Matt. xv. 21—29. Mark vii. 24—31.

What number did Jefus feed at his fecond

CATECHISM. 39

second miracle of that kind? Matt. xv. 32—39. Mark viii. 1—10.

Give an account of the transfiguration of Jesus. Matt. xvii. 1—13. Mark ix. 2—13. Luke ix. 28—36.

What miracle did Jesus perform on his descending from the mountain on which he was transfigured? Matt. xvii. 14—21. Mark ix. 14—29. Luke ix. 37—42.

In what manner did Jesus pay tribute for himself and Peter? Matt. xvii. 24—27.

What were the circumstances of Jesus's curing ten lepers? Luke xvii. 11—19.

Recite the history of the woman taken in adultery. John viii. 1—11.

In what manner did Jesus cure the man who had been blind from his birth, and what were the consequences of it? John ix. 1—41.

Relate the parable of the Good Samaritan. Luke x. 30---37.

What reproof did Jesus give to Martha? Luke x. 38---42.

Recite the parable of the prodigal son. Luke xv. 11---32.

Recite the parable of the rich man and Lazarus. Luke xvi. 19---31.

Relate the parable concerning the Pharisee and the publican. Luke xviii. 9---14.

What did Jesus say when they brought little children to him? Matt. xix. 13---15. Mark x. 13---16. Luke xviii. 15---17.

What reply did Jesus make to the person who asked him what he should do to inherit eternal life, and what observations did he make concerning riches upon that occasion? Matt. xix. 16---30. Mark x. 17---31. Luke xviii. 18---30.

Relate the parable of the housholder who hired labourers. Matt. xx. 1---16.

Recite the history of the resurrection of Lazarus. John xi. 1---57.

On what occasion did Jesus reprove the apostles James and John? Matt. xx. 20---29. Mark x. 34---45.

Relate what the evangelists say concerning Zaccheus. Matt. xix. 1---10.

Relate the parable of the ten pounds, and ten servants. Luke xix. 12--28.

What offended Judas Iscariot when Jesus supped at Bethany? Matt. xxvi. 6---13. Mark xiv. 1---9. John xii. 1---10.

In what manner did Jesus enter into Jerusalem? Matt. xxi. 1---11. Mark xi,

xi. 1---10. Luke xix. 29---40. John xii. 12---19.

What did Jesus do when he found the temple occupied with buyers and sellers? Matt. xxi. 12---22. Mark xi. 11---18. Luke xix. 45, 46. John ii. 14---17.

What did Jesus do with respect to a barren fig-tree? Matt. xxi. 17---22. Mark xi. 12---26.

Relate the parable of the housholder and the vineyard. Matt. xxi. 33---46. Mark xii. 1---12. Luke xx. 9---19.

What reply did Jesus make to those who asked him whether it was lawful to pay tribute to Cæsar? Matt. xxii. 15---22. Mark xii. 13---17. Luke xx. 20---26.

What question did the Sadducees put to Jesus, and what reply did he make to them? Matt. xxii. 23---33. Mark xii. 18---27. Luke xx. 27---40.

What did Jesus say to the lawyer who asked him which was the greatest commandment? Matt. xxii. 35---40. Mark. xii. 28---34.

On what account did Jesus reproach the Pharisees? Matt. xxiii. 1---39. Mark xii. 38---40. Luke xx. 45---47.

What observation did Jesus make concerning the poor woman who cast her

her mite into the treafury? Mark xii. 41---44. Luke xxi. 1--4.

What did Jefus prophefy concerning Jerufalem and the temple? Matt. xxiv. Mark xiii. Luke xxi. 5---33.

Relate the parable of the ten virgins. Matt. xxv. 1---13.

Relate the parable of the talents. Matt. xxv. 14---30.

What account did Chrift give of the day of judgment? Matt. xxv. 31—46.

Relate the circumftances of Jefus wafhing his difciples feet. John xiii. 1—17.

Give an account of the inftitution of the Lord's fupper. Matt. xxvi. 26—29. Mark xiv. 22—25. Luke xxii. 19, 20.

Relate the circumftances of Chrift's agony in the garden. Matt. xxvi. 36--46. Mark xiv. 32—42. Luke xxii. 40—46.

In what manner was Jefus apprehended? Matt. xxvi. 47—56. Mark xviii. 43—50. Luke xxii. 47—53. John xviii. 2—11.

What paffed when Jefus was examined before the high priefts? Matt. xxvi. 57—75. Mark xiv. 53—72. Luke xxii. 54—71. John xviii. 19—27. What

CATECHISM. 43

What became of Judas? Matt. xxvii. 1—10.

What were the particulars of the examination of Jefus before Pilate? Matt. xxvii. 2—25. Mark xv. 1--15. Luke xxiii. 1--25. John xviii. 28--40.

Relate the particulars of the crucifixion of Jefus. Matt. xxvii. 27—56. Mark xv. 16--41. Luke xxiii. 26--49. John xix. 1—37.

In what manner was Jefus buried? Matt. xxvii. 57—66. Mark xv. 43—47. Luke xxiii. 50—56.

Relate the particulars of the refurrection of Jefus, and his appearing to Mary Magdalene. Matt. xxviii. 1--15. Mark xvi. 1—11. Luke xxiv. 1--12.

In what manner did Jefus appear to two of his difciples, who were walking to Emmaus? Luke xxiv. 13—35.

In what manner did Jefus appear to all the apoftles, and efpecially to Thomas? Luke xxiv. 36—49. John xx. 19—31.

Relate the circumftances of Jefus appearing in Galilee. John xxi. 1--25.

Relate the particulars of Jefus's afenfion. Mark xvi. 19. Luke xxiv. 51—53. Acts i. 3—12.

ACTS.

ACTS.

IN what manner was Matthias chosen to succeed Judas Iscariot? i. 15--26.

Relate the circumstances which attended the descent of the Holy Ghost, on the day of Pentecost. ii.

What miracle was performed by Peter and John in the temple? iii.

What were the consequences of imprisoning Peter and John? iv.

What was the occasion of the death of Ananias and Sapphira? v. 1--11.

In what manner was Peter delivered out of prison, and what followed upon it? v. 12, to the end.

Give an account of the martyrdom of Stephen. vi. 8, to the end. vii.

What circumstances attended the planting of Christianity in Samaria? viii. 1--25.

In what manner was the Ethiopian eunuch converted to Christianity? viii. 26, to the end.

In what manner was Paul converted? ix. 1--23.

In what manner did Paul escape from the Jews, who lay in wait to kill him? ix. 23--31.

What miracle did Peter perform with respect to Tabitha? ix. 32, to the end.

In

In what manner was Christianity first preached to the Gentiles? x.

How was this event received by the Jewish converts? xi. 1--18.

What was the prophecy of Agabus? xi. 27, to the end.

What were the actions and death of Herod? xii.

What success had Paul and Barnabas in their preaching in Cyprus, and Antioch in Pisidia? xiii.

In what manner were they received at Lystra? xiv.

What did the apostles enjoin with respect to the Gentile converts? xv. 1---32.

What happened to Paul and Silas at Philippi? xvi.

What was the character of the Jews at Berea? xvii. 10---15.

In what manner was Paul received at Athens? xvii. 16, to the end.

How did Paul maintain himself at Corinth, and what was the issue of his accusation before Gallio? xviii.

What happened to some Jews who attempted to cast out devils in the name of Jesus? xix. 13---20.

What uproar was occasioned by Paul's preaching at Ephesus? xix. 23, to the end.

What

What accident befel Eutychus, and what was the iffue of it? xx. 6—11.

In what manner did Paul take his leave of the elders of Ephefus? xx. 17, to the end.

What intimation did Paul receive concerning the rifk that he would run in going to Jerufalem, and what effect had it upon him? xxi. 1—18.

In what manner was Paul delivered from the fury of the Jews, on his arrival at Jerufalem? xxi. 18, to the end.

What defence did Paul make for his conduct, and by what means did he efcape being fcourged? xxii.

By what ftratagem did Paul make a divifion among his enemies? xxiii. 1—10.

How did Paul efcape the confpiracy that was made againft him by the Jews? xxiii. 10, to the end.

How did Paul defend himfelf when he was accufed before Felix? xxiv.

In what manner did Paul extricate himfelf from the power of his enemies in Judea? xxv.

Give an account of the pleading of Paul before Agrippa? xxvi.

Relate the particulars of Paul's fhipwreck on his voyage to Rome? xxvii.

What happened to Paul after his landing

CATECHISM. 47

landing on the island Melite? xxviii. 1—11.

In what manner was Paul received in Rome? xxviii. 11. to the end.

The Apostolical Epistles.

WHAT account does St. Paul give of the state of the Gentile world before the promulgation of Christianity? Rom. i. 18, to the end.

What advice does St. Paul give with respect to things of an indifferent nature, as to moral virtue? Rom. xiv. 15.

What admonition does he give with respect to divisions and factions among Christians? 1 Corin. iii.

How did St. Paul advise the Corinthians to treat a person who had been guilty of incest? 1 Cor. v.

What account does the apostle Paul give of the resurrection? 1 Cor. xv. 1 Thess. iii. 13, to the end. v. 1—6.

Give an account of what St. Paul suffered in preaching the gospel from his own brief account of it? 2 Cor. xi. 23, to the end.

Into what dangerous opinions and practices had the churches in Galatia been seduced? Gal. i.

What

A SCRIPTURE, &c.

What did St. Paul prophesy concerning the man of sin? 2 Thess. ii. 1---13. 1 Tim. iv. 1, &c.

On what account does St. Paul commend Timothy? 2 Tim. iii. 14, to the end.

What was the occasion of St. Paul's writing to Philemon? The whole epistle.

What remarkable actions does the author of the epistle to the Hebrews ascribe to the principle of faith in God? Heb. xi.

What account does the apostle James give of pure and undefiled religion? James i. 26, 27.

What admonition does he give concerning a respect to riches? James ii. 1---9.

What are the genuine effects of faith? James ii. 14, to the end.

In what manner is this world to be destroyed? 2 Peter, iii.

In what manner are we to make it appear that we love God? 1 John, iv. 20, 21.

F I N I S.

A SERIOUS ADDRESS
TO
Masters of Families,
WITH
FORMS
OF
FAMILY-PRAYER.

By JOSEPH PRIESTLEY, LL.D. F.R.S.

The SECOND EDITION.

If ye, being evil, know how to give good gifts unto your children, how much more shall your Father who is in Heaven give good things to them that ask him. JESUS.

LONDON:
Printed for J. JOHNSON, N° 72, St. Paul's Church-Yard.
[Price NINE-PENCE.]

BT
1030
P7
1979

THE
PREFACE.

THE great end of religion is a good life, and the higheſt happineſs of man in conſequence of it. Chriſt came to bleſs us in turning us away from our iniquities, and to purify to himſelf a peculiar people zealous of good works. The connection between virtue and happineſs is evident. Without the due government of our paſſions, and of our conduct, we can neither be truly happy in this life, nor in that which is to come. If, therefore, we be wiſe for ourſelves, and be chriſtians in deed, and in truth, and not in name only, we ſhall ceaſe to do evil and learn to do well. We ſhall be careful to diſcharge

THE PREFACE.

the proper duty of every ſtation in which it ſhall pleaſe divine providence to place us. And if we have any concern for the welfare of others, we ſhall diligently exhort one another daily, while it is called to-day, left any of us be hardened by the deceitfulneſs of ſin. We ſhall, as the apoſtle directs us, conſider one another, to provoke unto love and to good works.

This is the trueſt friendſhip, and it was in order to fulfil this duty, of *a friend*, as well as of *a miniſter*, that the following addreſs was drawn up, at firſt, for the uſe of one particular congregation, and afterwards made more public. Happy will the author think himſelf if it at all contribute to make ever ſo few perſons more attentive to their duty, in ſo important a relation, on which the virtue and happineſs of others, as well as of themſelves, ſo much depend.

That other perſons may have an opportunity of exerciſing the ſame kind of benevolence,

THE PREFACE. v

nevolence, the addrefs is purpofely fhort, and the forms of prayer fubjoined to it few. By this means the price will not be confiderable, and more perfons may be induced to buy it, and give it to poor families, where there may be a profpect of its being ufeful.

The two firft prayers are very fhort, plain, and general, being intended for common and daily ufe. The third is the compofition of my worthy friend the Rev. Mr. Turner of Wakefield. I think it excellent for a rich variety of fentiment, and for propriety and force of expreffion. It is confiderably longer than either of the others, and therefore will, perhaps, be thought more proper for Sundays, when families have leifure for longer exercifes of devotion. The forms for *particular occafions* may be ufed along with any of them, at the difcretion of the perfon who conducts the fervice.

A 3   To

THE PREFACE.

To those persons who can afford to purchase books, I would recommend other *sets of family prayers*, containing a greater variety of forms, out of which they may be more likely to select such as particularly suit their own circumstances and turn of thinking. A sufficient variety will be found in those composed by Mr. Bourn, Mr. May, Dr. Leland and other ministers in Dublin, and especially a set lately published by the Rev. Mr. Enfield of Warrington.

It seems to me, that there is a great want of books of practical religion, free from superstitious notions, and recommending no superstitious practices. I earnestly wish that ingenious and pious persons would attend to this circumstance. They cannot employ their talents to better purpose than by enforcing, like our Saviour, the practice of genuine virtue and piety, and, at the same time, dispelling that unnatural gloom and horror, which weak or wicked men have thrown over those things,

THE PREFACE. vii

things, which, though truly serious, are in themselves so chearful and engaging. Treatises on these important subjects, respecting the supreme happiness of man, both in the present and future world, could not fail to be acceptable and useful.

Had we ever so many books of this kind, there would always be sufficient reason for publishing more. Old books will be neglected, and new ones, with no other recommendation but that of being new, will be bought and read. Besides, while every mode of false religion is continually presented to us in some new form or modification, should not their effects be counteracted by the exhibition of truth and virtue, in all the variety of dress they will naturally and easily admit of.

A 4   N. B. *In*

viii   THE PREFACE.

N. B. *In thoſe occaſional forms in this work in which particular perſons are referred to, it will be eaſy for the perſon who reads them to change the words* ſervant, he, him, *or* his, *into* ſervants, ſhe, *or* her, they, their, *or* them, *as the occaſion may require; and they are printed in Italics, to make them the more eaſily diſtinguiſhed, and, thereby, leſs liable to occaſion any embarraſſment to the reader.*

A SERIOUS

A SERIOUS ADDRESS

TO

MASTERS of FAMILIES.

My Christian Brethren,

I Take the liberty to address you at this time, under the respectable character of masters and heads of families; hoping that some good may be done by informing those who are ignorant, and exhorting those who are negligent, in the discharge of the important duties of that relation; and that no offence will be taken by those who are not unattentive to them, if they be hereby reminded of their obligations.

A serious Address to

Every family is a little society within itself, and has a system of government peculiar to itself, the laws and regulations of which are wholly in your own power. This is an authority which is, in its own nature (as far as the laws of our country permit it to extend) more absolute than that of any civil government in the world can possibly be; and in the administration of it you are accountable to none but to God, and your own consciences.

Be sensible, then, of the importance of your character and station, and be solicitous to fulfil the proper duty of it. And as the only true guide to discover what the duty of your station is, consider what *good* you are capable of doing in it, and what are the most probable means of producing this good. For a *power* of doing good, and an *obligation* to do it are, in the eye of reason and religion, of exactly the same extent; and it cannot be conceived to be otherwise, under the moral government

Masters of Families.

ment of God, who has given us all our powers for that, and no other purpose.

Think not, my brethren, that you have discharged your duty to you children and servants, when you have behaved towards them, and made provision for them in such a manner as law, or equity (as it is commonly understood) requires of you. There are transgressions and neglects of duty, of which human judicatories can take no cognizance, and duties of indispensable obligation in the sight of God. Nay, these duties are of more importance, with respect to happiness, and therefore of more indispensable obligation, than many of those of which men do take cognizance.

Yourselves, and the members of your families, have not only bodies, which must be supplied with food and raiment, and other conveniences of this mortal life; but you have immortal souls, which must be happy or miserable after death; and the discipline by which we are formed to that

that temper, and trained to that conduct, which will enſure everlaſting happineſs, is exerciſed to the moſt advantage in family relations. The influence of a maſter of a family, in this reſpect, is of far more importance than that of a miniſter or magiſtrate. Your children and ſervants are always under your eye. You ſee all their behaviour; and therefore may, in general, check whatever is wrong and vicious in both, before it be fixed into a habit.

With reſpect to your children, nature has given you an uncontrolled authority over them, at a time when their minds are exceedingly pliable; ſo that it is in your power, almoſt, to mold them as you pleaſe. By all means then improve this advantage, which nature, and the God of nature gives you, to the beſt of purpoſes. Be particularly attentive to every ſtep that may lead to a moral habit. Teach them betimes their duty to God, and to their fellow creatures. Inſpire them with an abhorrence of profane ſwear-

Masters of Families.

swearing, lying, and stealing. Encourage whatever you see, that is gentle, tender, and compassionate in their nature; and check every thing that may lead to cruelty, malice, and revenge.

This, in general, is no difficult, but an easy and pleasant task, when your children are young, and their minds apt to receive new impressions. It requires, indeed, an uniform and steady conduct; and sometimes a considerable degree of severity may be necessary; but consider, that if your authority be once lost, your child may be undone. If you indulge or neglect your children, till bad habits are formed, there will be a time when it will be too late to do them any real service, though you may earnestly wish to do it; and divine providence is often awefully just, in permitting wicked children to be a curse to their criminally indulgent parents.

Indeed

Indeed no pains you can take can absolutely infure fuccefs; for notwithftanding (to allude to our faviour's parable) you may fow good feed, an enemy may fow tares. Your children are fubject to a variety of influences, of which no perfon, and more efpecially a man of bufinefs, can be fufficiently apprized; and the foundation you have been laying for their virtue and happinefs may be fecretly undermined. But by proper attention, and the ufual blefling of God upon your good endeavours, this evil may, generally, be prevented. Solomon fays, *Train up a child in the way he fhould go, and when he is old he will not depart from it.*

But fuppofing the worft that can happen, there is a great difference with refpect to the peace of your own minds, between feeing your children turn out corrupt and vicious, notwithftanding your beft and moft vigilant endeavours; and the fame thing happening in confequence

Masters of Families.

of your manifest neglect. In the former case, you are disappointed indeed, and greatly disappointed; but still you have the satisfaction to think that you have done your duty, and that you could do no more. In the latter case, nothing can alleviate your distress. If you have a just sense of things, such an event, brought on in such a manner, must bring your grey hairs with sorrow to the grave.

The virtuous and religious education of your children, besides being the best method of providing for the peace and comfort of your own future lives, and the most important service you can do for your beloved offspring, is a duty which you owe to *God*, the father of their spirits, who hath, as it were, committed them to your care for their improvement; and, likewise, a debt you owe to *society*, and the civil government under which you live, to the good laws, and wise administration of which you owe the peace and

and fecurity of your lives. If your children be well educated, they will be an honour and an advantage to your country; but except they be well principled, and have acquired good moral habits, they may prove the greateft pefts to fociety; and it might have been better for the world, if they, or their parents had never been born.

Think not, my brethren, that you have difcharged your duty to your SERVANTS, when you have fulfilled, the legal contracts you have entered into with them. The authority and influence which all mafters have over fervants, and efpecially domeftic fervants, as they give you a *power* of doing more, do, therefore, according to the general rule above laid down, include an *obligation* to do more. Be attentive, therefore, to check any irregularities you may fee your fervants running into. Allow of no methods of fpending their time that are likely to lead them into bad company,

and

Masters of Families. 9

and make them contract bad habits. Take proper opportunities of discoursing with them about their moral conduct, and the consequences of it. See that they attend some place of divine worship. If they can read, put good books into their hands, and let them want no means of improvement, in any kind of knowledge proper for their station, that you can conveniently procure them.

When your servants see you thus attentive to them, and that you have their interest, their best interest, at heart, it is more probable that they will have your interest at heart, and serve you with more attachment and fidelity. The growing complaint, that servants have no care of their masters interests, may have a variety of causes; but it appears to me, that one of them is the little attention that masters pay to the interest, the morals, and the religious instruction of their servants. This last part of the duty of masters is much easier to discharge, when the servants are of the same religious persuasion with themselves. When the case is otherwise, servants who are at an age to judge for themselves, will less bear to be advised in any thing that has the least relation to religion. However, in this case, a great part of the duty above-mentioned may be discharged with the utmost strictness, without seeming to impose, in the least, in matters of religion.

I would observe in this place, that masters of families have many opportunities of making useful reflections upon *particular occurrences*, and that they ought carefully to improve them; in order to give young persons and servants a turn for thinking and reflecting themselves. In this manner the probity, good character, and success of some, and the profligacy, infamy, and ruin of others, of their neighbours and acquaintance, may be turned to good account. Moral instructions, thus exemplified, have a double force upon the mind. Also, by attending to particular events,

Masters of Families.

events, an habitual regard to God, both in gratitude for his mercies, and a fear of his judgments, may be most advantageously inculcated. In consequence of frequent reflections of this kind, persons may be taught to see the hand of God in every thing they observe or hear of, and so come to have *his fear at all times before their eyes*; and this great principle cannot fail to operate as a powerful motive to virtue, and a most effectual restraint against vice and wickedness.

In order to make your duty to your children and servants the easier, and more effectual, be careful, in the first place, to set them *a good example.* Let the strictest sobriety accompany your chearfulness and good humour. Let condescension go hand in hand with authority. Let integrity, and the strictest honour, appear in all your dealings between man and man; and let it be seen, that you make conscience of doing your duty to God, your father and master in heaven,

at

at the fame time that you require the duty of your children and fervants to you, as their father and mafter on earth. This duty of *example* alone is more than a thoufand exhortations. Thefe can only be repeated occafionally, whereas the other is feen, and has influence every day, and every hour of the day. This cannot fail to have the happieft effect upon a family, and operate equally to your benefit, and that of all who are under your care.

Befides this principal article, of good example, I fhall only recommend to your attention two things, which have fo good an effect with refpect to the religious inftruction, and improvement of your children and fervants, in every thing that is virtuous and good, that I do not fcruple to call them two important branches of family duty.

The firft is CATECHISING; but as I have urged this in the preface to my
fmall

Masters of Families. 13

small *Catechism*, I shall say nothing about it here.

The second is FAMILY-PRAYER, which, I am afraid, is growing into neglect with some of the politer part of this age, who have seen or heard so much of the appearance of religion in former times, that they seem ashamed to leave any trace by which it might be known, to their most intimate acquaintance, that they have any religion at all.

I do not pretend to produce any express scripture authority for the observance of this duty. One of the excellencies of our religion consists in the small number of its positive institutions. The observance of the *Lord's day*, for the purpose of religious worship, cannot be directly proved from the New Testament, but the moral and devotional tendency of the christian religion is evident; and therefore we ought, of ourselves, to adopt those customs, which, without being superstitious, perftitious, do really tend to promote the purpofes of virtue and devotion in our own minds, and the minds of others. And, in this rational view of things, the obfervance of family prayer feems to want no other recommendation.

"This practice," fays the excellent Archbifhop Tillotfon, " is fo neceffary to " keep alive, and maintain a fenfe of God " and religion on the minds of men, that " where it is neglected, I cannot fee how " any family can, in reafon, be deemed " a family of chriftians, or indeed to have " any religion at all." I do not join in all the feverity of this cenfure, but I think there is the greateft reafon in the remark which introduces it.

In a multiplicity of worldly affairs, we are certainly too apt to forget God, and the *one great bufinefs* on which we are fent into this world; but we cannot help being reminded of it, if it be our cuftom to affemble in families every day, to read fome useful

useful portion of scripture, and to join in an act of rational devotion, expressing the sense we have of our dependence upon God, our maker and benefactor, our reliance upon his mercy, our confidence in his providence, and our resignation to his will, in all the events of this transitory life, in which we are to be trained up for a better life after death.

This practice, my brethren, will naturally prevent much of the irregularity into which we are apt to be betrayed by the impetuosity of our passions. By this means we may have the fear of God always before our eyes, and walk with God all the day long. By this means we may go through the business of the day with greater pleasure, in humble expectation that, while we thus acknowledge God in all our ways, he will direct our paths, and make every thing that befalls us subservient to our real good. And, lastly, your children and servants, seeing you regular

regular and devout in the performance of this duty, cannot fail to conceive a greater reverence for religion; and by this means its sanctions, and the obligations of virtue in general, will have a stronger influence over them as long as they live. I may add, that you yourselves will appear more respectable in their esteem, and your authority will have greater weight on that account.

Every family is so much a separate and independent society, that no argument can be produced for *public worship* of any kind, that will not even more strongly enforce *family worship*. The connection between members of the same family is closer, and more intimate, than the connection between the members of the same political society, and the subjects of the same civil government. They are naturally more united both in interest, and affection. A family, therefore, being so much one person, the obligation to family worship approaches to the obligation
of

of private devotion. Moreover, the members of the fame family, having such intimate intercourse, and so many things in common, have, consequently, many relative and reciprocal duties; and the sense and obligation of all these must be greatly strengthened by joint prayer.

The difficulties attending the performance of this duty appear to me to be such, as might easily be surmounted, by men who are not altogether destitute of firmness of mind, and whose conduct in life would be no reproach to the forms of rational devotion. The service itself, when conducted with propriety, is a decent, and becoming thing, nor does it need to take up much time. Long prayers, we know, were particularly objected to by our Lord himself; and, in all cases, the benefit of the exercise must be derived from the propriety, and the fervour of our devotions, and not from the length of them. If it be inconvenient for the family to assemble for this purpose *twice*
every

every day, particularly in the morning, let it be done in the evening, after the bufinefs of the day is over. To avoid oftentation, which is fo hateful in religion, it may be deferred till any company that do not fpend the night in the family be gone home; or if it be omitted occafionally, ftill let it be done whenever nothing extraordinary prevents it, and when the family can be alone. The real good effect of family devotion will not be fenfibly leffened by thofe omiffions and interruptions, which are either cafual, or are evidently made to avoid the appearance of oftentation.

After all, I do not expect that I fhall be able to recommend this duty to thofe who give into the gaities of this luxurious and diffipated age. It will not fuit with a mafter of a family being much from home, with his generally keeping bad hours, and much lefs bad and rakifh company. It is a ferious thing, but it ought to be remembered, that we come into the world

Masters of Families. 19

world upon very serious business, and must give a serious account of the manner in which we acquit ourselves in it.

Religion, my brethren, is the great business of our lives. Our abode in this world is short and precarious. In the beautiful and expressive language of the scriptures, *We have here no continuing city, and are only strangers and pilgrims on the earth*; but we are to be some where else for ever, and our happiness or misery in a future and unknown state of being depends upon our behaviour here. In this situation, it is certainly our wisdom, *in this our day, to mind the things that relate to our everlasting peace and welfare, before they are for ever hid from our eyes*. If you be laughed at for the appearance of decent and rational devotion, consider who they are that ridicule you on this account, and of how short continuance, and of what little moment, is the *laughter of fools*. The beginning of any new, though laudable practice, may require some degree of courage;

A serious Address to

courage; but the exertion of that courage is virtue, and it is glorious for a man to be fingular in that which is good.

According to the maxims of the prefent age, it is poffible, that even for the common decencies of religion, you may be cenfured by fome, as precife, and righteous over much; and you may pafs for men of no fpirit or tafte; but confider the time is coming, when many of our prefent notions and maxims will vanifh like a dream; when he only will be accounted a man of true fpirit, to have acquired a juft fenfe of honour, and to have formed himfelf to a juft method of thinking and acting, who has had the refolution to fubdue his paffions, who has had the fortitude to refift the folicitations of bad company, and the fteadinefs to act a wife, moderate, and virtuous part through life; whereas he who has fuffered his vain mind to be carried away by the current maxims of a licentious age, who has fuffered himfelf to be feduced by the artifices

ces of his vicious and profligate companions, who could not stand the shock of ridicule and reproach, but has been laughed and bantered out of his virtue, will be ranked among the meanest, the most abject, and contemptible of all wretches. And this day, which will try every man's work what it is, and shew who have acted the truely sensible, wise, and spirited part, is not far off; for after *death* comes the *judgement*; and what is our *life, it is even as a vapour, which appears for a little time, and then vanishes away.*

I shall close this address with a few passages selected from various parts of the scriptures, expressing the duties of masters with respect to their families.

Gen. xviii. 19. *I know him* (says God concerning Abraham) *that he will command his children, and his houshold after him, and they shall keep the way of the Lord, to do justice and judgement.*

A serious Address to

Deut. vi. 6, 7. *And these words which I command thee this day shall be in thine heart, and thou shalt teach them diligently unto thy children, and shalt talk of them when thou sittest in thine house, and when thou walkest by the way, and when thou liest down, and when thou risest up.*

Joshua xxiv. 15. *As for me, and my house* (saith Joshua) *we will serve the Lord.*

Psalm ci. 2, &c. *I will behave myself wisely in a perfect way. I will walk within my house with a perfect heart. Mine eyes shall be upon the faithful of the land, that they may dwell with me. He that walketh in a perfect way he shall serve me. He that worketh deceit shall not dwell within my house, he that telleth lies shall not tarry in my sight.*

Job xxxi. 13—15. *If I did despise the cause of my man-servant or of my maid-servant, when they contended with me. What then shall I do when God riseth up; and*

when

Masters of Families.

when he visiteth, what shall I answer him? Did not he that made me in the womb, make him; and did not one fashion us in the womb?

Coloss. iv. 1.—Eph. vi. 9. *Masters give unto your servants that which is just and equal, knowing that ye also have a master in heaven, and there is no respect of persons with him.*

Prov. xxii. 6.—xiii. 24. *Train up a child in the way he should go, and when he is old he will not depart from it. He that spareth his rod hateth his son, but he that loveth him chasteneth him betimes.*

Eph. vi. 4. *Ye fathers, provoke not your children to wrath, but bring them up in the nurture and admonition of the Lord.*

To assist you in the proper conduct of family prayer, I shall subjoin a few forms composed for that purpose, with the addition of *shorter forms* for some particular occasions,

occasions, which may be introduced when they are found to be expedient.

As it will seldom be convenient to read more than one chapter at once on these occasions, I would advise, that, in general, choice be made of the *four gospels*, the *book of Acts*, and *the practical parts of the apostolical epistles.* These contain what is most fundamental and useful in christian knowledge, and in them the great duties of the christian life are inculcated with clearness and energy. Several of the *Psalms* may also be read with peculiar advantage at these devotional exercises.

PRAYERS

PRAYERS
FOR
FAMILIES.

The First Prayer.

Almighty and moſt merciful God, we thy dependent creatures preſent ourſelves before thee, under a deep ſenſe of our manifold obligations to thee, as our maker, preſerver, and benefactor. Thou art he who haſt made us, and not we ourſelves. We are the workmanſhip of thine hands, what thine own fingers have framed; and we are curiouſly and wonderfully made, every part of our bodies bearing evident marks of thine infinite wifdom and goodnefs. More efpecially do we rejoice in the rank which thou haft been pleafed that we fhould hold in thy creation, as rational and immortal beings, and thank thee for thofe powers whereby we are capable of attaining to the knowledge of thee our God, and of underftanding and doing thy holy will.

We thank thee for all thy goodnefs to us in this life, and that the earth, which thou haft given us to inhabit, is fo full of the riches of thy goodnefs. We thank thee for the bread that we eat, for the raiment with which we are cloathed, for the bleffings of fociety and friendfhip, and for every thing that contributes to make our fituation in this world comfortable and happy. But, above all, do we thank thee for, the

the revelation of thy will to mankind, in order to recover men from that ſtate of vice and miſery into which they were fallen, and for the gracious promiſes thou haſt made us, by thy ſon Jeſus Chriſt, of the free forgiveneſs of all our ſins, of a reſurrection from the dead, and a life of immortal happineſs in a future ſtate, if we repent of what we have done amiſs, and endeavour to live according to the precepts of his goſpel.

We are ſenſible that in many things we have all broken thy holy and righteous laws, ſo as juſtly to have incurred thy diſpleaſure; but do thou, we humbly intreat thee, according to thy abundant mercy declared to mankind in the goſpel of thy ſon, blot out all our tranſgreſſions, and receive us into thy divine favour; and may we be enabled, from the motives of

our

our holy religion, to walk more circumspectly and unblameably before thee for the time to come.

May we love thee, the Lord our God, with all our hearts, and our neighbour as ourselves, doing to others as we would that they should do to us; and may we in all things live righteously, soberly, and godly in this present evil world.

In a faithful and chearful endeavour to discharge this our duty, and to preserve our consciences void of offence so long as we shall live; may we be enabled, according to thy gracious encouragement, to cast all our cares upon thee who carest for us, depending upon thy promise, that if we, in the first place, secure that good part which can never be taken from us, all other things shall be added unto us; and that, after having seen thy
goodness

goodnefs in the land of the living, when we shall have fought the good fight of faith, and finished our christian courfe with joy, an abundant entrance will be adminiftered unto us into the everlafting kingdom of our Lord and Saviour Jefus Chrift.

[*In this place may any of the* occafional forms *be introduced.*]

Hear us, Almighty God, in thefe our requefts, as the difciples of thy fon Chrift Jefus, through whom to thee, O Father, be glory for ever. *Amen.*

The Second Prayer.

ALmighty God and heavenly Father, we adore thee as the greateft and beft of all beings, intitled to the higheft reverence, love, and confidence of all thy rational creatures..

creatures. Thou art the maker and preserver of all things. Thou spakest and it was done, thou commandedst and all things stood fast, and they still continue according to thy first wise appointment, for all are thy servants. As thou hast made all things, so thou hast abundantly provided for the supply of all the wants of thy creatures. They all have their eyes up unto thee, and thou openest thine hand, and satisfiest the desire of every living thing.

We also have largely shared thy bounty; yet, with shame and confusion of face, we acknowledge, that the God in whose hand our breath is, and whose are all our ways, have we not glorified. In many things we offend all. Shouldst thou be strict to mark iniquity, O Lord, who could stand! But it is our happiness to have to do with a God who is merciful and gracious, long fuffering, abundant in mercy, and goodnefs, and truth; who is not willing that any fhould perifh, but had rather that all fhould repent and live.

Being encouraged, in the gofpel of thy fon Jefus Chrift, to expect the free forgivenefs of all our fins, upon our fincere repentance, we would refolve, that wherein we are now convinced we have hitherto done amifs, we will, for the future, do fo no more, and endeavour to walk in all the commandments of God blamelefs. Do thou affift us to fulfil thefe our refolutions; and left the cares of this world fhould overpower the good motions of our minds, may we ever have prefent to our thoughts the moft important motives to a virtuous life and converfation. In a more efpecial
manner,

manner, may we live under a strong sense of thine universal presence; and while we consider that thine eyes are in every place, beholding both the evil and the good; that thou knowest even the thoughts of our hearts (for that all things are naked and open to the eyes of him with whom we have to do) and that, as thou now seest in secret, thou wilt one day reward openly, may we keep the strictest watch over our thoughts, our words, and our actions; and may no temptation seduce us from the path of our known duty.

Professing ourselves to be the disciples of Christ, may we make his instructions the rule of our lives, and carefully copy after his great example; that we, like him, may be holy, harmless and undefiled, intent upon fulfilling the will of him who sends us into this world, and finishing his work; and maintaining a perfect resignation to thy righteous will in all the events of life. Being chriftians, may we confider that, like our Lord and Mafter, we are not of this world. May we, therefore, as ftrangers and pilgrims on earth, be endeavouring to raife our affections from all things here below, that we may have our treafure in heaven, from whence alfo we look for a faviour, the Lord Jefus Chrift, who shall change thefe our mortal bodies, and fashion them like to his own glorified body, in that day when corruption shall put on incorruption, and this mortal be fwallowed up of immortality. Animated by this glorious hope, fet before us in the gofpel of thy fon, may it be our daily endeavour to abftain from all the corruptions of this world, and to cultivate that holinefs of heart and life,

life, without which no man can see the Lord.

[*In this place may any of the* occasional forms *be introduced.*]

These our petitions we humbly offer up to thee as the disciples of thy son Jesus Christ, who has taught us when we pray to say,

Our Father, who art in heaven, hallowed be thy name. Thy kingdom come. Thy will be done on earth, as it is in heaven. Give us this day our daily bread. Forgive us our trespasses, as we forgive them that trespass against us; and lead us not into temptation, but deliver us from evil: for thine is the kingdom, and the power, and the glory, for ever and ever. Amen.

The THIRD PRAYER.

Almighty God, and moſt merciful father! the maker, preſerver, and governor of all things; who neglecteſt nothing that thou haſt made. In thy hand is the life of every living thing, and the breath of all mankind. Thou giveſt food unto all fleſh; and we obſerve, with admiration, the ſuitable proviſion thou haſt made for the ſupport and comfort of all thy wanting creatures.

We deſire to be, at all times, very ſenſible of, and to rejoice in our own ſtate of dependance on thee; for we alſo are the work of thy hands, and under the care of thy providence. May we never fail to glorify thee, in
whoſe

whofe hand our life and breath are, and whofe are all our ways.

Deeply impreffed with this conviction, we defire to unite in grateful acknowledgments of thy manifold and great benefits to us. We praife thee for the gift, and prefervation of life; for the wonderful and ufeful frame of our bodies, for the excellence and foundnefs of the capacities of our minds, for that meafure of health which thy good providence continueth to us, and for the many comforts which flow from thence. We thank thee for a daily fupply of many things needful for our fupport and conducive to our delight.

We gratefully acknowledge the kindnefs of thy providence in all the comforts and fervices we derive from fociety, society, neighbourhood, and friendship; for the daily endearments of relative affections, and the good offices resulting from our domestic connections one with another, and also for the security to our persons and properties; together with the other manifold and great advantages we enjoy by means of our situation in this land of religious and civil liberty, and of the protection of the equitable constitution and good government under which we live. Surely, the lines are fallen to us in pleasant places, and we have a goodly heritage. Blessed be the Lord, who hath shewn us so largely of his goodness in the land of the living.

But, above all, would we praise thee, with our whole hearts, for thy great mercy manifested to mankind by thy son Christ Jesus; whom
thou

thou haft given, that whofoever believeth in him fhould not perifh, but have everlafting life. We thank thee for the heavenly inftructions, the holy precepts, and the exceeding great and precious promifes delivered to us in the gofpel. We thank thee for the benefits of our Lord's excellent and perfuafive doctrines; his amiable and perfect pattern; his plain and profitable inftitutions, his exemplary obedience, even unto death; his glorious refurrection, which is a pattern and affurance of that refurrection which he hath promifed to us; and for his triumphant afcenfion, now to appear in the prefence of God for us. Having fuch an high-prieft over the houfe of God, we would at all times draw near to thee, our Father in heaven, with pure hearts, in full affurance of faith; believing that thou art a bountiful rewarder of all them that diligently feek thee.

May

May it be the earneſt deſire of our hearts, and our continual endeavour, to walk worthy of the holy vocation wherewith we are called, as the children of thee, our God and Father, and the diſciples of thy holy and beloved ſon Chriſt Jeſus. To which end diſpoſe us diligently to read and conſider, and enable us to underſtand the word of thy truth, eſpecially, the goſpel of our Lord Jeſus. May we receive the good ſeed of thy heavenly word in the love of it, cheriſh it in good and honeſt hearts, and bring forth the proper fruits of it in all holy diſpoſitions, and a ſober, righteous and godly converſation.

Incline us to reverence and love thee above all things; to maintain a continual regard to thine authority and inſpection over us; to rejoice in our dependance on thy government;

to

to be satisfied with thy difpofals, thankful for thy mercies, patient under thy corrections, confiding in thy promifes, that all things fhall work together for good to them that love thee. In all the events and employments of life may we fet thee, the Lord, always before us; making thy perfections our confidence, thy precepts our counfellors, thy promifes the rejoicing of our hearts, and the hope of thine acceptance, and of glory, honour and immortality in thy heavenly kingdom, our animating motives to a patient continuance in all well-doing. And, O! that there may be fuch an heart in us, that we may fear thee, and keep all thy commandments always, that it may be well with us.

Affift us to cherifh all kinds and good affections towards all men; and to
fupprefs

suppress and root out of our hearts all bitterness, envy, hatred, malice and all uncharitableness. Enable us to maintain, at all times, truth in our words, sincerity in our professions, faithfulness to our engagements, and integrity and righteousness in all our dealings. Whatsoever we would that men should do unto us, may we do even so unto them, in serious expectation of thy righteous judgment, wherein there will be no respect of persons.

Animate us with a spirit of unconfined love and good-will, that we may be ready to do good and to communicate, as we have ability and opportunity, to whomsoever we can serve or oblige. Especially may we never fail in sincere gratitude to our friends and benefactors; and as we hope, that thou, our most merciful father,

father, wilt forgive us our fins, if we be penitent, may we alfo, from the heart, forgive thofe who have offended, or injured us, when they turn to us; in the mean time guarding againft malice, and forbearing revenge. May we be always ready to perform with chearfulnefs all good offices towards our neighbours and acquaintance; and, if it pleafe thee, make us inftruments of thy gracious providence for real benefits to thofe among whom we dwell.

We farther befeech thee, O moft pure and holy God, the father of our fpirits, to enable us to purify ourfelves from all filthinefs of flefh and fpirit, and to perfect holinefs in thy fear. May we continually preferve a due government over our affections and paffions, be watchful againft all pride, vain-glory and hypocrify, and
fupprefs

suppress all foolish opinions and hurtful lusts. May we regulate our spirits by humility and meekness, keep our bodies in purity and temperance, and use the good things of this world as not abusing them; but so, as that we may give a good account of them to our own reflections, and to the final judge. May we be prudent and circumspect in our conduct, contented in our lot, industrious in our callings, and both in our present and every future station of life, maintain consciences void of offence towards God and towards man; that we may adorn the doctrine of God our Saviour in all things.

May we at all times consider seriously, and feel the powerful influences of the prospects set before us by the gospel of thy son Jesus. Firmly persuaded of the truth of all thy promises delivered by him, may we behave as pilgrims and ſtrangers upon earth, where we have no continuing city; but ſeek for a better country, even an heavenly one, a city which hath foundations, whoſe builder and maker is God. May the ſupreme deſires of our hearts, and our unwearied endeavours, concur with the methods of thy providence and grace, to complete our meetneſs for the inheritance prepared for us.

Finally, O thou father of all the families upon earth, we commit ourſelves unto thee in our domeſtic capacity and family relations. Be thou the guardian of our common intereſts; beſtow upon us all needful ſupplies and bleſſings, and protect us from real evil. Aſſiſt us all to diſcharge the duties we ſeverally owe one to another, as the ſervants of God

our

our common master in heaven. With kind affections one towards another may we mutually share in prosperity and adversity, and be helpful one to another in every temporal and eternal interest. May we live in love and peace, and may the God of love and peace dwell with us; and, in the end, make us all sharers in eternal life and happiness, through our Lord Jesus Christ.

Now unto him who is able to keep us from falling, and to present us faultless before the presence of his glory with exceeding joy; to the only wise God, our Saviour, be glory and majesty, dominion and power, now and ever. *Amen.*

FORMS
FOR
PARTICULAR OCCASIONS,

To be ufed at the Difcretion of the Perfon who conducts the Service.

1. To be ufed in the Morning.

WE thank thee, heavenly father, for thy care over us the laſt night, that we were preſerved from diſagreeable accidents in the hours of ſleep, and that we are brought to ſee the light of another day in ſuch comfortable circumſtances. May we be in thy fear all the day long, and may this fear be an effectual reſtraint upon us, that we commit no ſin or folly.

2. To be used in the Evening.

WE thank thee, heavenly father, for thy goodness to us this day past. Through thy good hand upon us we continue hitherto; and we commit ourselves to thy care and protection this approaching night. May thy good providence be our guard, from all the dangers to which we are exposed in the defenceless hours of repose; and make us to awake in the morning, rejoicing in thy goodness, and refreshed with moderate rest, for the discharge of the duties of the day ensuing.

3. To be used on Sundays.

BLESS, we intreat thee, most merciful father, our attendance on the public worship of christians this day. We thank thee for the opportunity we enjoy of worshipping thee according to the dictates of our consciences, without any to molest us, or make us afraid. May we be careful to improve this great privilege in the best manner. May thy word, which we read, and which is explained to us, be a light to our feet, and a lamp unto our path. May it enter deep into our hearts, and bring forth fruit in our future lives and conversations. When, upon these occasions, we join with our fellow creatures, and fellow christians, in one common address to thee, the father of our spirits, expressing our joint sentiments, desires, and expectations, do thou hear in heaven, and grant us an answer of peace. And by worshipping thee here below, with reverence and godly fear, may our minds be formed for the delightful exercises and enjoyments of a future world.

4. For Relations, &c.

BLESS, we intreat thee, heavenly father, all our relations, our friends, neighbours, and acquaintance. May we so live together in thy fear, in a mutual intercourse of good and kind offices, and a regard for each other's best interests, that when we have been separated by death, we may meet again in thy glorious and everlasting kingdom; where we shall be happy in the enjoyment of thee our God, and of each other, to all eternity.

5. For Persons of different Conditions in Life.

CONSIDERING this world as a state of trial and probation, may we cultivate those virtues which our situation and circumstances peculiarly require,

quire, and learn wifdom and inftruction from all the difpenfations of thy providence. If we be rich in this word, may we confider every thing we enjoy as the gift of thy bounty, and endeavour to be rich in good works, ready to diftribute, willing to communicate, laying up for ourfelves a good foundation for the time to come. If it feem good to thy wife and righteous providence, that we be poor in this world, may we be humble and induftrious ; rich in faith, and heirs of an inheritance; incorruptible, undefiled, and that fadeth not away, referved in heaven for us.

6. For Perfons of different Ages.

TEACH thofe who are young to remember thee their creator in the days of their youth, to avoid the fnares of bad company, and to employ the morning of their life in acquiring that
knowledge

knowledge and virtue, which may make them uſeful members of ſociety, and fill them with pleaſing reflections when they come to die. Bleſs the aged. Support their minds under the decays of nature, that as their outward man grows weaker and weaker, their inward man may grow ſtronger and ſtronger; till, in thy due time, they obtain their difmiſſion from the infirmities and troubles of this mortal life, and be admitted to the joys of thine heavenly and everlaſting kingdom.

7. For Huſbands and Wives.

MAY thoſe who are engaged in the conjugal relation live in perfect love and harmony. May all their thoughts and actions tend to advance their common intereſt and happineſs. May they walk before their houſe in a perfect way, be examples of ſobriety, and every virtue, to their dependents;

and

and having faithfully difcharged all the important duties of the family relation on earth, may they be admitted members of the great family of thy children in heaven.

8. For Parents and Children.

TEACH parents, by a proper mixture of gentlenefs and feverity, to train up their children in the paths of wifdom and virtue, and thereby to make the beft provifion for their temporal and eternal welfare. And may children be taught to honour and obey their parents, and be the comfort and fupport of their age, in return for the obligations conferred upon them in their early years.

9. For Mafters and Servants.

INCLINE the hearts of mafters not to rule with rigour, but to give

to

to their fervants that which is juft and equal, remembering that they alfo have a mafter in heaven, with whom there is no refpect of perfons. And may fervants be obedient unto their mafters, not with eye-fervice, as men-pleafers, but in finglenefs of heart, fearing God; knowing that whatever good thing any man doth, the fame fhall he receive, whether he be bound or free.

10. For Perfons under Affliction in general.

SANCTIFY to us, heavenly father, the afflictive difpenfation of thy providence, with which thou haft vifited us. We blefs thy name, that, in the midft of judgment, thou rememberest mercy, and afflicteft us lefs than our iniquities deferve. We would endeavour to humble ourfelves under thy mighty

mighty hand, and to learn patience and obedience by the things which we ſuffer. By all the viciſſitudes of this mortal life, may we learn to raiſe our affections from all things here below, and be taught to look for our chief portion and happineſs in a future and better world. If it be thy pleaſure, remove this ſtroke from us, that we may again rejoice in thy goodneſs, and bleſs thy name.

11. A Thankſgiving for the Removal of Affliction in general.

WE thank thee, heavenly father, for the favour thou haſt ſhewn to this family, in removing the afflictions under which we laboured. What ſhall we render to thee the God of our mercies, who crowneſt our lives with thy goodneſs! Bleſs the Lord O our ſouls, and all that is within us bleſs
his

his holy name. Write upon our hearts a law of love and gratitude, and may our lives be devoted to thy service.

12. In case of dangerous Sickness.

DO thou, our most merciful God and father, who art a present help in time of trouble, and who hast, in thy word, particularly encouraged those who are afflicted to pray, have compassion on thy *servant*, on whom thou hast laid thine afflictive hand. Thou sayest to diseases, Go, and they go; Come, and they come, to answer the wise and gracious purposes of thy providence. If it be thy pleasure, restore thy *servant* to *his* health, and a capacity of usefulness in life. But, above all, do thou fit *him*, and all of us who are concerned for *him*, for thy holy will;

will; and whatever be the iſſue, may all theſe afflictions, which are but for a moment, be a means of working out for us a far more exceeding, even an eternal weight of glory, by making us to look not ſo much at the things which are ſeen, and temporary, as at thoſe things which are unſeen and eternal.

13. A Thankſgiving for Recovery from Sickneſs.

WE join with thy *ſervant* in returning thee thanks for the great mercy thou haſt ſhown to *him*, in *his* recovery from a dangerous diſorder. May a grateful ſenſe of this thy goodneſs deeply impreſs *his* mind, and all our minds; and may *his* life which thou haſt ſpared, and may our lives, which thou preſerveſt by the watchful care of thy providence over us, be devoted to thy ſervice.

14. To

14. To be used after the Death of a Relation, or, in the Time of great Sickness and Mortality in the Neighbourhood.

DO thou, who hast, in great wisdom and justice, appointed unto all men once to die; who hast said to the children of men, Dust ye are, and to dust ye shall return; grant that when we see this aweful sentence put in execution; when we attend our friends, relations, and acquaintance, to their last and silent habitations, we may be seriously reminded of our own mortality; and considering the uncertainty, as well as the shortness of our abode in this world; considering that we cannot tell what a day or an hour may bring forth, that, perhaps, even this very night our souls may be required of us, may we be excited to

use

use all diligence in working the work of God while it is day, knowing that the night of death comes (and may surprise us) in which no man can work: for there is no work or devise, or knowledge, or wisdom, in the grave, whither we are hasting.

Duly influenced by these considerations, may we be enabled to live the life of the righteous, that so our latter end may be like his, full of hope and joy. Having retained our integrity so long as we live, at the hour of death may not our hearts reproach us; but on leaving this world, may we be able to sing the christian triumphant song, O death, where is thy sting? O grave, where is thy victory? and finally, when we, with the rest of mankind, shall stand before thy righteous tribunal at the last day, may we hear this joyful sentence pronounced upon us,
Well

Well done, good and faithful servants, enter ye into the joy of your Lord.

15. To be used before a Journey.

DO thou, who preservest man and beast, protect thy *servant*, who is undertaking a journey, from all the dangers to which *he* may be exposed in the course of it. Teach *him* to acknowledge thee in all *his* ways, do thou direct *his* paths, and cause *him* to return in health and safety to *his* family and friends.

16. A Thanksgiving after a Return from a Journey.

WE join with thy *servant* in returning thee thanks, for preserving *him* from all the dangers to which *he* has been exposed in a journey, and for restoring *him* to *his* family and friends

friends in health and safety. While we rejoice in thy goodness on this account, may we be careful to express the sense we have of our obligation to thee, by a suitable life and conversation.

17. To be used before a Voyage.

DO thou, who sayest to the sea, Be calm, and its waves obey thy commandment, preserve thy *servant*, who is undertaking a voyage, from the dangers to which *he* will be exposed on that unstable element; and give *his* friends an opportunity of rejoicing with *him*, and praising thy name, on *his* safe return.

18. To be used after a Voyage.

WE thank thee, Lord of heaven and earth, who raisest, and stillest the waves of the sea, that thou hast
graciously

graciously preserved thy *servant* from the dangers to which *he* has been exposed in *his* voyage. May *he* be duly sensible of *his* obligation to thee, the author of all good, and live to thy praise.

19. For a Woman near the Time of Delivery.

MAY thy favour and blessing attend thy handmaid, who is expecting the painful hour of child-birth. Bring her to her proper time, and make joy and gladness succeed to anxiety and pain.

20. A Thanksgiving after a safe Delivery.

WE join with thine handmaid, in returning thee thanks, for delivering her in the perilous hour of child-bearing, and making her the living

mother

mother of a living and perfect child. Do thou perfect her recovery, and may a sense of this thy great goodness to her deeply imprefs her mind, and all our minds. May thy servants be enabled to educate their child in the nurture and admonition of the Lord, and may it live to be the joy of its parents, and a blessing to society.

21. Another Form, to be used when the Child is dead.

WE join with thine handmaid in returning thee thanks, for delivering her in the perilous hour of childbearing, though it hath seemed good to thy wise providence not to spare the life of the child. Sanctify the affliction. Perfect the recovery of thy servant, and may a sense of this thy goodness deeply imprefs her mind, and all our minds.

22. For

22. For the whole World.

DO thou, who art the father of all the families of the earth, extend thy compaſſion to all our brethren of mankind. May the great bleſſings of thy ſon's goſpel be univerſally diffuſed. Purify chriſtian churches from every thing that debaſes their religion, and obſtructs its efficacy on the minds of men; and may it finally prevail, to the extirpation of idolatry, Mohammedan deluſion, and Popiſh ſuperſtition. May thine antient people the Jews be at length brought within the pale of the church of Chriſt, together with the fulneſs of the Gentiles; that, in thy due time, all thy rational offspring may be worſhippers of thee, the only living and true God, by Jeſus Chriſt whom thou haſt ſent.

23. For our Country.

SHEW thy favour to this land of our nativity, the kingdoms of Great Britain and Ireland, and all our colonies and plantations abroad. Pardon our many fins, which might juftly bring down upon us thy heavy judgments. Promote the great work of reformation among all ranks and degrees of men among us; and may we continue to be a people highly favoured of thee our God, in confequence of our being to thee a peculiar people, zealous of good works. Blefs thy fervant our fovereign king George. Eftablifh his throne in righteoufnefs, and may the prefent reigning family be the inftruments, in thy hands, of continuing to us our invaluable liberties civil and religious. Blefs the queen, and every branch of the royal family,

family, and make them as eminent for their princely virtues and accomplifhments, as they are for their high ftations in life. Give peace in our times, O Lord, or grant fuccefs to our arms, in every juft and neceffary war. May our manufactures and commerce flourifh. May we have proper weather for bringing to perfection, and for gathering in the fruits of the earth. Thus may our poor be fatisfied with bread; and while we live in the enjoyment of every temporal bleffing, may we not abufe thy goodnefs by indulging to luxury and excefs, but may we exprefs our gratitude to thee, the giver of all good, by the temperate and generous ufe of all our bleffings.

24. For

24. For the Parliament and the King's Minifters.

BLESS, O Lord, we intreat thee, the great council of the nation, and make all their confultations to iffue in the public good. May thofe who are intrufted with the conduct of national affairs be endowed with wifdom and integrity, proper for their important ftations. Succeed their juft and good defigns, and overrule all their meafures for the real good of this people.

THE

INDEX.

	Page
THE First Prayer,	25
The Second Prayer,	29
The Third Prayer,	35

OCCASIONAL FORMS.

1. To be used in the Morning, — 46
2. To be used in the Evening, — 47
3. To be used on Sundays, — 47
4. For Relations, &c. — 49
5. For Persons of different Conditions in Life, — 49
6. For Persons of different Ages, — 50
7. For Husbands and Wives, — 51
8. For Parents and Children, — 52
9. For Masters and Servants, — 53
10. For Persons under Affliction in general, — 53
11. A Thanksgiving for the Removal of Afflictions in general, — 54

THE INDEX.

Page

12. In cafe of dangerous Sicknefs, — 55
13. A Thanfgiving for Recovery from Sicknefs, — 56
14. To be ufed after the Death of a Relation, or, in the Time of great Sicknefs and Mortality in the Neighbourhood, — 47
15. To be ufed before a Journey, — 59
16. A Thankfgiving after a Return from a Journey — 59
17. To be ufed before a Voyage, — 60
18. To be ufed after a Voyage, — 60
19. For a Woman near the Time of Delivery, — 61
20. A Thankfgiving after a fafe Delivery, — 61
21. Another Form to be ufed when the Child is dead, — 62
22. For the whole World, — 63
23. For our Country, — 64
24. For the Parliament and the King's Minifters, — 66

THE END.

FREE ADDRESS

TO

Proteſtant Diſſenters,

AS SUCH.

By a DISSENTER.

The SECOND EDITION, enlarged.

After the manner which they call hereſy, ſo worſhip I the God of my fathers. PAUL.

LONDON:
Printed for J. JOHNSON, No. 72, in St. Paul's Church-Yard.
MDCCLXXI.

BT
1030
P7
1779

PREFACE.

THE prefent fituation of the diffenting intereft makes any apology for this addrefs fuperfluous. If the author be blamed for reflecting on the church of England, when he can plead no particular provocation for it; let it be confidered, that this has been done only *indirectly*, and when his fubject unavoidably led to it. As the addrefs is directed to *diffenters* only; the members of the eftablifhed church have no bufinefs with it; and if they never look into what is not addreffed to them, or intended for their infpection, no offence can be taken. If notwithftanding this, they cannot refift a curiofity to pry into the concerns of their neighbours, themselves only are answerable for the consequences, not the author.

If, in this case, they do not find this performance to be written in the tame and humble stile of an *apologist*, they should consider that the writer does not think there is any thing in the principles of the dissenters as such, so palpably open to objection, as to require an apology.

The things that seem to want an apology are the doctrines of original sin, predestination, trinity in unity, satisfaction by vicarious punishments, &c. a hierarchy, consisting of persons with names and powers altogether unknown in the New Testament; ecclesiastical persons, as such, invested with civil power, contrary to the very genius of the religion of Jesus Christ, whose kingdom was not of this world; and civil officers assuming a power to decide concerning articles of faith; subscriptions to creeds of human composition;

the

the impofition of ceremonies by the authority of men, in a church, of which Chrift alone is the head; and the abfolute enjoining of rites, which are the remains and badges of popifh fuperftition; fuch as the wearing of a furplice, the fign of the crofs, with god-fathers and god-mothers, in baptifm; confirmation by the impofition of the hands of a bifhop; wheeling about to the eaft, and bowing at the name of *Jefus*, as if it was a mere found that was worfhipped, and the enjoining of the pofture of kneeling at the lord's fupper, &c. &c. &c. Such as thefe are the things that look as if they wanted fome *apology*; for, certainly, their reafonablenefs is far from being evident at firft fight.

If it be afked, why the author chofe to conceal his name, he frankly acknowledges, that it was not becaufe he was apprehenfive of making himfelf obnoxious to the members of the church of England. If they underftand him right, they will perceive that his intentions towards them are far from being unfriendly; and if they underſtand him wrong, and put an unfair and uncandid conſtruction upon what he has written; he truſts that, with a good meaning, and in a good cauſe, he will never be over-awed by the fear of any thing that men may *think* of him, or *do* to him.

Neither was it becauſe he was apprehenſive of giving offence, either to the *miniſters*, or to the *people* among the diſſenters, becauſe he has ſpoken with equal freedom to both; but, in reality, becauſe he was unwilling to leſſen the weight of his obſervations and advice, by any reflections that might be made on the perſon from whom they come. An anonymous author is like the abſtract idea of a man, which may be conceived to be as perfect as the imagination of the reader can make it.

If,

If, however, notwithstanding all the author's precautions, any of his readers should find him out; he hopes that, along with so much *sagacity*, they will at least have the *goodness* to forgive what was well intended, and excuse imperfections in one who is, at least, desirous to render others free from them.

If any person, who is not a dissenter, should take it into his head, that by reading this Address, he will become possessed of a great secret, and be acquainted with the real sentiments and views of the dissenters, as a body, he will miserably deceive himself. Dissenters *as such* have nothing in common but a dissent from the established church; and it by no means follows that they, therefore, agree in any thing else. The majority of the dissenters will be more offended at this performance than any member of the church of England; and even that part of the dissenters to whom it is more particularly addressed will be far from being universally pleafed with it. The author is a fingle perfon, who writes without the concurrence of any other perfon whatever, and is therefore anfwerable only for his own private fentiments and conduct.

If it be faid that this addrefs was written purpofely to gain converts from the church of England; though in an indirect manner, the author can only reply by faying, that he really had no fuch views or expectations. At the fame time, he would have no objection to acknowledge it, if that had been either a primary, or a fecondary object in this publication. It is certainly no crime in a man to write in defence of what he thinks to be a good caufe, or to endeavour to gain converts to it from what he thinks to be a bad one.

He, no doubt, like the reft of mankind, fincerely wifhes that other perfons would enter into his views, and adopt his fentiments; but having no *dragoons* to employ for this purpofe, and no *acts of parlia-*

parliament to second him, he must be content to do what he can by the help of reason and argument alone; and these spiritual weapons, are by no means so certain in their effects on the *minds*, as carnal weapons are on the *bodies* of men; so that no person need be apprehensive, especially in this age, in which riches, fashion, and power have such influence, of any great execution being done, or any great changes being brought about by *books* only, which, few persons read, and fewer regard.

Though this address was certainly written with a serious desire to make dissenters think, and act in a manner worthy of their profession; it is not, however, any part of the author's intention to revive the spirit of a *party*; except, primarily, so far as the party has *religion*, that is the interests of its members in another world, for its object; and, secondarily, so far as the interest of this particular party, in *civil matters*, is the interest of the whole society of which they are members; having

for

for its object the cause of *liberty*, and all the valuable rights of Englishmen.

The author of this work is not much concerned about the *civil privileges* of the diffenters as such, and as a separate body in the state; but he most earnestly wishes that their liberal and generous views, with respect to civil and religious liberty, may be so fully imbibed by themselves, and so far diffused among others, as that all their countrymen, without excepting their most violent enemies, may reap the benefit of them. This performance is certainly intended to make one particular part of the commonwealth more respectable; but this part is of such a nature, that the author conceives that the necessary consequence of their being more respectable would be a great increase of glory to his country at large, from which that part would derive no particular advantage, except the honour of having contributed to it.

If

If the author appear to wish for a farther reformation in the established church, it is with no interested views, derived from his expectation of a comprehension of the dissenters in it. Were he himself permitted to new model the ecclesiastical establishment of his country, he would do it according to his best judgment, and according to his present ideas of perfection in things of that nature; but he would not be a member of it himself so long as it was a *national establishment*; because he thinks it is more for the interest of christianity, that particular societies of christians should be as free and independent as private persons. He does not apprehend that any greater inconvenience would arise from unbounded liberty being given to every man to think and act for himself in all matters of religion, than there is found to arise from the same liberty with respect to medicine. It appears to him that individuals would provide better for themselves, in both these respects, than their civil governors ever have done, are disposed, or are able to do for them. To

To *dissenters* the author recommends a candid and serious attention to the subject of this address. He was very serious in writing it, and will rejoice exceedingly if it have any good effect on ever so few of the members of that body to which he belongs. Gladly would he contribute to render them in any degree more respectable as *men*, as *Englishmen*, and as *christians*; that, unfettered as they are by any laws, but those of *their one only master, even Christ*, they may exhibit a specimen of a truly christian temper and conduct, by joining the religious zeal of their ancestors to their own enlarged views, and liberal sentiments; things which are so far from being incompatible, that they have, naturally the closest connection.

Earnestly does he wish that *ministers*, being free from the impositions of men, would apply with more assiduity to the faithful and chearful discharge of their proper duty, in enlightening the minds, and improving the hearts and the conduct of
their

their hearers; fetting them an example of unbounded confidence in divine providence, under the circumftances of a fcanty and precarious provifion, of a confcientious and fearlefs integrity in afferting *the truth as it is in Jefus*, of a generous contempt of the pleafures and pains of this life, when they tend to lead men from the path of their duty; and, univerfally, of the prevailing influence of thofe confiderations which are drawn from their character, as *citizens of heaven*, over thofe which refult from their intereft in this tranfitory world. Earneftly, alfo, does he wifh that *the people* may be duly influenced by fuch examples, and inftructions; that, though they are more engaged in the bufinefs and commerce of this world, they may not lofe fight of their relation to another.

May minifters and people jointly ftrengthen each others hands in the great work of reformation, and bear a noble teftimony againft all antichriftian errors and
fuper-

superstition. Instead of being discouraged by the reproaches and hardships to which their profession exposes them, may they rather *rejoice that they are counted worthy to suffer shame* in so glorious a cause. By their peaceable and inoffensive behaviour may prove themselves worthy of the protection of the civil government, how much soever they may disapprove of the maxims, or the administration of it. May they excite the honest emulation of the members of the established church, and of christians of every other denomination, by their zeal to promote all kinds of useful knowledge, by their attention to the advancement of the best interests of society, and by their exemplary care to understand their religion, and to live according to the rules of it; that, whatever treatment they may meet with in the world, they may secure the approbation of the great judge of hearts and actions, and, at least, *deserve well* of their country and of mankind.

ADDRESS
TO
Proteſtant Diſſenters,
AS SUCH.

My Chriſtian Brethren,

I AM a Proteſtant Diſſenter, I glory in the name, and it is with a view to render you, in general, more ſenſible of its dignity, and importance, that I take the liberty to make this free addreſs to you. Sorry I am, from a regard to the intereſts of truth and liberty, to ſee the zeal of many to cool in ſo noble a cauſe, for which our heroic anceſtors ſacrificed ſo much; when the reaſons for our diſſent are ſo far from having been leſſened, in number or weight, in the interval

be-

between their times and ours, that, in proportion to the improvements in religious knowledge, thefe reafons have been greatly multiplied, and continue to grow in number and ftrength every day. Yet, paradoxical as it may appear, thofe of us, who have thefe growing reafons to be fatisfied with this caufe of truth and liberty, are generally lefs ftrongly attached to it, and more eafily and frequently defert it, than thofe whofe opinions are fuch, that they have lefs reafon than ever to feparate from the eftablifhed church. It is to the former clafs of diffenters, therefore, that I would be underftood to addrefs myfelf in a more particular manner; and I beg nothing more, my brethren, than your candid attention, while I argue this matter with you, confidering you both in *a religious*, and *a civil* capacity. I promife you I will take up as little of your time as I can help, and ufe as few words as poffible, to make you fully fenfible of what I have to propofe to your confideration.

SECTION

SECTION I.

Of the importance of the diffenting intereft, with refpect to religion.

IF I confider the fubject of our diffent as a matter purely *religious*, I cannot help thinking it of the utmoft importance, even to the caufe of chriftianity in general. That grofs corruptions have been introduced into this moft excellent fcheme of religion, corruptions which began very early, and which have been confirmed by long continuance, corruptions which totally disfigure it, and defeat the principal ends of its inftitution, is a lamentable truth, univerfally acknowledged by proteftants. If chriftianity itfelf, therefore, be of importance, it muft be of importance to free it from thefe corruptions : for whether it be better for men to be chriftians at all, or to continue papifts, is very problematical, and a queftion which many fenfible perfons would not hefitate to determine

in

in the negative. But to whom are we to look for the advancement of this neceffary work of reformation from the errors and abufes of popery ? I anfwer, without hefitation, it is to *diffenters* only, of whatever denomination, in every chriftian country.

Can it be fuppofed that the princes of this world, or *mere ftatefmen*, who are the perfons that erect or model, according to their pleafure, all ecclefiaftical eftablifhments, will ever have this bufinefs at heart ; or that, if they fhould undertake it, they are duly qualified for the conduct of it. It cannot be expected that religion fhould ever be a primary object with civil governors. They may make ufe of it as an engine of ftate policy, to promote their own fecular ends ; but, in general, they are too much *men of this world*, to concern themfelves about a fcheme, the great object of which is *a world to come* ; and, provided religion give them no great interruption in their plans of civil policy, it cannot be thought that they will ever voluntarily promote any reformation in it.

Their intereſt is, generally, beſt anſwered by the quiet continuance of all things of this nature, which are foreign to their immediate province, in the condition in which they are, and have been, let that condition be ever ſo wretched; and they are ready to take the alarm at every thing that may hazard their tranquility, or create diſturbance in the ſtate: and reformation in religion, eſpecially when it has been violently attempted, and when corruptions and abuſes (by means of the injudicious interpoſition of government) have been confirmed by long continuance, is known to have this tendency.

I ſeemed to lament that the princes of this world are not difpoſed to concern themſelves about reformation in religion; but, indeed, it is rather a happineſs that they are not; for all the ſervice they can do to religion is not to intermeddle with it it at all, so as to interrupt the reformations which might take place in it from natural and proper causes; and for this *negative assistance* the friends of religion would think themselves under the greatest obligation to civil government.

✓ Civil power is a very improper engine to be employed in work of this nature; and, whenever employed, can hardly fail to defeat its end. Wherever *opinion* is concerned; *force* of all kinds, and all motives of *interest* (both of which will ever accompany the civil magistrate) ought to be removed to the greatest distance; and spontaneous, disinterested, and calm reasoning, have the field entirely to herself. Jesus Christ and his apostles asked no aid of the civil powers, nor gave the most distant hint of their desire of any alliance with them.

Non tali auxilio, nec defensoribus istis.

VIRGIL.

The

The kingdom of Chrift is not reprefented by any part of the metalick image of king Nebuchadnezzar, which denoted all the empires of this world; but is the *little ftone cut out of the mountain without hands.* It is a thing quite *foreign* to the image, and will at laft fall upon it, and deftroy all the remains of it. All that true chriftianity wifhes, is to be un-✓ molefted by the kings and rulers of the earth, but it can never fubmit to their regulations. No chriftian prince before the Reformation ever interfered in the bufinefs of religion, without eftablifhing the abufes which had crept into it; and all that chriftian princes have done fince the Reformation, has tended to retard that great work; and to them, and their interference, it is manifeftly owing, that it is no farther advanced at this day.

There needs to be no greater evidence of this, with refpect to England, than a comparifon between the reformation propofed by Wickliffe, fo early as the year 1460,

1460, and the church of England as by law eftablifhed, from the year 1559, in the reign of queen Elizabeth, to the prefent year 1769,* and as it will probably continue fo long as our civil and ecclefiaftical governors fhall be able to maintain it, in its prefent imperfect ftate, notwithftanding the increafing light of the age.

Wickliffe admitted of no more than two degrees in the minifterial office, viz. *deacons*, and *prefbyters*, or *bifhops*. " Thefe " two," fays he, " were known in Paul's " time, and the others are the invention of " imperious pride." The church of England has *archbifhops*, *bifhops*, *archdeacons*, *deans*, *canons*, *prebendaries*, &c. &c. &c. Wickliffe fays, that " civil government " fhould not be committed to the clergy." We fuffer the feat of all the bifhops in the higheft houfe of parliament, and give them power in ecclefiaftical courts; in which they have cognizance of civil matters, and in which punifhments are inflicted

* When the firft edition of this addrefs was publifhed.

flicted that affect the perfons, liberties, and fortunes of Britifh fubjects, though the proceedings are contrary to thofe which are in ufe in the civil courts, and repugnant to the free conftitution of this government.

Wickliffe would have abolifhed all ceremonies in religion not prefcribed in the fcriptures. He fays, that " confirmation, " giving orders, and the confecration of " places, were referved to the pope and " bifhops for the fake of temporal gain " and honour; that it is not lawful for a " chriftian, after the full publication of " the law of Chrift, to devife, himfelf, " any other laws for the government of " the church;" and he condemns a fet of prefcribed forms of prayer, as derogatory from the liberty God had given them. How confonant, in every article, is all this to reafon, chriftianity, and good fenfe; but how oppofite to this, in every article, are the maxims of the church of England, as by law eftablifhed.

Had

Had not our civil governors (among whom, let it be obferved, I include the bifhops, and all the members of the hierarchy) taken the alarm, and oppofed the attempts of Wickliffe and his partizans, there is no doubt, but that a reformation would fpeedily have taken place upon his enlarged plan. And fince, without the interference of the civil magiftrate, he himfelf could not have formed any other eftablifhment, more light would have continued to be thrown upon religious fubjects; and not only would the *difcipline*, but the *doctrines* of the church, have been reformed more and more. Whereas, fuch have been the bleffed effects of the interference of the civil magiftrate in the religion of this country, that, inftead of feeing things in this glorious train, all that has been effected hitherto, is a miferable compromife between popery, and the imperfect plan of reformation propofed by Wickliffe.

If

If the errors and abuses which Wickliffe discovered have not yet been reformed, how can we expect a reformation of those errors which he never suspected, but which he retained, as the most sacred of all truths, and which he would have been shocked to have heard called in question? And yet, I have heard of no christian establishment in Europe, in which the grossest corruptions of the most fundamental doctrines of the gospel are not retained; corruptions which entirely pervert the whole scheme, and are so repugnant to our natural notions of God and virtue, that, so long as they are known to be maintained by christians in general, and considered as essential parts of the scheme of christianity, they must necessarily prove an insuperable obstacle to its propagation in the world, and especially to the conversion of the Jews and Mohammedans.

With them the belief of the *divine unity* is, and, indeed, justly, a fundamental article of faith. This is also the clear doctrine

doctrine both of the Old and New Testament; but, not being the faith of the generality of those who pretend to derive their religion from them, *all* christians are unavoidably considered by them as guilty of *po'ytheism* and *idolatry*. And who can acquit them of the charges, so long as they profess to pay divine honours to *three persons*, and address their most solemn prayers, not to *one God, the Father*, but to *Father, Son, and Holy Ghost ?* Many other corruptions might be mentioned connected with this, which, altogether, make the whole system of modern christianity less like the christianity of the New Testament, than it is to the religion of the Brachmans of Indostan.

What I am saying is, perhaps, no news even to the generality of the members of the established church. Many of them *feel*, and *lament* the wretched state of things among them; and some of the clergy have, now and then, the courage to *propose* a reformation; but so long as the
civil

civil power continues to be the *supreme head* of this church, the first effectual motion must come from thence; and till there be some *state necessity* for setting about a reformation, the remonstrances of a thousand *candid disquisitors*, followed by as many *confessionalists*, will signify but little.

This *state necessity*, which alone can make our civil governors think of a reformation, must arise from the difficulty of carrying on the business of our present *politico-ecclesiastical constitution* without it. And so long as the laity are content with their clergy, and their *statute duty*; and so long as clergymen can be found, who are content to do this duty, and are satisfied with the *terms* on which they are required to do it (and without which they cannot receive the *reward* for doing it) it is very unlikely that the houses of parliament, who have business enough, of other kinds, upon their hands, will ever take this affair into consideration.

In order to engage their attention to this subject, therefore, both the clergy and the laity must *act*, as well as *think* and *write*. The laity must *dissent*, and quit those places of worship in which they are convinced that divine service is not conducted according to truly christian principles; and the clergy must throw up the preferments which they *received*, and which they, therefore, *hold* upon their solemnly declared assent to doctrines which they disbelieve, and upon their approbation of a ritual which they dislike.

Should either of these two events happen (both of which, however, are, to the last degree, improbable) that the laity, in general, should be so far enlightened, as to see the errors of the established religion, and at the same time so strictly conscientious, as to think it their duty not to give any countenance to those corruptions of christianity by their presence at the service, and their concurrence in it; or should the generality of the clergy, for the

the fame juft reafons, relinquifh their preferments, to teach a purer religion, without expecting their recompence from man; the king of England, and the two houfes of parliament, would fee it to be high time to attend to this fubject, and a reformation of the greateft abufes, at leaft, would immediately take place.

But my bufinefs is not with the *eftablifh-ed church*. I thank God, the caufe I am pleading is not quite fo hopelefs. I have not to do with fettered churchmen, but with *free diffenters*; and it is, confeffedly, not fo difficult to perfuade men to continue as they are, as to engage them to change their fituation.

While there are diffenters from civil eftablifhments of religion; that is, while there are men who are not *hired*, and who do not lie under any temptation to proftitute their confciences in the fupport of falfehood, there will be freedom of inquiry, unchecked by the apprehenfion of confequences; freedom of inquiry will produce its natural offspring, truth; and truth has charms, that require only to be feen and known, in order to recommend itfelf to the acceptance of all mankind. Darknefs and prejudice cannot always involve the minds of men; and if truth once begin to dawn upon them, it will be as the *morning light, which fhineth more and more unto the perfect day.*

Learn, then, my proteftant diffenting brethren, to regard your fituation with refpect; when you confider, that among you alone, in this country, is the worfhip of the only living and true God known, and the purity of the chriftian doctrine and difcipline exhibited. Errors, no doubt, and perhaps great ones too, ftill remain among the moft enlightened of us, but we have no reafon to be alarmed at the fufpicion. We are at liberty to make the moft rigid fcrutiny into the foundation of our religious principles. We may inftantly rectify what we find amifs, and may, without

out restraint, use our endeavours to enlighten the minds of others. We have subscribed to no systems, or articles of faith; and therefore have no formal recantation to make upon the occasion. We enjoy no emoluments in consequence of our assent to any religious opinions or practices; and, therefore, are under no temptation to equivocate with our consciences (which are apt to prove intractable, and are seldom perfectly easy under that kind of treatment) to avoid the disagreeable alternative of giving up a church living, when we are convinced that the doctrines we have subscribed to, upon our induction into it, are erroneous, and that the discipline we have conformed to, is inexpedient, or dangerous.

This last circumstance, I am sensible, chiefly affects *ministers*; but if you, gentlemen of the *laity* among dissenters, think yourselves unconcerned in it, you are greatly mistaken. Being men of a liberal turn of mind in other respects, condemning

demning no man for his religious opinions, and being fully fatisfied that honeft men, of all profeffions, cannot but ftand well in the favour of their maker, you are apt to purfue thefe juft fentiments too far; and to think that, becaufe there is no harm to *them* in their worfhip, there is no harm to *you* in it; fo that by joining in what is good, and neglecting what is bad, you may, without the violation of your confciences, and without any inconvenience, join in a conftant way with any fect of proteftants whatever, in the celebration of divine worfhip. But confider, that, upon the very fame principles, you might join with any fect of chriftians, and even join in the fervice of the *mafs* in a conftant way. Upon the fame principles, alfo, you might neglect all the forms of chriftian worfhip, and join yourfelves to the Jews, or the Mohammedans; for it cannot be denied, but that there is fomething good to be found among them, and this you might pretend to take, and neglect the reft.

In

In short, this specious principle, founded, in appearance, on generous sentiments ✓ of moderation and candour, is a most fallacious and dangerous one. By the help of it the primitive christians might have joined the worship of the heathens, there needed to have been no martyrs in the christian church, and all *persecution for the cross of Christ* would have ceased.

Many of the old Puritans, indeed, constantly attended divine worship in the church of England; but there were no other places of public worship open; and they thought it their duty to give their testimony in favour of religion and christianity in general, by joining in the best forms that they conveniently could. Besides, it should be considered, that the old puritans did not object to the doctrines of the church of England, or to forms of prayer, but only to ceremonies, and matters relating to discipline; nay, many of them had no great objection to the ceremonies *in themselves*, but only to the

im-

impofition of them; which they juftly thought was owning a power, which Chrift had not committed to man. But, my brethren, your objections now lie much deeper, and affect the very effentials of the eftablifhed worfhip.

Do not fay that I inherit the rigid fcrupulofity of my anceftors. On the contrary, I think it extreme bigotry never to indulge a liberal curiofity, fo far as, in the character of a *fpectator*, to fee in what manner perfons of other denominations conduct divine worfhip. I have frequently gone to church myfelf, and do not fcruple to go fometimes ftill, though I am fhocked at what I hear there; but, certainly, by joining *habitually* with any one denomination of chriftians, we declare our preference of it to any other, efpecially to any other that it would be as convenient for us to attend; and whatever errors and irregularities there are in that church, more than in any other, we, by our conduct, give our fanction to them, and, as

far

far as our influence extends, recommend and enforce them.

If, therefore, you be a believer in the one true God, *the Father*, and, in other refpects, maintain the purity of the gofpel principles; you not only expofe your own minds to perpetual difquiet and uneafinefs, by habitually joining in the fervice of the eftablifhed church; which is, throughout, founded on principles very different from yours; but chriftianity in general is offended at your conduct, as you virtually oppofe all reformation, and contribute to entail all its errors and abufes upon it. Indeed I cannot help thinking, that a man who is properly in earneft in religion, who confiders of what importance genuine chriftianity is, and how exceedingly unlike to it is the whole fyftem on which the Englifh hierarchy is founded, muft be ftaggered when he weighs thefe things in his own mind.

Going.

Going to church in a conftant way, is not going in the character of a *fpectator*. If you be obferved to be there conftantly, you will be fuppofed to *prefer* that method of worfhip. You will, likewife, be fuppofed, not only to be *feeing* what is done there, but alfo to have fomething to *do* yourfelves. You are fuppofed to join in the prayers of the church; and, therefore, to pay divine worfhip to inferior and derived beings, as if they were the *true and very God*; which is certainly undifguifed impiety and idolatry.

Think not that this fpecies of idolatry, though not fo malignant as fome other fpecies of it, is, therefore, *innocent*; and that it has no *practical confequences*. The afcription of divine honours to Jefus Chrift, befides robbing *his God and our God* of the honour that is due to himfelf alone, and of *the glory which he will not give to another* is a dangerous depravation of the idea of God. By making more Gods than one, you unavoidably make a diftribution

of

of divine attributes; fo that the all-perfect character of deity will be found in none of them, and no being will be left poffeffed at the fame time of all the venerable and amiable attributes that we ought to afcribe to him; by which means the purity and genuine fpirit of devotion will be greatly debafed. And there is, no doubt, a near connection between this opinion of the proper divinity of Chrift, and other notions held by fome Chriftians, which imply the greateft reflection upon the moral government of God; and, as far as they operate, muft be prejudicial to virtue among men.

So unlike to genuine primitive chriftianity are all the ecclefiaftical eftablifhments in Europe, and fo much in the fpirit of this world are they conducted, that it is no wonder that perfons who inquire but little, and who judge of chriftianity by what they fee, are, fo many of them, unbelievers. By joining thefe corrupt eftablifhments, therefore, you promote the caufe of infidelity; whereas by
joining

joining with a fociety of chriftians, who profefs the gofpel in its original fimplicity; or, at leaft, are in a fituation in which they are at liberty to bring it to that fimplicity, you bear your teftimony againft all the corruptions of this divine religion; you reprefent it in an amiable light to mankind; and, without fpeaking or writing in its defence, are advocates for the truth, and preachers of righteoufnefs in the world.

If this be to be a diffenter, it is certainly a refpectable and important character. Learn then, my brethren, to reverence your profeffion, and confider it as a thing that is as much fuperior to any ecclefiaftical eftablifhment, as a fcheme which has an eternal world for its object, is fuperior to all fchemes of worldly policy; as much fuperior to them, as Chrift, whom alone you acknowledge to be your legiflator, is fuperior to the princes and powers of this world, whom thofe who adhere to eftablifhments acknowledge, as their legiflators. Diffenters

Diffenters in England are often confounded with the Prefbyterians of the *kirk of Scotland*; and time was when thofe who go by the name of *Prefbyterians* in England entertained the fame principles, and would have been glad, either to have united with them, or to have formed themfelves upon the fame, or a fimilar plan. Mr. Pierce dedicated his *Vindication of the Diffenters* to the paftors and minifters of the church of Scotland, calling them *Brethren*, and faying that the diffenters in England were united to them in the fame *faith, worfhip, form of government, defign,* and *brotherly love.* But divine providence happily prevented the execution of what our forefathers earneftly defired, and has brought the diffenters in England into a fituation infinitely more favourable to the interefts of truth and chriftianity, than they had any idea of themfelves.

We are, now, far from admitting that the members of the church of Scotland are

are any more our brethren, than the members of the church of England. A charge of any alliance with the Scotch prefbyterians would now be confidered as a calumny; and if we were difpofed to conform to an eftablifhment, we fhould not look fo far North. The two eftablifhments in the ifland differ in little more than matters of *difcipline*, which we now think to be of little confequence, in comparifon of thofe errors in *doctrine*, which lie at the very foundation of the chriftian fcheme; errors in which they both agree, and which they both enforce with the fame unrelenting rigour. And there is not much more profpect of things growing better in the one, than in the other.

The great advantage which the church of Scotland enjoys over the church of England, arofe from this fingle, but important circumftance, that the former was prompted and conducted by the *people*, who had nothing but religion in view, and who carried their fcheme as far as they

thought

thought proper; whereas the latter was conducted by the *civil magiſtrate,* who went no farther in the reformation than he could help, and modelled the government of the church, fo as to make it ſubſervient to the purpoſes of the ſtate.

Hence the Scotch miniſters have all decent and moderate ſalaries; they have little or no civil power, and pluralities are unknown among them; while there remains a ſhameful inequality in the proviſion for the Engliſh miniſters, fome living in affluence in palaces, and adding one large benefice to another, while others of them are abſolutely ſtarving on miſerable curacies; and, notwithſtanding an ample ſufficiency in the revenues of the church, are obliged to depend upon the voluntary contributions of their pariſhioners, for a neceſſary ſupport. Here, alſo, the biſhops, along with the revenues of princes, have an extenſive *juriſdiction,* and great civil power; and while the biſhopricks, and, in a manner, all the great benefices

benefices are, directly or indirectly, at the
disposal of the court, a ministry, be they
ever so corrupt, can never want tools to
assist them in carrying on their most iniquitous and oppressive schemes. Witness
the slavish and absurd doctrines of *passive
obedience* and *non-resistance*, so furiously
inculcated by, I may say, the body of the
English clergy, in the arbitrary and accursed reigns of the Stewarts.

SECTION II.

*Of the importance of the dissenting interest,
with respect to the civil interests of the
community.*

HAVING considered the importance
of the dissenting interest with respect to *religion*, I shall now briefly treat of
it as it respects *civil policy*. Mr. Hume
acknowledges, that whatever civil liberty
is now enjoyed in this country, it is owing to our ancestors the Puritans, who
were

were equally friends to the civil and religious rights of their countrymen. For my own part, I cannot say that I consider them as having been uniform and consistent friends to either; but their schemes being thwarted by the court, they were necessarily engaged in the opposite interest; and thus, from the mere force of oppression, without any greater enlargement of mind, or superior merit, they became advocates for liberty. But still it was only liberty for themselves, and their own party, that they aimed at; and, could they have carried their point, they would have exercised as severe a tyranny over the consciences of men as their antagonists. Were they now in power, I myself should expect to be one of the first victims to their bigotry and rage. It must be acknowledged, however, in favour of these *heroes*, that intolerance was the error of their times, and that no other professors of christianity had any more liberal, or enlarged views than themselves.

But

But whatever were the views of the diffenters originally, tho' they were extremely narrow and confined at firft, they have been fo long the weaker party, and confequently in an intereft oppofite to the views of tyranny and arbitrary power; that, at length, they have begun to underftand their fituation, and have found the true and juft principles, on which the caufe of *univerfal liberty* may be beft fupported. On thefe principles, my brethren, I truft you will always act, without troubling yourfelves to make any apology for the maxims and conduct of our anceftors. If they were culpable, let them bear the cenfures they deferve. We muft think, and act for ourfelves.

So long as we continue diffenters, it is hardly poffible that we fhould be other than friends to the civil liberty, and all the effential interefts of our fellow citizens. The friends of this great caufe may always depend upon us; but ftatefmen who have other views may juftly be jealous of us;

us; and they cannot give a clearer proof of their hoftile intentions towards the liberty of their country, than by ufing us with rigour. Witnefs the fevere perfecutions we fuffered in the arbitrary reigns of the Stewarts, the meafures that were taking with us towards the clofe of the reign of queen Ann, and the indulgence that has been fhown us fince the happy revolution, under king William of glorious memory.

In all this, we claim no particular merit. Diffenting minifters, being chofen by their people, will naturally enter into the views of their people, in civil as well as religious matters; and the diffenting laity, not being noblemen, or men of very large fortunes, will have in general, the fame intereft with the bulk of their fellow fubjects. Diffenting minifters, therefore, as far as their influence in a political light is of any confequence, will naturally enter into the intereft of the people at large. It is for the fame reafon that the
eftablifhed

established clergy may be supposed to favour the court, as it has the disposal of bishopricks and rich benefices. The maxim *No bishop, no king,* i.e. no arbitrary king, might justly have had weight with wiser princes than our James the first.

It is also natural for the dissenters to wish well to every mild administration, which secures to them their privileges, and opposes the attempts of a bigoted and headstrong multitude, of clergy or laity, to oppress them. For the same reason, too, when the country, by its established laws, favours the interest of the dissenters, so that they have a *legal right* to their privileges, they naturally consider *their country*, and *its laws*, as their guardians, and will strenuously oppose all the encroachments of the prerogative on the constitution, and on the rights of the subjects in general. For they must be sensible, that the established laws of a free community must be a better security for their privileges, than the will of any single

single man whatever. They have too much at stake to be willing to hold it on so precarious a tenure.

It also clearly follows, from the same principle of *self-interest*, independent of gratitude, that the more indulgence dissenters meet with from the government, the stronger will be their attachment to it. Tho', therefore, it should seem proper to the legislature to give a preference to one mode of religion, by a legal provision for the maintenance of its ministers, it is clearly for its interest to attach all dissenters to it, as much as possible, by a participation of *civil privileges* ; and it is both injustice, and bad policy, in civil governors, to debar themselves from the service of men of ability and integrity, and, at the same time, to alienate their affections, by such an *opprobrious exclusion* from civil honours.

Yet, tho' I think it right that these things should be publickly said, that they

may

may have weight with thofe whom it may concern, far would I be from encouraging the leaft tendency towards difaffection in the diffenters to the prefent conftitution of England. Imperfect as it is, and hard as the prefent laws bear upon us diffenters in fome refpects, our fituation in England is, upon the whole, fuch as we have great reafon to be thankful to divine providence for, being abundantly more eligible than it would be in any other country in the world; and it is not fo defirable to obtain even a juft right by clamour and contention, as by the continuance of a prudent and peaceable behaviour.

This may convince our legiflators, that we are deferving of their indulgence. Men who harbour no refentment, though under a reftraint, of the injuftice and unreafonablenefs of which they are fully fenfible, muft be poffeffed of generofity enough to be capable of the moft grateful and firm attachment to the hand that frees them from the reftraint. If a man
have

have magnanimity enough not to bear malice againſt an enemy, much more will he be ſuſceptible of a generous zeal for his friend.

Beſides, though, from a regard to the honour and intereſt of our country, it is to be wiſhed that diſſenters might be admitted to all civil offices of honour and truſt, in common with others, their fellow-ſubjects, who have no better title to them in other reſpects: yet a perſon, who ſhould conſult the intereſt of the diſſenters only, as a body of men who ſeparate themſelves from a principle of *religion*, without regard to the intereſt of the community at large, might, perhaps, heſitate about taking any ſteps to procure an enlargement of their privileges.

Profeſſing a religion which inculcates upon us that we are *not of this world*, but only in a courſe of diſcipline, to train us up for a better, it is worth conſidering, whether a ſituation, in which more ſcope would

would be given to ambition, and other paſſions, the tendency of which is to attach us to this world, is to be wiſhed for by us. Should not a chriſtian, as ſuch (though he ſhould by no means, ſecrete himſelf from ſociety, or decline any opportunity of ſerving his friend, or his country, when divine Providence ſeems to call him out to the ſphere of active life) be content to paſs unmoleſted in the private walks of life, rejoicing, as his maſter did, in doing all kind offices to his fellow creatures, without aſpiring at civil power, and thoſe honorary diſtinctions, with which the hearts of the men of this world, are ſo much captivated, and, very often, ſo fatally inſnared.

As our Lord warned his diſciples, that *the world would love its own*, and would hate them, becauſe they were not of the world; and that he who would follow him, muſt *take up his croſs* to do it; is it not, *cæteris paribus*, more probable, that we are theſe diſciples, when we ſuffer ſome
degree

degree of perfecution, and are rather frowned upon by the powers of this world, than if we had free accefs to all the emoluments of it? Certainly, fuch a fituation is far more favourable to our gaining that fuperiority of mind to the world, which is required of all chriftians,. whatever be their ftation in it. We know that *if per-fecution should arife, on account of the word*, we muft be ready to forfake houfes, lands, relations, and all the endearments of life, rather than make fhipwreck of faith and of a good confcience; and that, in thofe trying times, if we deny Chrift, he will alfo deny us. Then he that would fave his life, fhall lofe it, and he only that is willing to lofe his life, fhall fave it to life eternal. This, chriftians, is the tenure on which we hold all the bleffings of the gofpel.

Now, if this be the temper to which we are to be formed, whether perfecution fhould actually arife, or not, what kind of a fituation fhould we (from the knowledge we have of human nature) prescribe, as the most favourable for the purpose? Certainly, not one in which we should have nothing to bear or to suffer, and where every thing should be just as we could wish it. A mind accustomed to this treatment would be ill prepared for encountering the various hardships of the christian warfare, in a time of persecution. In a situation in every respect favourable to the pursuits and enjoyments of this life, it would not be easy for a man to attain to any thing like a satisfactory conviction, that he had the proper temper and disposition of a christian. Habits of mind are not acquired by *putting cases* (which, however, persons would little think of doing, when the cases were not likely to occur) but by actual experience and feeling. A habit of caution can never be given to a child by admonition only. It is by frequent hurts that he learns to take care of himself. So likewise courage and fortitude are acquired by being frequently exposed

posed to pains and hardships, by exerting our powers, and feeling the benefit of such exertion.

All these things duly considered, a man who entertains the truly enlarged sentiments of christianity, and is sensible how momentary and insignificant are all the things of this world, in comparison with those of a future, will, in proportion to the influence of these views, be less impatient of the difficulties and restraints he may lie under in a civil capacity. He will more easily acquiesce in a situation not perfectly eligible, when he is prepared even to bear the greatest sufferings that can befall him in this life with christian fortitude, patience, and resignation; at the same time that the benevolence of his heart is always ready to take the form of the most generous patriotism, whenever there occurs a clear, and great cause to exert it. If a true christian be conscious that he is engaged in a good cause, he, of all men, has the least reason to fear *what man*

man can do unto him, and therefore he is more to be depended upon, in any critical emergence, than any other perfon whatever.

A diffenter, then, who is fo *upon principle*, who has, confequently, the jufteft notions of the nature and importance of civil and religious liberty; who is, on many accounts, thoroughly fenfible of the bleffings of a mild and equal government, and, therefore, heartily attached to the intereft of that conftitution which allows him the rights which he values fo highly; whofe mind is prepared to bear *irremediable* hardfhips with patience, but whofe active courage, in cafes in which the great interefts of his country call him to exert himfelf, may be depended upon, is a very valuable member of civil fociety. Such a man will fcorn the mean arts of court intrigue. If he can gain his laudable ends, and be admitted to his natural rights, as a loyal Britifh fubject, by fair and open means, he will not defpife it;
but

but he will rather continue to suffer unjustly, than prostitute his interest to a corrupt, profligate, and oppressive administration.

SECTION III.

Of the manner in which Dissenters ought to speak or write concerning the Church of England.

SO long as persons are *sincere* in their profession of any form of religion, they are certainly intitled to our candour and respect. Integrity is the chief excellence of every moral agent, and claims our esteem and veneration even in a papist, a mahometan, or a heathen. The man who loves and seeks after truth, and who conscientiously obeys it, wherever he but thinks he has found it, will, no doubt, be accepted of God, though his faith should happen to be ever so erroneous, and his practice, founded upon it, ever so absurd.

And without the chriſtian virtues of mutual love, candour, and forbearance, the foundeſt chriſtian faith will ſtand for nothing.

The truth of theſe ſentiments is acknowledged, felt, and contended for, by the author of this addreſs; and by ſome he will be blamed for extending the benefit of them to papiſts and infidels. But let us, with a due regard to truth and ſincerity, conſider in what manner they ought to influence our conduct with reſpect to thoſe who differ from us in religious principles and practices.

If the truth which we hold, and which others deny, appear to us to be of importance, and eſpecially of practical importance (as certainly thoſe opinions are which divide the rational diſſenters from the church of England) our love of truth, and of mankind ſhould concur to make us zealous in taking every prudent method to convince them of their errors, and

and make them converts to the truth; by
setting the evidence and importance of
the latter in its just light, and by no means
concealing the abfurdity and dangerous
tendency of the former.

Upon every fair occasion, therefore, let
the rational diffenter speak and write with
the simplicity and fearless integrity of a
christian, openly afferting the great doctrines of the proper unity of God, and
the equity of his moral goverment, in opposition to what is in reality *tritheism*, and
the doctrines of absolute predestination
and reprobation by whomsoever they may
be held; and let us claim for ourselves
and others that equal *liberty*, to which we
have a natural and a divine right, of thinking and acting for ourselves in all religious matters, whoever they be that would
abridge us of it, by assuming authority
in matters of faith. In every other respect, also, in which our opinions and
practices are different from those of others,
let us, if we have occasion to mention

them at all, fpeak or write with perfect freedom, and with a degree of zeal pro- portioned to their importance.

Many of the modern friends of church power in England affect to allow diffenters to *think* for themfelves, but deny them the liberty of *writing* againft the eftablifhment; and many diffenters alfo feem to enter into the fame abfurd diftinction. If they can be permitted quietly to enjoy their own opinion and mode of worfhip, they think it wrong even to fpeak difrefpectfully of the religion of their country, notwithftanding the greateft infults and provocations. They even take upon themfelves to be offended with any perfon who fhall fo much as make the leaft comparifon with refpect to the ftate of religious knowledge in the two parties, in order to fhew the advantage of the fituation of one of them, for improvements in religion, above that of the other. But what does common fenfe, the practice of the primitive chriftians, and that of the reformers

reformers from popery fay upon this fubject?

Can any man maintain the truth of his own opinion, without shewing the absurdity of that which is directly contrary to it, and especially if he be in such a situation, that he must expressly deny what another has previously afferted? How then can I exhort diffenters to value their situation, *as fuch*, if I do not shew them how much it is preferable to that of those from whom they diffent? It may, perhaps, be possible for a person exceedingly well skilled in the art of writing and *fineffe*, to do the one without the other; but it is impossible he should do the one without *thinking* of the other, and even keeping it constantly in view; and certainly to supprefs what a man thinks, especially when it is that which alone can give any weight, energy, or even propriety, to what he is saying, must be a mode of writing constrained, artificial, unnatural, and ineffectual.

The

The primitive chriftians appear to have known nothing of this refined diftinction, but in their apologies for chriftianity inveighed with the utmoft freedom againft the eftablifhed religions of the countries in which they lived. St. Paul did the fame, without the leaft fcruple or referve, upon all occafions; as alfo did his and our great mafter; who never fpared the abfurd and mifchievous doctrines that prevailed in his time, to the corruption of a true and divine religion. And the reformers from popery followed their example, in expreffing upon all occafions, their honeft indignation againft the abfurdities and ufurpations of the church of Rome.

Why then fhould not we, who diffent from the church of England, as they did from the church of Rome, take the fame liberty, in proportion to their importance, with her abfurdities and ufurpations. If we think that the church of England is *not* chargeable with fuch things, we are not diffenters, and ought not to continue

the

the feparation. On the other hand, if we think that the church of England *is* chargeable with great errors, and unjuftifiable ufurpations, and fcruple to fay fo, we have not that zeal for truth and liberty that becomes diffenters; I may add that becomes chriftians.

But the prefent age, verging to infidelity, and an indifference to all the forms of religion, and to religion itfelf, brands with the cenfure of *unpolitenefs*, every thing that looks like molefting the religious opinions of others, be they ever fo erroneous or dangerous; and the man who thinks, feels, and writes like a chriftian; who loves his religion, and values the purity of it; and who expreffes his generous indignation at the ufurpations of fome, and the fervility of others with refpect to it, muft be called a *bigot*, and an *illiberal minded* perfon. With fuch may I ever be deemed a bigot. I fhall be proud of the character, and fhall begin to think bigotry to be a term fynominous to integrity, honefty, nesty, generosity, and every thing that is manly and liberal belonging to human nature.

These specious principles, which have their source in *infidelity*, have infected many members of the church of England, and dissenters also, who are not, at least, *not yet* unbelievers. But certainly such dissenters are least acquainted with the true principles of their dissent, and must be the least *valuable*, and the least *stable* part of the interest. Accordingly, we see that those dissenters, who speak with this extreme tenderness, charity, and respect concerning the church of England, notwithstanding, if they were asked, they could not deny their disbelief of more of her principles than any other denomination of dissenters, find the least difficulty in conforming to the church; and for the same reason, would find as little difficulty in joining the church of Rome, the church of Mahomet, or any church in the world; and their minds would be as

little

little shocked with the idea of even *constant conformity* to any of them. For it supposes only the same disregard to religious truth, and the rights of conscience.

But let such persons consider how, as I have observed before, and cannot repeat too often, with this excess of candour, and suppleness of conscience, any of the primitive christians could ever have died *martyrs* to their religion; or whether there could have been any such thing as *persecution for the cross of Christ* ?

The doctrine of toleration and religious liberty is now maintained on two very different, and even opposite grounds. The one is an *indifference to all religion*, and an opinion of the absolute insignificance of all the distinctions of it; and the other its exceeding great *importance* to every man singly considered ; so that every thing belonging to it is held sacred with him, and he cannot, upon any consideration, surrender his own right of determining concerning

cerning it, to any man, or body of men upon earth.

Thofe who are advocates for toleration upon the former ground, are *unbelievers in chriftianity*, and perfons who are governed by political confiderations only; who think it folly to difturb the peace of fociety for the fake of trifles, and who have feen in hiftory how much feveral ftates have been injured by adopting perfecuting meafures. But, upon the fame principles, thefe perfons would not fcruple to give up all regard to thofe infignificant opinions, and pretended rights of confcience, if they faw that the outward fplendor, power, and wealth of the ftate required it. Thefe unbelieving ftatefmen have, therefore, within them the principles of the cooleft and moft unrelenting perfecution; and, without believing one fyllable of the matter, are capable of conforming themfelves, and of enforcing the ftricteft obedience in others, to any fcheme of religion in the world. Nay the

the Bifhop of Gloucefter, Dr. Balguy, and others, who are not infidels, avowedly go upon this ground, and maintain even the *obligation* of the civil magiftrate to eftablifh the religion of the majority of his fubjects, without making any diftinction with refpect to the poffibility of its being ever fo impious or abfurd. Certainly fuch principles as thefe are highly dangerous and alarming, and yet they are fpreading every day.

On the other hand, thofe who are advocates for religious liberty upon the other ground, namely an opinion of the exceeding great importance of religious principles, are fincere *believers* of chriftianity, and the fartheft in the world from thinking that religion is a thing to be regulated by, and made fubfervient to civil policy, when no confiderations relating to this world are worthy to be named with it. In a thing fo interefting, it is their opinion, that every man, for himfelf, fhould be the fole umpire of his own judgment

ment and practice, acknowledging *no master upon earth*, since *one is their master, even Christ*. And least of all will they submit their faith and practice in matters of religion to the decision of men, who, on account both of their education, and situation in life, must be very incompetent judges of the subject, and who, in fact, have never had its interest at heart; but, in all their ecclesiastical constitutions, have been solely influenced by political and worldly considerations. To those who assert their religious liberty upon these principles, the authority of the Pope, or that of the king of England, with the impious titles of *supreme heads of the church*, are held in equal contempt.*

These principles can never, like the former, degenerate into persecution, for, with such men, the conscience of every individual

---

* This is by no means intended to deny the authority of temporal sovereigns over all persons within their dominions, ecclesiastical as well as others.

individual of their fpecies will be as inviolable as their own; and upon the fame principles that they feel for themfelves, they cannot but feel for others.

Formerly religious liberty had no proper advocates upon either of thefe grounds: Even the diffenters, who thought religion to be of importance, imagined that it was, on that very account, not to be deferted by thofe who were in poffeffion of the civil power, and that the beft interefts of mankind ought to be taken care of in fpite of themfelves. But of late, the abfurdity and dangerous tendency of this principle has been acknowledged, at leaft by the rational Diffenters; and they have become advocates for religious liberty upon the true, broad, generous, and chriftian principles above mentioned.

But forry I am to fee too many of thofe who are called *rational diffenters*, talk more like *infidels* than *chriftians* upon this great fubject, and treat the moft important religious

ligious truths with the fame contemptuous indifference. They are forward to acknowledge, upon all occafions, that all the difference between them and the eftablifhed church is a mere trifle; that the belief of *three,* or *three hundred gods* is only a metaphyfical fubtlety, of no practical confequence whatever; and that even the doctrines of abfolute election and reprobation are well enough for the common people, who will always be foolifh and fuperftitious, and whom it is not worth the while to take any pains with, or to run any rifque to fet right. With this declared indifference to fyftems of religion, it is no wonder that they are difpofed to think favourably of eftablifhments in general, and of that of their own country in particular; and that they are offended when any perfon, more ferious and in earneft than themfelves, afferts the true diffenting principles, with a warmth and zeal fuited to their importance.

I was

I was in hopes, that this difpofition, fo unworthy of chriftians, and efpecially of proteftant diffenters, had been confined to a few, who might have learned their principles of toleration from Voltaire or Rouffeau; but feveral circumftances have occurred of late, and particularly the reception which the former edition of this *Addrefs* has met with, which give but too much reafon to fufpect, that the evil has fpread farther than I had imagined. For I cannot conceive that any perfons fhould be much offended either at the *fentiments*, or the *manner* of this addrefs, except thofe who (though, perhaps unknown to themfelves) are influenced by fuch principles as I have here animadverted upon. In this view the unpopularity of this addrefs, among thofe diffenters for whofe ufe it was particularly intended, gives me ferious concern. For their fakes it is that, in this edition, I have added the reflections which are the fubject of this fection, and to which I wifh they would give their attention, with the fame ferioufnefs with which they were written. If

If there be no weight in what I have observed, do you, with equal plainnefs, produce your own *ftrong reafons* againft me; but, for God's fake, do not, my brethren, in a cafe of this importance, determine and act without thinking, or influenced by fuch fuperficial fentiments, as have weight with none but men of *pleafure* and *fafhion*, who never properly think about religion; who, confequently, know nothing of the fubject, and therefore can be no judges of its importance, or of the manner in which it ought to affect the hearts and the conduct of reafonable beings.

Believe me, I feel nothing for the credit of a fhort *and anonimous compofition*, but, if I know my own heart, I feel for *you*, I feel for the *caufe to which you give your names*; and I hope that I feel ftill more for that *great caufe*, from its relation to which only every inferior denomination of religion derives its value and importance. And the turn of thinking, the preva-

prevalence of which I lament, appears to me to be diametrically oppofite to the genuine fpirit of chriftianity; and would be fo far from leading a man to do and to fuffer what Chrift, and his immediate followers did, that it would rather difpofe him to ridicule them, as men who *turned the world upfide down* for the fake of mere *fpeculative opinions*, and who could not be content *to think with the wife, and act with the vulgar*. This, which is known to have been the fpirit both of the *heathen philofophy* of old, and of *infidelity* in modern times, is too like the principle of many profeffing chriftians, and even thofe who call themfelves rational diffenters. They are fo much alike, that one of them is certainly the parent, and the other the child.

But, my brethren, if there be any thing facred in *religious truth*, let it infpire the breafts of us who profefs to maintain it; and if any religious truths be of importance, as affecting a man's heart and

life

life, or as comprehended under any definition that can be framed of *important truths*, several of them will certainly be found among those which we profess *as dissenters*, the very contrary of them being asserted among the 39 articles of the church of England. If you have no zeal for the dissenting interest, *as it now stands*, you must think your ancestors fools and mad, to have set such a value upon it as it stood *in their times*. For, certainly, you cannot think the business of *a surplice*, to be equally worth contending for with the doctrine of the *Divine Unity*, or that we ought to object to *kneeling at the Lord's supper* as strenuously as against the doctrines of *absolute predestination and reprobation*, and others connected with them; and the principles of *liberty* among the old puritans were certainly narrow and confined in comparison with ours. As the cause of the dissenters has so greatly improved in *real value*, we ought certainly to encrease in our zeal for it and attachment to it; and to be more indifferent in
thefe

these circumstances, as is apparently the case with many, must argue a want of thought, a want of knowledge, or of love for truth.

I do not write this to exasperate any man. I hope I shall not exasperate any serious member of the church of England. If he be serious and in earnest himself, he will excuse another, who thinks that he has equal cause to be serious and in earnest; and it is not with the truly *pious* and *worthy*, that even an intemperance of zeal, and *single expressions* that may appear inconsiderate and unjustifiable, that will make a man the object either of *anger*, or of *ridicule*. Warm and ingenuous hearts will compare their own feelings with mine, and will make those allowances for me, which they would wish to have made for themselves.

With numbers in the established church, I believe, my heart is in perfect unison. With some of them I know, and feel it to be fo. They are men who, if they do not approve of the whole fyftem, make the beft ufe of their fituation, in employing their moft earneft endeavours to bring about a reformation of whatever they are convinced is amifs in it; though their pious labours are counteracted by thofe *who yet lett*, but who, it is to be hoped, will, in due time, be *taken out of the way*. With thefe perfons notwithftanding we may, in fome refpects, fee each others fituation in different lights, it is not poffible that I fhould have any difference of confequence. It can only confift in the choice of means to gain the fame great ends; fo that, though the parts we are acting be confiderably different, we muft mutually rejoice in each other's fuccefs; and that fympathetic union of heart and objects, that has commenced here, will, I truft, be completed, and be a fource of mutual congratulation and happinefs hereafter.

SECTION

SECTION IV.

Observations on the expence attending the dissenting interest.

SOME of you, my brethren, I am afraid, are discouraged, and are ready to quit the dissenting interest, because it is *expensive* to you. You think it hard to be taxed by the government very high, and contrary to all principles of equity, in order to maintain the ecclesiastical establishment of your country, and at the same time raise salaries for the maintenance of your own ministers, besides being frequently called upon to contribute towards building meeting houses, houses for ministers, funds for the education of ministers, for the relief of their widows, &c. &c. &c. I own that all these things are incident to you as dissenters; they are necessarily expensive, and, I think the times

are

are such, that these necessary expences must rather increase than diminish. But this is not a thing to be complained of, if the cause be worth supporting at the expence; and I hope enough has been said already, to put that beyond a doubt.

I trust there are none among us of so sordid a disposition, as to think that nothing is worth money, but money itself, or such things as may be bought with it, in the ordinary method of traffic. The gift of God, said St. Peter to Simon Magus, is not to be purchased with money; but is was a thing of unspeakably more value. And, certainly, useful truth of all kinds, and especially *religious truth*, though not to be bought with money, is of infinitely more value than money; and to be sparing of money, in a cause in which religion and truth may be promoted, is the most contemptible parsimony. *Liberty*, also, together with the other great natural rights of mankind, is to be ranked in the same class. They are things
in

in which price has no concern, but they are *above all price*; and in a cause in which they are so clearly concerned, no man of a generous mind will ever repent of his expences, though he be not able to demonstrate what he has gained, by the method of *profit and loss*, in his books of accompt. You may not be so *rich* after such expences; but yourselves, and your posterity, may be more *wise*, *free*, and *happy*.

Consider, my brethren, in what manner christianity operated upon the minds of men when it was first promulgated. Of so little value did the primitive christians think the things of this world, in comparison of the great cause of christianity, that, without any command from God, they made no difficulty of throwing every thing they had into a common stock, to be applied to the advantage of the common cause, at the discretion of certain stewards, chosen by themselves for that purpose. They were men so detached from this world, and had their views so much fixed upon another, that they thought the best use they could make of all their possessions here, was to make them subservient to their interest hereafter. They set no bounds to the application of this rule, concerning *the true use of riches*. They gave *all they had*, and kept nothing back. And did the circumstances of christianity at present require it, we should not deserve the name of christians, if we hesitated a moment about doing the same.

But tho' there be no occasion to do what they did, let us follow the same rule. They did what their times required; let us do what our times require, and do it without grudging. You can never dispose of your wealth in a manner that will give more satisfaction to a mind that sees things in their true light, than by making it subservient to the interests of truth, liberty, and genuine christianity; and this, I believe, is the cause I am pleading, when I plead that of the protestant dissenting interest in England and Ireland. I

I do not, however, suppose that the circumstances the dissenting interest is in at present, by any means require, that you should materially injure your fortunes, or your families, in its support. It will be abundantly sufficient, if your expences on this head only come near those you actually do make on other accounts, which yourselves, if you were asked, would acknowledge to be of less use; and *so far* the dissenting interest has a just claim upon you; and you are debtors to the cause of truth and liberty, if you have hitherto done less. The obligation to contribute in cases of this nature, is, by no means, the less, because it can never be defined what particular sum, or what proportion of your fortune, you ought to expend. In this respect, no person has a right to tax you, nor may you be able to fix any exact bounds to yourselves. It is the same in cases of common charity, and a variety of other things, of which instances occur every day, which are all of *unquestionable*, tho' of indefinite, and various obligation;

and,

and with respect to which, the generous will act generously, and the mean-spirited will, like themselves, act meanly.

It may assist you to feel, and act with propriety upon this occasion, to consider what your heroic ancestors did and suffered in the same cause, and how much you owe to their liberality. How many hundreds and thousands of the old puritans, men *of whom the world was not worthy*, bore with chearfulness *the spoiling of their goods*, and submitted to heavy fines and confiscations, till they were absolutely impoverished, rather than relinquish what they were persuaded was the cause of *truth and liberty*, and therefore *the cause of God*.

Consider how many years they bore cruel imprisonments, under which numbers of them languished and died, in the imperious reign of queen Elizabeth, and the more oppressive reigns of the Stewarts; so that many men of opulent fortunes, who were qualified to make a figure

gure in their native country, were glad to take refuge from the ftorm of perfecution, on the then inhofpitable coafts of *North-America*, expofed to an inclement climate, and the fury of intractable favages, (but who had more compaffion than the hackneyed tools of a wicked adminiftration at home) glad, at this rifque, to procure what they thought the invaluable privilege of worshipping their maker according to the dictates of their confciences, unmolefted.

Confider the glorious fcene that was exhibited on the ever memorable St. Bartholomew, A. D. 1662, a fcene which few countries befides England can boaft of, when *two thoufand* minifters did not hefitate to throw up their church preferments, many of them without any other refource, rather than violate their confciences, by complying beyond their fentiments in religious matters. And this they did, though many of the things impofed upon them were acknowledged to

D 5   be,

be, in themselves, matters of indifference. Of so much consequence did they justly think it, not to admit a *right* in any men, or body of men, whatever, of prescribing and imposing any thing, with respect to that religion, of which Christ alone is the supreme head ; so as by law to make that necessary, which he left indifferent. What would they have felt, and how would they have acted, had their minds been enlightened as ours are now ; and, consequently, had they been persuaded, that they were not only required to submit to the impositions of men in matters of religion, but to the imposition of a form of worship, which, besides containing many articles of faith, the very reverse of the most important doctrines of genuine christianity, as delivered in the New Testament, derogated from the sacred rights of the only living and true God, and was therefore *idolatrous.*

Consider, my brethren, the vast sums your ancestors began to expend, the moment

ment they gained a little refpite from the perfecution above mentioned, exhaufted as they then were, in erecting places of worfhip, in the liberal fupport of their minifters, and alfo in the endowments they made, of lands and houfes, in order to provide for the continuance of that method of worfhip which they approved; and the benefit of which we enjoy at this day.

If you afk how they were able to fupply thofe expences, I anfwer, that they thought the intereft in which they were engaged, of fo much confequence, that they were hardly at any other extraordinary expences. They were men who had no tafte for the fafhionable and expenfive pleafures of the age in which they lived. From the higheft to the loweft, they were men of the greateft frugality, and the moft indefatigable induftry in their feveral employments; which, through the bleffing of God, proved a never-failing refource for the many and large demands that were

made

made upon them, for the common caufe. For thefe virtues your anceftors were fo greatly diftinguifhed in thofe times, that though they were almoft all of them concerned in trade, a bankrupt was not known among them for many years. When inftances of this kind did happen, fo ftrict was their church difcipline, and fo heinous did they confider the vices which they thought to have been inftrumental in bringing men's affairs to that cataftrophe, that excommunication certainly followed upon it; nor could the bankrupt be reftored to church communion, till he had clearly demonftrated, that he had not been guilty of fraud, extravagance, or want of induftry; but that his misfortune was the act of God.

I wifh, my brethren, you would review the hiftory of the great worthies, from whom you have the honour to be defcended. Warm your hearts with the recollection of what they did and fuffered, imitate their laudable induftry, adopt their generous

generous zeal; retrench, like them, the superfluous expences of a frivolous and luxurious age; and be liberal, as they were, in the cause of religion, liberty, and truth.

Give me leave to represent to you those circumstances, in the present state of the dissenting interest, and particularly of its ministers, which make a considerable expence absolutely necessary to support the cause, and without which that part of the interest which is most liberal, and worthy of support, must necessarily decline. The interest in which you are engaged cannot be respectable, unless your ministers be men of a liberal education, and feel themselves in a situation, in which they may freely think and act, as themselves shall judge the cause of christianity, and your interest demand. This, you must be sensible, requires not only a liberal education, but likewise a *liberal support*.

If,

If you fay that the minifters of the laft age had fmaller falaries than thofe of the prefent, you fay what is true, but you deceive yourfelves at the fame time. They did not receive fo much as a *fixed ftipend* ; but, in many cafes, their families were almoft wholly maintained by the bounty of their hearers.

In fhort, minifters, in thofe days, being free from all anxiety about the things of this world, either on their own account, or that of their families, were at liberty to give their whole attention to the proper duties of their function; and notwithftanding minifters feem to have been more dependent upon their people, there never was a time in which minifters had more influence, and when their reproofs and cenfures were more feared. That this was very much the cafe formerly, I can appeal to the memory of many perfons now living, or even to what is now the fact, in fome parts of the kingdom where the old cuftoms have been religioufly kept up.   At

At prefent, though the falaries of minifters have been confiderably advanced, in comparifon of what they were formerly, all other advantages are, in general, very inconfiderable, and, from the fame caufes, muft be expected to grow more fo.

Add to this, that the price of all neceffary provifions is prodigioufly advanced all over England. Moreover the tafte of living is much higher than it was, fo that the expences which *cuftom*, at leaft, if not *nature* have made neceffary, in their cafe, are more than double of what they were in the memory of man. On this account, the largeft income of any diffenting minifter is barely a decent maintenance for a family, without a poffibility of laying up any thing for the ufe of a widow, or children, after his death. Indeed, a genteel congregation would think themfelves difgraced by the mean houfekeeping, drefs, and appearance of their minifter, or his family. It is unfortunate, alfo, that minifters,

nifters, by being invited to the tables of their richer hearers, too often acquire a tafte for high living themfelves, a tafte which it would be ruinous to them to gratify at home.

The confequence of thefe difcouragements is a circumftance, which already begins to be very alarming to the diffenting intereft. Formerly, when the miniftry was more reputable, perfons of fome rank and fortune educated their fons for it. Many of thefe minifters, being eafy in their circumftances, took no care about their falaries, and were fo far from making a gain of godlinefs, or even being fupported by the intereft, that they contributed to its fupporr, by preaching in places, in which the falary kept dwindling, till, after they died, a minifter could not be fupported. Many places have been intirely fhut up in this manner.

So well known are the ftraits to which minifters and their families have often been

been reduced, that few are now educated with a view to it, except young perfons, who have a turn for learning, and whofe parents are unable to make any other provifion for them. Even perfons educated in this manner are fewer every year; for it is a low way of life indeed, that will not produce more *money*, which is the the thing that the generality of parents chiefly confider; fo that it is now no eafy matter to find young perfons to educate for the miniftry, though it coft the parents little or nothing.

What, then, is likely to be the confequence of this deficiency of minifters liberally educated among the diffenters? The intereft muft grow lefs refpectable, lay preachers, and perfons of an enthufiaftic turn of mind, and fuperficially inftructed, will grow more numerous, or vacancies among us muft be fupplied from Scotland; and *how* they are fupplied from this quarter, let the ftate of the diffenting intereft in the north of England teftify.

What

What religious principles are they, that we can expect to have brought among us by men who have subscribed *the Scotch confession of faith*, and *the Assembly's catechism?* Besides that, in general, only the very refuse of the country, and such as can get no preferment at home, can be expected to migrate into England. When I say this I leave room to suppose, and I know there are, many exceptions.

The only method by which these evils can be remedied, is to make the dissenting ministry an object worth the attention of persons of a liberal education, and this is only in the power of gentlemen of fortune to do. Exert yourselves, my brethren, for this purpose. Revive the zeal of your ancestors, and dispose of your superfluous wealth in this *good old cause*. Behave towards your ministers, not with a superstitious reverence, but with that respect which a regard to virtue, learning, and religion ought to enforce. Treat them with generosity, and exact no
servile

servile compliances from them; but consider them as your superiors with respect to office, whatever your rank in life may be, your equals as men and gentlemen, and your inferiors in nothing but what will always make fools and knaves superior to men of sense and virtue. There are many congregations of dissenters, which fully answer this description, nay which exceed whatever can be reasonably expected of them.

SECTION V.

Advice to Ministers.

WITH the same freedom with which I have treated the *laity* among us, I would subjoin a word of advice to the *ministers*. Propriety of conduct on your side will go a great way towards replacing your order in that respectable situation, in which I most heartily wish to see it. Imbibe

bibe the spirit of your religion and of your office. Without adopting all the austerity of your predecessors, whose minds were made more severe by the hardships they had suffered, refrain from giving into the levities of the age in which we live. Let it be manifest that you are no lovers of what is called *pleasure*, or given to dissipation; that you are no slaves to your *appetite*, and have nothing of *conceit*, or *vanity*, with respect to your persons, your dress, or your talents. Avoid, also, all expensive shew in furniture and ornament of every kind.

This caution against giving into an excessive love of pleasure, and indulging a turn for gaity and dissipation, which are so prevalent in the present age, is strongly enforced by a regard to your particular situation, as persons who pretend to *think* more freely than others. You are not unacquainted, that the popular cry against you is, that you *act* more freely too, and are less scrupulous with respect to propriety,

ety, decency, and moral strictness of behaviour; and the suspicion is not, altogether, without foundation. Such is the nature of man, that we are prone to run into extremes; so that, having once called in question the principles of our ancestors, we are too apt to think them to have been absurd and wrong in every thing. Indeed a great deal of their external strictness was certainly superstitious, and some of the good customs they kept up were, with respect to them, built on false principles. These, therefore, being thrown down, whatever rested upon them, how good soever in itself, falls with them.

But, being aware of this, let us, my brethren, be upon our guard against the licentiousness of reformation. Let us not be precipitate, but endeavour to separate the *wheat* from the *chaff*; and, before we absolutely reject any thing, let us consider whether other, and better reasons may not be given for it, than those by which it has been enforced upon us. Having discarded ed every thing of fuperftition, and what is falfe and ufelefs in religion, let us be the more zealous in the obfervance of what appears, upon examination, to be genuine and ufeful.

I cannot help thinking that, in this cafe, the apoftles example, *to become all things to all men*; and his advice about the conduct of thofe who are ftrong towards thofe who are *weak*, fhould engage us to a conformity, at leaft for a time, in every thing that is innocent, to the prejudices of others. This we fhall certainly do, if we mean to give to others a favourable opinion of ourfelves, and of our principles, if we have any thoughts of winning upon them, and do not intend to exafperate them againft us, and to induce them, from the mere fpirit of oppofition, to perfift in obftinately holding their errors and prejudices.

Do not fail to inculcate thefe confiderations upon the *laity*, whofe fituation and
cir-

circumstances lay them under less restraint than yourselves ; and whose freedom, from the prejudices of their ancestors is, in many cases, by no means to be placed to the account of a love of truth, or can be called the result of mature and serious examination. Many of them laugh at the strict observance of the sabbath, and regularity in the times of public and private devotion, as *superstition*, and not necessarily connected with moral conduct. They sneer at the doctrines of a trinity in unity, original sin, predestination, and atonement, &c. because, at first view, they are mysterious and unintelligible; but, from the same superficial turn of mind, they neglect the Lord's supper, discard family prayer, never catechize their children, and are apt to neglect devotion in all its forms. Because they think they need not *extirpate*, they will not so much as *restrain* their appetites, and dreading the imputation of precisenes and rigour, they abandon themselves to absolute licentiousness; so that having nothing about

bout them whereby they can be diftinguifhed as *chriftians*, they refemble, in all refpects, the mere *men of this world*, and fome of them even thofe *whofe God is belly, and whofe glory is fhame, who mind earthly things only*,

Too many of thefe modern freethinkers, having indulged themfelves, without referve, in laughing at every thing they cannot comprehend, take it into their heads to be offended at the *Jewifh religion*; they make no fcruple to ridicule the divine miffion and miracles of Mofes; and after this it will not be wondered at, that they often reject the chriftian revelation alfo. To trace this fatal *unthinking* progrefs a little farther: ftill they will pretend to expect a future ftate of rewards and punifhments, from the principles of the light of nature; but when once they have advanced thus far in infidelity, they are generally foon content to rank themfelves with the beafts that perifh; that is, they are, in fact, at leaft to all practical

pur-

purposes, *Atheists*. And though they may themselves, through the influence of good principles, and early habits, continue to live sober and respectable lives; their posterity, not having the same advantage; but, on the contrary, being brought up in great ignorance with respect to religion, and frequently hearing the great sanctions of virtue treated with ridicule, may be expected, in many cases, (especially considering the bias of the present age) to be utterly profligate and abandoned.

When persons have, in this manner, thrown off all regard to religion, can it be supposed they will have any strong attachment to the *dissenting interest*? Some of them may continue to rank among us, from a regard to the principles of liberty, and other political considerations; but when *religion* makes no part of the tie, it may be expected, in general, that the laity will be governed by their own secular interest; and if, through the influence of the fame caufes, a minifter have become an unbeliever in the religion he profeffes to teach, I do not fee why he may not, with equal confiftency, officiate in the church of England, the church of Rome, or among the Mohammedans, as among the diffenters.

This, however, is too often the progrefs of infidelity with the thoughtlefs and half thinking laity; and to keep them in a proper medium, muft be owned to be of great importance, and a matter of great difficulty. I know of nothing that is fo likely to be effectual for this purpofe, as the prudent conduct, and true moderation of minifters. Let it appear, by the whole of your behaviour, that you are *ferious chriftians*, and not afhamed of any practices which are of real ufe to form a chriftian and devout temper. Let it be feen, that the doctrines of chriftianity have a real and happy effect upon your hearts and lives, and that, by virtue of a practical faith in its great principles,
you

you are poffeffed of an uniform chearfulnefs of mind, are enabled to live in a firm confidence in divine providence, under all the events of life, and are prepared to die with compofure and good hope.

Carefully avoid infulting or ridiculing thofe who differ from you in opinion, efpecially thofe who retain the principles you yourfelves once held. This fhows as much bigotry and want of real candour as their cenforioufnefs, and readinefs to pafs a fentence of damnation upon you. Nay, it may be faid, in excufe for their zeal in condemning your opinions, that they confider them as inconfiftent with falvation; whereas you do not pretend that their opinions are fo dangerous to them. There may, therefore, be the fincereft friendfhip in their anger, but there is wanton cruelty in your laughter.

Let it appear that the principal object of your attention is the proper duty of your profeffion, and let no tafte you may have for any of the *polite arts*, as mufic, painting, or poetry, nor a capacity for improvements in *science*, engage you to make them more than an *amufement* to you, or, at the moft, any more than an object of fecondary confideration. Let not even the ftudy of *fpeculative theology* prevent your applying yourfelf chiefly to the advancement of *virtue* among your hearers. Let your conduct demonftrate, that you confider one foul reclaimed from vicious habits, or even one perfon's mind confirmed in any good refolution, as a greater acquifition to you, than the detection of any fpeculative error, the illuftration of any known truth, or the difcovery of any new ones.

With refpect to your general manner of behaviour, let not a fenfe of your inferiority to your hearers, in point of fortune, lead you into any mean and fervile compliances with their foibles and opinions; nor, on the other hand, let a fenfe of the dignity of your office, or your advantage

in

in point of fenfe and learning, betray you into pride, arrogance, and an overbearing decifive manner in converfation, which cannot fail to give offence. Study human nature and mankind, but with no other view than to do them good. Endeavour to be chearful, polite, (as far as that term conveys the idea of a reafonable defire to pleafe) and free from affectation. Take no pains to conceal any natural peculiarity of manner, that is innocent in itfelf, and not offenfive to others; for, above all things, *fimplicity of character*, and the greateft freedom from artifice and difguife, becomes the teachers of the religion of Jefus Chrift.

Let it appear that, in confequence of being much converfant with fubjects fuited to your profeffion, you have acquired a fuperiority of mind to this world, and all the things of it; that you are chiefly folicitous about the faithful and impartial difcharge of your duty, which is to inculcate upon others the fame chriftian temper
and

and conduct, of which you exhibit an example in yourselves; and let it appear, that this conscioufness of doing your duty, gives you a practical and habitual reliance on the providence of God, for the supply of your wants, and the care of your families after you are dead.

If, however, you have a fair opportunity of making provision for futurity, by no means neglect to do it; and I sincerely wish that every student for the christian ministry among the dissenters would, in the course of his education, give attention to those branches of knowledge, by which he might be of use to society, independent of his profession as a minister. This would prove a resource to him in a day of adversity, and, in the mean time, would make him be regarded by his people, with more of that respect, which is always paid to persons that are independent of them.

It

It was not my purpose to descend to *particular advises*, but there are two subjects, on which I think I ought not to omit this opportunity of addressing you. The first, and the most important is, that you take proper measures to promote *religious knowledge* among your hearers, by no means neglecting to ground them well in the true principles of our dissent. It is notorious, that along with the spirit of controversy the *love of truth* has, in too great a measure, left us; and that many of our youth, particularly in genteel and opulent families, are brought up in great ignorance.

Family prayer, and consequently the regular reading of the scriptures, being laid aside, the younger branches of the family have a very imperfect acquaintance with the contents of the sacred books; and it is to be feared that their posterity, being of course still more ignorant, will know little or nothing of the difference between one mode of christianity and another,

nother, or concerning christianity itself; and that a very trifling circumstance may convert the nominal dissenter into a nominal churchman, and the nominal christian into an unbeliever, and of the most profligate kind. Whereas, if men actually will read, and *study* their bible, and consequently understand their religion, there must be some uncommon fatality in their circumstances, if they disbelieve it, or become indifferent to it; and if a man really knows the ground of our *rational dissent* from the church of England, I will venture to say, that, if he has been educated in it, he must bid adieu to virtue, and the prime of virtues *integrity*, before he can desert the dissenting interest.

2 The second subject of my advice respects your *manner of preaching*, or the delivery of your sermons. It appears to me that there are two extremes in this case, and that both of them are too prevalent among us. Some ministers, whose discourses are excellent, deliver them with a shame-

a shameful carelessness and unconcern, with no force or energy, suited to their importance. This manner of preaching can never engage a suitable attention. The discourses of the same persons are also, generally, too refined for the common people. Such preaching, therefore, can neither be *understood* nor *felt* by the hearers. How then can it profit them? For the same reason, it cannot please. And how can a man expect to be well attended, who communicates neither *profit* nor *pleasure* ?

On the other hand, some of our ministers seem to study nothing but the art of harranguing the populace. Not content with speaking with that earnestness and dignity which becomes the importance of the things they have to deliver, their principal object is merely to excite a *temporary emotion*; if they be not seeking their own praise, and emolument.

With thefe views it becomes a maxim with them that every difcourfe muft be ftriking or affecting; which neceffarily begets a falfe tafte in eloquence, and gives them a habit of flourifhing or bawling upon the moft indifferent fubjects. Till at length, infenfible of the change in themfelves, they come never to fpeak from juft and *real feelings*; but their whole fervice is a *piece* of artifice, vifible to every man of fenfe, and who is acquainted with human nature, and pleafing to none but thofe who are dupes to the groffeft illufions; who are charmed with every noife, and agitated with every motion of the limbs, or contortion of the features.

To guard againft both thefe extremes, was, one would think the eafieft thing in the world; but in fact, it is by no means fo. The foundation, however, of a good and juft delivery is to be truly ferious, to underftand and feel every thing a man fays, and to exprefs himfelf in the moft natural manner. The former of thefe belongs

longs to the virtues of the heart, but the latter muft be acquired by the ufe of proper means; more efpecially great pains muft be taken to form the voice for fpeaking to a large company. Otherwife, a perfon who has been ufed to fpeak only to a few people, in a room of an ordinary fize, will have no idea of making himfelf heard by a large audience, without lofing his natural emphafis, cadence, and tone of voice. He, is therefore, fure to contract fome aukward and abfurd habit, even though he be ever fo ferious and in earneft, and confequently have no affectation.

The art of public fpeaking, therefore, muft be ftudied, and the inftructions of a mafter muft be accompanied with frequent exercife. But when this is done, and when practice has made it *habitual*, a *juft temper of mind* is all that is requifite to form the moft perfect fpeaker; by which I mean not one whofe talents will ftrike the bulk of mankind, or gain him the

moft

most noisy applause, but whose manner will command the attention of those who are disposed to think.

If a man have not reputation in view, if he aim at nothing besides making converts to truth and virtue, and will content himself with endeavouring simply to convey his own *just*, and sometimes *warm* conceptions to others, he will speak so as to inform or animate them as occasion will require. He will make them think of, understand, and act upon what he says. And the reputation he *indirectly* acquires, though it will be less than that of many who less deserve it, will be *sufficient*; and if he be a good man, and a good christian, it will content him.

SECTION

SECTION VI.

Of the low *state of the dissenting interest, and the causes of it.*

IT is possible that some of those who are called *rational dissenters* may be discouraged by the *smallness of the party*, and the seemingly declining state of the interest. But this is an objection that will hardly bear to be avowed, and can only have weight with weak minds. The cause of *truth and liberty* can never cease to be respectable, whether its advocates be few or many. Rather, if the cause be just and honourable, the smaller is the party that support it, the fewer there are to share that honour with us. It can never be matter of praise to any man to join a multitude, but to be singular in a good thing is the greatest praise. It shows a power of discernment, and fortitude of mind,

mind, not to be overborne by those unworthy motives, which are always on the side of the majority, whether their cause be good or bad.

That there are few dissenters of exceeding large fortunes, especially in the country, is very true; but it may be accounted for, in a manner that is far from reflecting any dishonour on the interest. Many dissenters have been born to great fortunes, and many others have themselves acquired large fortunes by trade; but when this has been the case, as the possession of wealth naturally tends to make men more worldly minded, and exposes them more to the influence of worldly views; and as men naturally aspire to rank with their superiors, rather than their inferiors in fortune, they have not been able to find proper persons to associate with, except in the established church; and the consequence of such connections is evident. Many persons, also, have left the dissenters after marrying into families

that

that go to church. But thefe are motives intirely foreign to the *merits* of the caufe, and therefore will never have the leaft influence with men of reafon and religion. Let a number of perfons be produced who will gravely fay, they left the diffenting intereft, and went to the eftablifhed church, from real *conviction of mind*, and after mature confideration; and if even their new acquaintance believe them, this objection fhall be confidered again.

It will be faid the diffenting *minifters*, and efpecially thofe who are called *free* in their fentiments, frequently conform to the church of England. It is acknowledged; but, at the fame time, it is apprehended, that when the members of the eftablifhment confider all the circumftances attending thefe *converfions*, they will fee little to boaft of in the acquifition. It is well known that many of them have been men of profligate lives, or defpicable characters, who were difmiffed with ignominy from the fervice of the diffenters;

others,

others, there is reason enough to suppose, found nothing among the dissenters suited to their ambitious views. It may perhaps be true, that some could not get a decent maintenance by their labours; however the class of dissenters to which they are acknowledged to have belonged (viz. those who, in their sentiments, differ the most from the principles of the church of England) is a sufficient indication of *what kind* must have been the motives of their conformity. For, as it can never be pretended, that they have changed their sentiments concerning those articles, which the rational part of the dissenters object to the most in the church of England, the motive could not be *serious conviction*; but their subscription to articles which they do not believe, but which they continue to preach against, and even to laugh at, must either have been a subscription to them as *articles of peace*, or as far as they are *agreeable to the scriptures*, or with some other of those *miserable equivocations*, the futility of which has been so clearly exposed

exposed by the author of the Confessional.

If, however, any dissenting minister has really, from full conviction of mind, *ex animo*, subscribed his assent and consent *to all, and every of the thirty nine articles* of the church of England, and also to all, and every thing else that a clergyman is required to subscribe, (the possibility of which I do not absolutely deny) I think the loss is by no means to be regretted. Let the bigots to the church set a high value upon him. He is *rara avis in terris, nigroque simillima cygno*.

Persons who are descended from members of the church of England, who are educated by clergymen, who are introduced into the ministry at an English university, where *theology*, if I be rightly informed, makes no part of their study, and where it is the custom to subscribe at a time of life, when it cannot be supposed they have reflected on the nature of the action;

action; who see that they do no more than all their friends and acquaintance do, and continue to do, without the least scruple; and who, perhaps, never heard any objection made to it, are to be considered in a very different light from dissenting ministers, who generally study theological subjects with great care; who also, in consequence of hearing the business of subscription frequently discussed, cannot but have reflected on the nature of solemnly subscribing to what they do not believe, and of repeating, in acts of divine worship, what their consciences disclaim. Every allowance may reasonably be made for the former; but, I own, that I can make no apology for the latter, except such an apology as may be made for sacrificing, in any other case, the sacred rights of conscience to some other consideration.

I cannot help considering the clergy of the *church of Scotland* as more criminal in the article of subscription than the clergy of of the church of England; becaufe the courfe of their ftudies neceffarily brings the fubject more frequently in their view. Indeed, with refpect to all matters of theology, the minds of the Scotch minifters are certainly, of late years, much more enlightened, and yet their practice is not more reformed, Numbers of the young minifters avow their difbelief of the Scotch confeffion of faith, &c. they fee the bufinefs of fubfcription to it in its juft and odious light; they cannot help feeling, or forbear complaining of the impofition; and yet I cannot fay that I have heard of of many of thefe *bold freethinkers* refufing to fubfcribe, and for fo paltry an advantage as a Scotch living. I call it *paltry* when I confider the *price* that is paid for it. As a falary for a minifter, I think it fufficient, and refpectable. But certainly it argues a bafer foul in a man, to facrifice his confcience for a *fmall* than for a *great* confideration.

Upon

Upon the whole, when the reasons of the small number of dissenters are such as have been represented the smallness of their number is far from being a matter of reflection upon them, or what they need to be ashamed of. Besides, there are many important ends which the existence of the dissenting interest answers, even with respect to the established church itself, which make it well worth supporting. It necessarily operates as a check upon the clergy, and prevents them from sinking into that indolence, luxury, ignorance, and arrogance, to which, as men, with little or no controul, they would otherwise be more subject; and their literary pride must be kept within bounds by seeing, among the dissenters, men equal to themselves in genius, application to study, and an acquaintance with all the branches of useful science.

This circumstance cannot fail also to rouse a laudable emulation, which will be of unspeakable advantage to the interests,

both

both of polite literature, and of real knowledge of all kinds. And without a diffenting intereft of fome kind, there would hardly be a poffibility of any *reformation in the church*; an event which the wifeft and beft among the clergy earneftly wifh for, and are labouring to bring about. Light always breaks out by degrees, and it is only from feeing a variety of *experiments*, as they may be called, of reformation, that the nation in general can be able to judge what are real improvements, and felect fuch as will beft fuit themfelves.

If, therefore, there be any, who are friends of the church of England, on any other account than the profpect of providing for fome of their relations and dependents by its emoluments, they cannot fhew a truer regard to it, than by favouring the diffenting intereft; becaufe, whatever is decent and refpectable in the church is, in fome meafure, owing to the diffenters. So long as the diffenting intereft terest is a nursery for men of liberal and enlarged minds, who make it their study to restore christianity to its primitive simplicity, (and many such it can boast at present) so long as it is the cause of civil and religious liberty (which it can never cease to be) and so long as it is a check upon the disorders into which the established clergy would otherwise sink (which, also, it can never cease to be) it must appear a truly *respectable* interest, in the eyes of all men who are capable of entertaining just and generous views of things, though it be ever so inconsiderable with respect to numbers.

As to the number of dissenters in England, it must be considered, that, notwithstanding the seeming declension of what we call the rational part of the dissenters, there is, perhaps, rather an increase than a decrease upon the whole. Those who are called *Independents*, retain all the zeal of the old puritans; and though several of their societies are become

come what we call more *free* in their sentiments, they receive daily recruits from the *Methodists*; and many very numerous focieties of Independents have been formed entirely out of that body. Even thefe new made diffenters will, by degrees, neceffarily come to think freely, and fupply the places of thofe rational, but lukewarm diffenters, who are daily abforbed either in the *church* or in *irreligion*; and thus may the *circulation*, at leaft, be kept up.

I cannot help confidering the *Methodifts* as raifed up by divine providence, at a moft feafonable juncture, as a barrier againft the encroachments of ecclefiaftical tyranny, in the declenfion of the old diffenting intereft. For whatever be the real views of their leaders, one great point, in favour of the diffenting intereft, is gained with all the Methodifts; which is, that though they communicate with the church of England, they are no longer attached to the hierarchy as fuch. That blind

blind and bigoted attachment, which is the great hold that the clergy have on the minds of the common people, is broken, the moment they can chuse to worship God without the walls of the parish church, and without the use of the common prayer-book. Their minds are, from that time, at liberty to consider the expediency of different forms of worship, and to adopt that to which their judgment shall give the preference; and as public worship is universally conducted among them, in the same manner as among the dissenters, they are already *in the way* to us, from the established church. When such a spirit of reformation is raised, it will not be in the power of those who have the most influence among them to say, *Hitherto shall it go and no farther*. It is not improbable, that a great revolution may take place in their affairs, when the heads of two or three of their present leaders shall be laid in the grave.

SECTION

SECTION VII.

Of the divided state *of the diffenting interest.*

I AM aware of another circumstance, which may make the diffenting interest appear despicable in the eyes of some; and I shall not conceal, but consider, and reply to the objection that arises from it. We are split into such a number of *sects* and parties, (some of which discover a mean, contracted, and illiberal spirit, treating their antagonists with hatred and abhorrence, while others treat theirs with a supercilious contempt) that some persons may be ashamed of having any thing to do with us. The charge is, in a great measure, true; but this *divided state* of the diffenting interest is inseparable from the *freedom* we all profess and enjoy, and, consequently, from the great good that evidently arises from the exercise of that freedom.

F Besides,

Besides, it is wrong to consider the dissenters as *one body*. They have nothing necessarily in common, but their claim to worship God according to the dictates of their own consciences; and those consciences, being the consciences of different men, dictate very different things; and no person is responsible for more than his own sentiments and conduct. I cannot but say, however, that I heartily wish all the sects of dissenters would consider, that, in consequence of their agreement in this one circumstance, concerning their natural right to worship God according to the dictates of their own consciences, they have great interests in common; and, that they would, for this reason, entertain less animosity against one another, on account of the things in which they differ.

Though it happen, that in the town in which you live, there be no society of dissenters that you can intirely approve of, it can hardly happen, but that there will be some, which, if you consider seriously, you

you may more confcientioufly join with, than with the church of England. If we take in every thing relating to doctrine, difcipline, and method of worfhip, I think there is no fect or denomination among us, that is not nearer to the ftandard of the gofpel than the eftablifhed church; fo that, even in thofe circumftances, you will be a diffenter, if reafon, and not paffion, or prejudice, be your guide.

If when you refide for any time in the country, you chufe to go to church rather than to the diffenting meeting-houfe, becaufe the diffenters happen to make no great figure in the place; if you feel any thing like *fhame*, upon feeing the external meannefs of the intereft, and fecretly wifh to have your connections with it concealed; conclude, that the *spirit of this world* has got too much hold of you, and that *religious motives* have loft their influence.

If this be your general practice (and I wifh I could fay it was not fo, with many of the more opulent among us)' you are but half a diffenter; and a few more worldly confiderations would throw you intirely into the church of England, or into any church upon earth. With this temper of mind you would, in primitive times, have been afhamed of *chriftianity* itfelf, and have joined the more fafhionable and pompous heathen worfhip. But confider what our Lord fays, with a view to all fuch circumftances as thefe, *Whofoever fhall be afhamed of me, and of my words, of him alfo fhall the fon of man be afhamed, when he cometh in the glory of his father with his holy angels.*

General, alas! and fatal is the influence of fafhion in what it ought to have the leaft concern with, matters of *religion*. Members of the reformed churches on the continent, who are generally prefbyterians, feldom fcruple to join the epifcopal church of England, evidently for no other reafon, than becaufe it is the moft illuftrious of the proteftant churches in the

the ifland; and because, in this connection, they are more in the way of being taken notice of by perfons of figure and diftinction, and thereby advancing themfelves in life. Rapin, the hiftorian, acknowledges himfelf to be a prefbyterian, but at the fame time, avows his conftant communion with the church of England when he refided here.

If you be an *unitarian*, and, in other refpects, one of thofe who are called the free-thinking party among the diffenters; and if there be no diffenting place of worfhip that you can conveniently attend, except one belonging to thofe who are of the rigid Independent party; and if you think that, in joining with them, you countenance many antichriftian errors; ftill, you fhould confider that, in going to the eftablifhed church, you not only countenance the very fame *antichriftian errors*, but an *antichriftian hierarchy* alfo, and a number of other abufes, which can never fubfift among any fect of diffenters

what-

whatever. And it appears to me, that every man is under an obligation to support the public worship of God, in that manner which he most approves upon the whole, notwithstanding it may contain many things which he cannot approve; provided that it be so circumstanced, that his attendance upon doth not imply his joining in any thing that is sinful.

If you be of the other party of dissenters, I need say nothing to persuade you to adhere to the interest. Though you are much nearer to the established church than any other party of dissenters, you justly consider the points in which you do differ from it, to be of so much importance, that you will maintain the separation in the lowest state possible, rather than give it up intirely.

Besides, as you do not lay so much stress upon a *learned ministry*, a number of you, so small as not to be able to support a regular minister, can meet together, and
edify

edify one another, after the manner of the primitive church; which I mention not with ridicule, but with real approbation. Christianity may, surely, exist without the aid of human learning; and the notion of the validity of the administration of christian ordinances, depending upon any particular order of men, who must subsist wholly by the ministry, is, I think, exploded by us all.

Divisions among dissenters cannot afford any better foundation for an objection to the dissenting interest, than divisions among christians in general afford for an objection to christianity itself. Indeed this circumstance cannot supply a just and reasonable objection to any scheme of religion; for there are sects and parties in them all.

To conclude, I do not know that I have concealed any thing relating to the dissenting interest, that can afford any person a pretence for deserting it; and recommend-

commending what I have said in reply to the various objections to it, and concerning the difficulties and discouragements attending it, with what I have farther advanced in favour of it, to your deliberate and candid attention,

I am, Gentlemen,

Your very humble Servant,

A DISSENTER.

POSTSCRIPT.

POSTSCRIPT.

I CANNOT conclude this ADDRESS without mentioning a circumstance, which may be thought to be trifling, but which has an evident connection with things that are of considerable consequence, and which did not immediately fall under any of the heads of the preceding sections. It is the growing neglect of *attendance on public worship*, among those who are called *rational dissenters*. This is, at the same time, a *cause*, and an *effect* of the prevailing indifference both to religion in general, and the dissenting interest in particular.

When a number of persons consider themselves as having great interests in common, they will be fond of appearing in their common and public character; and, indeed, upon other occasions, their common sentiments, views, and expectations will be the subject of their common conversation.

It gives me concern to obferve, that not only *religious*, but almoft all *ferious* difcourfe, except on fubjects of worldly policy, or bufinefs, is, in a manner, banifhed from polite company; in fo much that the whole conduct of many perfons profefling chriftianity, under the denomination of *proteftants*, and *rational diffenters*, I am afraid, might be obferved with the utmoft attention, for weeks and months together, without a poffibility of difcovering, from any circumftance (except a few matters of mere form, which cuftom has not yet abolifhed) whether they made profeffion of any religion or not. Certainly, then, the leaft that can be concluded is, that it is not a matter of the firft confequence with them.

Confiderable allowance, however, muft be made for the influence of modefty, or rather of a falfe fhame. Many perfons, I am willing to hope, *think* of religion, are influenced by the motives of it, and confcientioufly practice its moft fubftantial duties,

duties, who are seldom heard to *talk* upon the subject. But a just zeal will break through this false shame, which, if it be not injurious to a man's self, is greatly so to others; who will necessarily conclude that he either believes nothing of religion, or that he has very little value for it, when he does not discover it by his conversation; so that the influence of our *example*, in favour of religion is altogether given up by this conduct.

The least that you can do, my brethren, towards reviving a just zeal in matters of religion, is conscientiously to attend public worship yourselves, and to see that your children and servants do the same along with you; unless they give you reason to think that they object to your mode of worship on a principle of conscience. Admit, therefore, of no excuse, except real sickness, and works of absolute necessity, either for your own non-attendance, or for theirs.

You.

You juftly diftinguifh between duties that are properly of a *moral* nature, and thofe that are in themfelves *indifferent*, as the obfervance of days and times muft be acknowledged to be. But, in confequence of fome perfons over-valuing pofitive inftitutions, many of you greatly undervalue them, to the injury of yourfelves and others. In things of acknowledged divine appointment, and that are known to have been appointed for the fake of their fubferviency to moral purpofes, as the inftitution of a *day of reft*, and of the *Lord's-fupper*, the difference between a regard to them, and to the morality to which they are fubfervient is not fo exceeding great. So nearly are they of equal obligation, that the man whofe rule of life is an impartial obedience to the will of God, will not neglect the one, but for the fake of the other; and the cafes in which a regard to moral virtue will really interfere with the obfervance of pofitive duties, are very few.

Travelling

Travelling on Sundays is now become fo common, that if many perfons, who call themfelves chriftians, and rational diffenters, be taking a journey of a few days, it may with certainty be concluded, that the *day of reft* will be one of them ; and if it be confined to a fingle day, and can poffibly be thrown upon that, it is almoft fure to be fo.

I am no advocate for the very rigorous manner in which many of our anceftors obferved this day; but certainly, if we pay any regard to the original defign of the inftitution, it fhould be made, as far as poffible, a day of reft for all the creation of God. We ought therefore confcientioufly to refrain from doing bufinefs ourfelves, or making our cattle labour on that day. Befides, if there be any propriety in attending upon public worfhip on the Lord's-day, it muft be agreeable to reafon, that we fpend the day in a manner confiftent with that ufe of it; and therefore that we abftain from all fuch exercifes exercises and diversions as would tend to defeat the purpose of religious worship, by erasing the effect of moral and religious instruction.

But whether business, pleasure, or mere indolence and indifference be the *cause*, the *effect* is manifest, and is growing every day more alarming. Consider that the decent and reverent attendance upon public worship on the Lord's-day, is almost the only means of promoting the knowledge and practice of christianity among the lower ranks of people, who are confined to labour all the rest of the week. And how can their attendance be effectually inforced, but by the example, influence, and authority of their superiors?

The interest of any particular party or denomination of christians is certainly trifling, in comparison with the greater considerations of religion and morality just now mentioned; but if you wish well to the dissenting interest, you should consider fider how much it fuffers in confequence of your neglect of public worſhip.

Your miniſters are diſcouraged by this means, and your children and fervants get a habit of indifference, or of roving from place to place; whereby their attachment to the cauſe is continually leſſening. Your remiſſneſs, therefore, in attending public worſhip promotes a defertion of the intereſt, by making the tranſition as eaſy to them as poſſible. For when things have been in this train, to abandon the intereſt intirely is breaking no eſtabliſhed cuſtom, or confirmed habit; ſo that thoſe perſons who have been very indifferent to public worſhip, can have little or no difficulty with reſpect to themſelves; and the thing being done almoſt without the notice of others, the difficulty on that ſide is alſo obviated. When the change is ſo gradual, it is, at length, no ſurpriſe to any body, to hear that thoſe who attended the diſſenting-meeting-houſe but ſeldom, ceaſe to attend there at all. Otherwiſe, wife, the difficulty that arifes from the force of cuftom, is fo great, in many cafes, that though a man might wifh to change his mode of worfhip, he would not chufe to expofe himfelf to fo much of the notice and cenfure of his friends and acquaintance, as, by fuch a ftep in his conduct, he is fenfible that he neceffarily muft do. But, by being lefs frequently in company with diffenters, their opinion and cenfure have lefs weight with him.

I MUST extend this Poftfcript, in order to exprefs my earneft wifhes, that, in this age, in which fo many diffenters are runing into *enthufiafm* on one hand, and *infidelity* on the other, thofe who have at heart the caufe of truth, chriftianity, and religious liberty, would endeavour to draw the attention of mankind to thofe fubjects, and others that are connected with them.

There can be no doubt, but that thefe great interefts will be taken care of by him who is conftituted *head over all things*
to

to that church, against which *the gates of hell shall not prevail*; but it appears to me that this end is to be accomplished by natural and human means, and that the judicious and zealous *labourers in this vineyard* are but few. The real friends of the cause of religion and virtue ought, therefore, to exert themselves; and it cannot but give us encouragement, and raise our generous emulation, to think that success in these glorious attempts is, to a certain degree, infallible. And what just reason will a man have to be *ashamed in the day of Christ*, who might have been among the foremost in supporting this cause, and yet, through indolence and inattention, let others carry away that palm, which will then be esteemed the most honourable.

On the other hand, it must be acknowledged, that the greatest care should be taken, not to injure the best of causes, by injudicious or unseasonable attempts to serve it. In this case, however, there will be the praise of honest zeal, and good intention

tention. Besides, it must be a very poor and weak manner of address indeed, that is calculated to do no good; and if one were written by an angel from heaven, it would offend and disgust many. Since there is such a variety in the previous dispositions and tastes of readers, let writers also indulge their own natural taste and manner. The man who means well can hardly fail to instruct and edify some, though he must lay his account with displeasing, and perhaps injuring others; and as the calculation of the probability of doing the most good or harm seems to be, in this case, too difficult for human comprehension, our best rule is to sow what we apprehend to be *good seed*, and leave the issue to the great *Lord of the harvest*; that is, strenuously to urge whatever appears to us, upon mature deliberation, to be favourable to truth and virtue, and to leave the consequences to him who knows them, who is interested in them, and who will attend to them; so as to bring good out of all the evil that we may

may inadvertently occasion. *Let us, therefore, consider one another, to provoke unto love and to good works. Let us exhort one another, and so much the more as we see the day approaching. For yet a little while, and he that shall come will come, and will not tarry.* Heb. x. 24, 35, 37.

As to the contempt of the world, I had almost said, happy are they who have the greatest share of it. This, at least, is true with respect to all the unthinking and vicious part of it. And there certainly will be cases, to the end of this state of trial and discipline, to which the following words of our Lord will be applicable. *Wo unto you when all men shall speak well of you.* Luke vi. 26. But *blessed are ye when men shall revile you, and persecute you, and say all manner of evil against you falsely, for my sake. Rejoice, and be exceeding glad, for great is your reward in heaven.* Matt. v. 11, 12. It will always, I doubt not, be true, in some measure, that *all who would live godly in Christ Jesus, must suffer persecution.*

perfecution. And perfecution unto death is by means the only, or perhaps the moft difficult to bear of all the modes of trial to which we are expofed. Of the number who *make shipwreck of faith and a good confcience,* there are probably but few who have been in thefe circumftances.

Confider what was obferved by the apoftle Paul, at the firft promulgation of the gofpel, viz. that *not many wife men after the flesh, not many mighty, not many noble were called.* 1 Cor. i. 26. and that the influence of *wealth, power,* and *fafhion,* is the very fame at this day, that it was in his time, and will probably continue to be fo to the end of the world. It cannot, therefore, but be a fufpicious circumftance with refpect to truly chriftian fentiments, maxims, and conduct, that they are *fafhionable,* or that they render a man more acceptable to thofe who have not their *converfation in heaven,* but who *mind earthly things only.* I do not fay that a popular religion cannot be a true one, but that

that the man who finds himself popular on a religious account; I mean popular with those persons whose interests and prospects are foreign to christianity, should suspect himself, and carefully re-examine his religious principles, and not pursue them, and act upon them, but with the greatest caution and deliberation.

It is happy, however, that our religion does not leave us without consolation under this contempt of the world, which we incur by adhering to it. For besides the assurance that, if *we suffer with Christ, we shall also reign with him, and be glorified together*; and that if we *overcome the world*, in imitation of him who has done it before us, we shall *sit down with him on his throne, as he also has overcome, and is now set down with his father on his throne*; we can balance our loss of the esteem of the world, with the acquisition of the much more valuable love and esteem of our fellow christians, of the few whose sentiments and views are the same with

our

our own, and whofe countenance will be more than fufficient to fupport us under all the odium that we can lie under, on account of the opinions of thofe, whofe judgments we defpife. And if a man have but a tolerable fhare of comprehenfion, and ftrength of mind, he cannot hefitate what part to chufe. He will eafily make light of *fuffering fhame* for the prefent, in a caufe that is fure to be crowned with everlafting glory hereafter.

N. B. The principal *additions* to the fecond edition of this ADDRESS are Section III, on the manner in which diffenters ought to fpeak and write concerning the church of England; the advices to minifters concerning the inftruction of youth, and the delivery of fermons at the end of Section IV (which were added at the requeft of an anonymous correfpondent) and this poftfcript.

I beg leave to refer to Dr. Prieftley's *Letters, in anfwer to fome Remarks on his Pub-*

Publications, and on this Addrefs, for a more particular account of the nature of *chriftian idolatry* than is given p. 36; and to his *View of the principles and conduct of the proteftant diffenters, with refpect to the civil and ecclefiaftical conftitution of England*, for many other particulars relating to them, not treated of here. I, alfo, cannot help expreffing my wifhes that what he has obferved on the fubject of *church difcipline*, may be ferioufly confidered by thofe who call themfelves *rational diffenters*; that, whether any of his propofals for reformation be approved of or not, fomething, at leaft, may be attempted, in order to obviate, the manifeft inconveniences, which he has pointed out, and which have been long felt and complained of, by ferious and thinking perfons, in our prefent fituation.

F I N I S.

BOOKS written
By JOSEPH PRIESTLEY, L.L.D.F.R.S.
And Sold by
J. JOHNSON, Bookseller, at No. 72, in St. Paul's Church-Yard, London.

AN Essay on the first Principles of Government, and on the Nature of Political, Civil, and Religious Liberty, including Remarks on Dr Brown's Code of Education, and on Dr. Balguy's Sermon on Church Authority, the Second Edition, corrected and enlarged, Price 5s.

2. A Free Address to Protestant Dissenters, on the Subject of the Lord's Supper, the Second Edit. 1s.

3. Considerations on Differences of Opinion among Christians; with a Letter to the Rev. Mr. Venn, in Answer to his Examination of the Address to Protestant Dissenters, 1s. 6d.

4. Additions to the Address to Protestant Dissenters, on the Subject of the Lord's Supper, with some Corrections of it, and a Letter to the Author of the Protestant Dissenter's Answer to it, 1s.

5. A Catechism for Children and Young Persons, 6d.

6. A Serious Address to Masters of Families, with Forms of Family Prayer, 9d.

7. A View of the Principles and Conduct of the Protestant Dissenters, with Respect to the Civil and Ecclesiastical Constitution of England, the Second Edition, 1s. 6d.

8. A Free Address to Protestant Dissenters on the Subject of Church-Discipline, 2s. 6d.

Also published, In Numbers,
(Under the Direction of Dr. PRIESTLEY.)
The THEOLOGICAL REPOSITORY; consisting of Original Essays, Hints, Queries, &c. calculated to promote Religious Knowledge.
N. B. Two Volumes, price 6s. each, are already compleated.

AN

APPEAL

TO

The serious and candid Professors of Christianity,

On the following SUBJECTS, viz.

I. The Use of Reason in Matters of Religion,
II. The Power of Man to do the Will of God,
III. Original Sin,
IV. Election and Reprobation,
V. The Divinity of Christ,

AND,

VI. Atonement for Sin by the Death of Christ.

By a LOVER of the GOSPEL.

The FIFTH EDITION, with Improvements,

To us there is one God, the FATHER; *and one Mediator, the* MAN CHRIST JESUS.   1 Cor. viii. 6.—1 Tim. ii. 5.

Printed for J. JOHNSON, No 72, Saint *Paul's* Church-yard. 1775.

PRICE ONE PENNY.

Published by the Author of this Pamphlet, and sold by Mr. JOHNSON, No. 72, St. *Paul's* Churchyard.

I. The Triumph of Truth; being an Account of the Trial of Mr. E. *Elwall*, for Herefy and Blafphemy, at *Stafford* Affizes, before Judge *Denton*, &c. Pr. 1d.

II. A Familiar Illuftration of certain paffages of Scripture relating to the Power of Man to do the Will of God; Original Sin; Election and Reprobation; the Divinity of Chrift; and Atonement for Sin by the Death of Chrift. Pr. 4d.

Advertifement.

THE Writer of thefe fmall Pieces will think himfelf obliged to any Perfon who will reprint them; efpecially in fuch a Manner, as that they may be fold *very cheap*, or that thofe Perfons who think them calculated to do Good, may afford to buy a Number of copies to diftribute *gratis*.

An Appeal to the serious and candid Professors of Christianity.

My Christian Brethren,

PERMIT one, who professes obedience to the same Lord, and faith in the precious promises of the same gospel with yourselves, to address himself to you, with all freedom and plainness of speech, upon subjects relating to our common salvation. I need not tell you that these subjects are interesting. In reality, nothing else is interesting in comparison with them. For what is this world compared with the future! What is time compared with eternity! Believe me, my brethren, it is nothing but the deepest concern for the honour of a religion which is the most valuable inheritance of the human race, and which sets us above all the follies and vices, all the weaknesses and troubles of life, by giving us the most solid hope in death, that has induced me to solicit your attention. But I am confident that you will not think it ill bestowed, because it is upon a subject that is near and dear to you, and the consideration of which cannot but please and profit you.

If, by the blessing of God upon our common endeavours to *lead* and to *be led into all truth*, I shall be so happy as to bring you to entertain the same views of these things with myself, we shall rejoice together; and if, after all that I may be able to advance, you should still think differently from me, I trust you will, at least, be disposed to think with more candour of some of your fellow-christians, who love the gospel, and are zealous for its honour, though you may think them mistaken in their conceptions concerning it. Let me intreat you, therefore, my brethren, to give me a patient and candid hearing. Attend, in the spirit of meekness, to what I shall say from the earnestness of my heart; and exercise the reason which God has given you upon this occasion, which is the noblest on which it can be exercised, and for which you may, therefore, conclude, that it was principally given you.

I. *Of the Use of Reason in matters of religion.*

BE not backward, or afraid, my brethren to make use of your reason in matters of religion, or where the scriptures are concerned. They both of them proceed from the same God and Father of us all, who is the giver of every good and every perfect gift. They cannot, therefore, be contrary to one another, but must mutually illustrate and enforce one another. Besides, how can we distinguish one scheme of religion from another, so as to give the preference to that which is the most deserving of it, but by the help of our reason and understanding? What would you yourselves say to a Mahometan, whom you would persuade to abandon the imposture of Mahomet, and embrace christianity, but bid him use his reason; and judge, by the help of it, of the manifest difference between the two religions, and the great superiority of yours to his? Does not God himself appeal to the reason of man, when he condescends to ask us, *Whether his ways be not equal?* Ez. xviii. 29. Does not the apostle exhort us that, *in understanding we be men?* 1 Cor. xiv. 20. Are we not expressly commanded to *prove all things, and then hold fast that which is good?* 1 Thess. v. 21. Also, when we are commanded to *search the scriptures,* John v. 39, more must be meant than merely *reading* them, or *receiving implicitly,* the interpretations of others. *Searching* must imply an earnest endeavour to find out for ourselves, and to *understand* the truths contained in the scriptures; and what faculty can we employ for this purpose, but that which is commonly called *reason,* whereby we are capable of thinking, reflecting, comparing, and judging of things?

Distrust, therefore, all those who decry human reason, and who require you to abandon it, wherever religion

religion is concerned. When once they have gained this point with you, they can lead you whither they please, and impose upon you every absurdity which their sinister views may make it expedient for them that you should embrace. A Popish priest would require nothing more than this, to make you believe the doctrine of transubstantiation, and that a man is infallible; or to persuade you to commit the most flagrant wickedness, as a means of *doing God service*. For the first of these articles they do not fail to urge the words of scripture, which expressly say, concerning the bread that is used in the Lord's supper, that it *is the body of Christ*; Matt. xxvi. 6. and there is no possibility of replying to them, but by appealing to reason, as the necessary and proper judge of the sense of scripture. The Papist, therefore, as might well be expected, is forward, on all occasions, to vilify human reason, and to require men to abandon it; but true Protestants will not part with it. It is by the help of reason, in conjunction with the scriptures, that we guard ourselves against the gross delusions of the Papists, who, after relinquishing reason, have been *made to believe a lie*; and by the diligent and continued use of the same power, let us endeavour to combat every remaining error, and trace out and reform every corruption of christianity, till we hold the pure *truth as it is in Jesus*, and *obey it in the love thereof*.

Do not think that, by recommending the use of reason, I am about to decry the scriptures. My appeal shall be to both, upon every subject upon which I address you; and I think you cannot but see that the plainest and most obvious sense of the scriptures is in favour of those doctrines which are most agreeable to reason. A good man will rejoice to see them thus go hand in hand, mutually illustrating, and enforcing one another.

II. *Of the power of man to do the will of God.*

ONE of the subjects, with respect to which I earnestly wish that you would attend to the voice of reason and the scriptures, and with respect to which, one mistake will be followed by many others, and miftakes of great confequence, is concerning *the power of man to do the will of God.* It is a favourite opinion with many teachers of religion, that men have *naturally* (or by that conftitution and frame which God their maker hath given them) no power at all to do any thing that is good, not even to think a good thought, much lefs actually to obey any of the commands of God; fo that, if men were left to themfelves, they could do nothing but fin, and muft be under a neceffity of aggravating their condemnation, by every thought, word, and action of their lives. But, my brethren, how does this doctrine agree with the fcriptures, and particularly with the manner in which the Divine Being conftantly expoftulates with the finful fons of men, as when he fays to the Jews, *Turn ye, turn ye from your evil ways, why will ye die, O Houfe of Ifrael.* Ez. xxxiii. 11. *Wafh ye, make ye clean; ceafe to do evil, learn to do well, &c. &c. &c.* Ifa. i. 16.

Is it not plain from this, that it depends upon men themfelves, whether they will repent and turn to God or not? And how can it depend upon themfelves, if they have not, naturally, a fufficient power to do it? You cannot think that God would command, and expect obedience, when he had not given power to obey; and much lefs that he would urge men to provide for their own fafety and happinefs, when himfelf had put an effectual bar in the way of it.

Suppofe that any man's children were fhut up in a building that was on fire, while he himfelf was without, and had the key: and that, inftead of opening the door to favour their efcape, he fhould only call out to them to flee out of the place, in order to avoid inftant deftruction; and that, as the neceffary confequence of this, they fhould all perifh in the flames before his eyes; what would you think of fuch a father? You would want words to exprefs your abhorrence of his cruelty; and yet in this very light do many chriftian divines reprefent the conduct of that God *whofe tender mercies are over all his works,* and who has folemnly declared, *that he hath no pleafure in the death of a finner, but rather that he would turn from his way*

and

and live. Ez. xxxiii. 11; yea, *who would have all men to be saved.* 1 Tim. ii. 4.

The conduct of our *merciful God and Father*, is certainly far different from this, and more agreeable to reason and equity. If he designed us to be accountable creatures, and treats us as such, we must have *talents* given us, which we may either improve or misimprove. If we be the subjects of his *moral government*, we must be in a condition either to *observe* or to *break* his laws. A power to do the one, necessarily supposes a power to do the other; and without this power we should not be the proper subjects of religion; as, in that case, it would be vain to propose to us either rewards for obedience, or punishments for disobedience.

Nor is the supposition of a power in man to do the will of God, any foundation for *pride*. For we must still say, with the apostle, *What have we that we have not received? and how then can we glory, as if we had not received it? Every good and every perfect gift comes from God*; and, knowing this, the more we receive of his bounty, the more thankful, and the more humble we should be. I shall, certainly, be more solicitous to exert myself in doing the will of God, when I believe that I have a talent to improve, than if I believe that I have no talent intrusted with me at all; so that I cannot do even so much as the *wicked and slothful servant, who hid his talent in a napkin.*

Some of those persons who believe that all mankind are absolutely incapable of doing any good, are sometimes heard to invite sinners of all kinds to come to Christ, *as they are*, and to say, that the viler they are, the more welcome they will be to him; as if he was, after this, to cleanse them by some miraculous power. But, my brethren, the invitation of the gospel runs in very different terms. It is, *Repent, and bring forth fruits meet for repentance.* Mat. iii. 8. *Repent and be converted, that your sins may be blotted out.* Acts iii. 19. And none are invited *to come to Christ*, but those who *labour and are heavy laden*; nor can they *find rest for their souls*, till they have actually *learned of him to be meek and lowly in heart.* Matt. xi. 28.

What can be more contrary to the maxims above-mentioned,

mentioned, than the whole tenour of that serious expostulation with the children of Israel in the prophet Isaiah, part of which I quoted above? *Wash you, make you clean, put away the evil of your doings from before mine eyes, Cease to do evil, learn to do well. Seek judgment, relieve the oppressed, judge the fatherless, plead for the widow, Come now* (and not before) *and let us reason together, says the Lord. Though your sins be as scarlet, they shall be white as snow; though they be red like crimson, they shall be as wool.* Isa. i. 16, &c.

Others, who entertain the same opinion of the utter inability of man to do the will of God, act more consistently with those sentiments, but far more inconsistently with the scriptures, in never preaching to sinners at all; though to *call sinners to repentance*, was the chief end of Christ's coming into the world. *Matt.* ix. 13.

Whatever represents a state of acceptance with God, as a thing that may be brought about without any efforts of our own, and especially if it may be done in a moment, or in a very short space of time, is sure to be a popular doctrine. Mankind in general care not how little is expected of them, or how little they themselves have to do, in order to get to heaven. But true religion, that alone which affords solid ground of hope towards God, consists in a change of heart, affections, and habits; which can only be brought about by serious resolution, and a vigorous and constant exertion of our powers. Nay, unless a course of virtue be begun, and good habits formed early in life, there is very great danger that the *thorns*, *briers*, or *bad soil*, will prevent the good seed from ever coming to maturity.

To believe, as the same persons do, that faith and repentance are nothing that we ourselves are capable of, but altogether the miraculous operation of the Spirit of God in us and upon us, supposes that this great and sudden change may as well take place at the last hour of life, as at any other; which certainly encourages the most unwarrantable and most dangerous presumption, and is far from having any countenance in the scriptures. The word of God always represents a safe and *happy death* as the consequence of

nothing

nothing but a good and *well-spent life*. Some indeed, are said to have been called at the *eleventh* hour, but none at the *twelfth*, when the time for labouring in the vineyard was quite over; and not one of the foolish virgins, who had neglected to provide themselves with oil, was admitted to the marriage supper.

III. *Of original sin.*

AS a foundation for this strange doctrine, of the utter inability of men to do what God requires of them, a doctrine so injurious both to our Maker and ourselves, it is said that our first parent Adam was the representative of all his posterity; so that when he sinned, we all sinned; and, every sin being an offence against an infinite God, we all became, from that moment, liable to an infinite punishment, even the everlasting wrath and curse of our Maker. And they say, that, on this account only, it would have been just in God to have made us all suffer the most exquisite and endless torments in hell, even though we had never sinned in our own persons; and, moreover, that, by this one offence, Adam, and all his posterity, lost all power of doing any thing acceptable to God for the future.

But, my brethren, you find nothing like any part of this in your bibles. For there you read, *The soul that sinneth, it shall die*. Ez. xviii. 4. And long after the transgression of Adam, and to this very day, God is continually calling upon men, to *cease to do evil, and learn to do well:* which certainly supposes, that men always have had, and that we now have, a power to do so. It is allowed that we *suffer* by the sin of Adam, as any child may suffer in consequence of the wickedness of his ancestor; but it is not possible that we should have *sinned* in him. Wherever there is *sin*, there is *guilt*, that is, something that may be the foundation of *remorse* of conscience; something that a man may be *sorry for*, and *repent of*; something that he may wish he had not done; all which clearly implies, that sin is something that a man has given his *consent* to, and therefore must be convinced of the reasonableness of his being punished for. But how can any man repent of the sin of Adam, or feel any thing like remorse of conscience for it; when he cannot but know that he never gave his consent to it, and could not possibly have been, in the least degree, accessary to it? Good and bad conduct are, in their own nature, *personal*, and cannot possibly be transferred from one to another. Whatever some divines pretend, nothing of this kind can be *imputed* in this sense of the word. We may receive harm by means of one person, and benefit by means of another (which is St. Paul's meaning, where he speaks of *imputation*) but no sin of the former, or righteousness of the latter, can be considered as ours, in the eye of an equitable and just God. The contrary is as much the language and the plain meaning of the scriptures throughout, as it is agreeable to the common sense and reason that God has given us.

IV. *Of Election and Reprobation.*

SUpposing that all mankind became liable to the everlasting wrath and curse of God for the sin of one man, some divines say, that it was mercy in God to save any, though by an *arbitrary decree*, which left all the rest of the human race under an inevitable necessity of perishing. But certainly, my brethren, such *tender mercy is cruelty*. All the creatures of God must look up to him as the author of their being, since it was undoubtedly, in his power to give, or to withhold it, at his pleasure; and, surely, a good and merciful God would have put a stop to the propagation of such a race of creatures, rather than suffer them to be born in such shocking circumstances; in which he infallibly foresaw, that the greatest part of them must be exposed to, and even actually suffer remediless destruction. As surely as I derive my being from a just and merciful God, I conclude that the terms on which I come into the world are advantageous to me; and therefore, that it must be my own fault only, if I have not reason to rejoice in it, and to be thankful for it. But, indeed, I can hardly think that any

any man ſeriouſly believes, that the greateſt part of his fellow creatures are born into the world under a predetermined neceſſity of being for ever miſerable. For, in that caſe, it muſt appear probable that any children which he himſelf may be the means of bringing into the world will be for ever miſerable; and ſurely no man of real goodneſs or compaſſion would wiſh to have children, or be acceſſary to their being born in ſuch circumſtances.

If this doctrine be true, what motive can any man have to endeavour to *flee from the wrath to come*, Mat. iii. 7. when, if it is to be his lot at all, nothing that he can do will enable him to eſcape it, or what motive can a man have to exert himſelf to *lay hold on eternal life*, 1 Tim. vi. 12. when, if he is to enjoy it at all, he cannot poſſibly miſs of it, or of any thing belonging to it, or that is neceſſary to prepare him for it? What reaſon had the apoſtle Paul to exhort chriſtians to *take heed leſt they ſhould fall*, 1 Cor. x. 12. when none that ever did ſtand could poſſibly fall, and what reaſon had he to *labour, leſt after having preached to others, he himſelf ſhould be a caſt-away*, 1. Cor. ix. 27. when, being certain of his converſion, he muſt have known that that conſequence was impoſſible?

This doctrine, of abſolute election and reprobation, is certainly a doctrine of *licentiouſneſs*, and not a *doctrine according to godlineſs*; and let divines employ all the ingenuity they are maſters of, it is impoſſible for them to clear this opinion from being the cauſe of fatal deſpair in ſome, and as fatal a ſecurity in others. If this opinion were true, and men were really aware of their ſituation, I ſhould think it impoſſible to prevent their falling into abſolute diſtraction, through terror and anxiety. It would be like a man having his *all*, his *life*, nay infinitely more than his life, depending upon the caſt of a die; the decree of God being a thing that he has as little power to command. Beſides, this doctrine certainly repreſents the God and Father of us all in ſuch a light, as no man would chuſe that he himſelf ſhould appear in.

A 6　　　　　　　　　　　V. *Of*

V. *Of the divinity of Christ.*

SO fatal have the consequences of the sin of Adam been represented, that you have been told, that nothing but the blood of God himself could reverse them; and therefore you have been taught to believe, that Jesus Christ, whose proper title is *the son of man,* as well as *the son of God,* was not *man,* but very and eternal *God* himself, without considering that, by thus making more Gods than one, you are guilty of a breach of the first and most important of all the commandments, which says expressly, *Thou shalt have no other Gods besides me.* Exod. xx. 3. But whatever such divines may say, the apostle Paul says, in direct contradiction to them, *To us there is but one God, the* FATHER, *of whom are all things, and one Lord Jesus Christ, by whom are all things, and we by him.* 1 Cor. viii. 6. And again, after saying that we have *one Lord, one faith, one baptism,* he adds, *one God and Father of all, who is above all, and through all, and in you all.* Eph. iv. 5, 6. The creed of all christians, therefore, ought to be, *There is* ONE GOD, *and one mediator between God and men, the* MAN *Christ Jesus,* 1 Tim. ii. 5.

The *Father* is frequently stiled *God,* even with respect to Christ, as well as other beings. *The God of our Lord Jesus Christ, the Father of glory, give unto you, that ye may know the exceeding greatness of his power, which he wrought in Christ, when he raised him from the dead, and set him at his own right hand, &c.* Eph. i. 17, &c. Christ himself uses the same language, *I ascend unto my Father, and your Father, and unto my God and your God,* John xx. 17. *My God, my God, why hast thou forsaken me?*

Christ who was *the Image of the invisible God,* and the *first-born* (or *most excellent*) *of all his creatures,* Col. i. 15, and *in whom dwelt all the fullness of the Godhead bodily,* Col. ii. 9, acknowledged that *his Father was greater than he,* John xiv.

xiv. 28, and, indeed, upon all occasions, and in the clearest terms, he expressed his dependence upon God his father, for all his power and glory; as if he had purposely intended to guard his disciples, against forming too high an opinion of the dignity of their master. *Verily I say unto you, the Son can do nothing of himself*, v. 19. *I can of mine own self do nothing. As I hear I judge, and my judgment is just, because I speak not mine own will, but the will of the father who sent me.* v. 30. *The words that I speak unto you, I speak not of myself, but the Father who dwelleth in me, he doth the works.* xiv. 10. *I live by the Father.* vi. 57. *The Father hath given to the Son to have life in himself; and hath given him authority to execute judgment.* v. 26, 27. *All power is given unto me, in heaven and in earth.* Matt. xxviii. 18. He even calls his Father *the only true God.* John xvii. 3. *that they might know thee, the only true God, and Jesus Christ whom thou hast sent.* It appears to me not to be in the power of language to exclude the idea of the divinity of Christ more expresly than by these solemn words.

Notwithstanding, the divine communications with which our Lord was favoured, some things are expresly said to be withheld from him. For he himself, speaking of his second coming, says, Mark xiii. 32, *But of that day and hour knoweth no man, no not the angels which are in heaven, neither the Son, but the Father:* in Matthew xxiv. 36, where the same observation is repeated, *but my Father only.*

The apostles, notwithstanding their attachment to their Lord and Master, always preserve the idea of his subordination to the Father, and consider all his honour and power as derived from him. *He received from God the Father, honour and glory,* 2 Peter i. 17. *It pleased the Father, that in him should all fullness dwell,* 1 Col. i. 19. *The revelation of Jesus Christ, which God gave unto him,* Rev. i. 1. *We are Christ's, and Christ is God's,* 1 Cor. iii. 23. *The head of Christ is God,* 1 Cor. xi. 3.

The reason why Christ was so much distinguished by God the Father, is frequently and fully expressed in the scriptures, viz. his obedience to the will of God,

God, and especially his submitting to die for the benefit of mankind. *Therefore doth my Father love me, because I lay down my life,* John x. 17. *He humblea himself, and became obedient unto death, even the death of the cross. Wherefore God has highly exalted him, and given him a name which is above every name; that at the name of Jesus every knee should bow, of things in heaven and things in earth, and that every tongue should confess that Jesus Christ is Lord, to the glory of God the Father,* Phil. ii. 8—11. *Who, for the joy that was set before him, endured the cross, despising the shame, and is set down at the right hand of God.* Heb. xii. 2.

Our Lord says, that *he and his Father are one.* John x. 30. but he sufficiently explains himself, when he prays that all his disciples may be *one with him, ana his Father, even as they two are one.* ib. xvii. 11. *ana he gives them the same glory which God had given to him,* ver. 22. Besides, at the very time that our Lord says, that he and his father are one, and in the very sentence preceding it, ver. 25, he says, that *his Father is greater than all.* But how could the Father be greater than all, if there was any other, who was so much *one* with him, as to be, in all respects, *equal* to him.

The mere term *God* is, indeed, sometimes used in a lower and inferior sense in the scriptures, denoting *dominion* only; as when the Divine Being himself says that *he will make Moses a god to Pharaoh,* Exod. vii. 1; but, surely, there can be no danger of our mistaking the sense of such phrases as these; or if it were possible, our Lord himself has sufficiently guarded against any misconstruction of them when applied to himself, by the explanation he has given of them; informing us, that, if, in the language of scripture, *they are called gods to whom the word of God came,* John x. 35, (though, in fact, they were no other than mere men) he could not be guilty of blasphemy in calling himself only *the Son of God.* Now if Christ had been conscious to himself that he was the *true and very God,* and that it was the utmost consequence to mankind that they should regard him in that light, this was certainly a proper time for him to have declared himself, and not to have put his hearers off with such an apology as this. But *of Christanity.* 15

But even this power and dominion, to which Christ is advanced by God his Father, who *gave all power into his hands,* and who *made him head over all things to his church,* Eph. i. 22, this *mediatorial kingdom* of Christ, (as it is sometimes, and with sufficient propriety, termed) is not to be perpetual. For the apostle Paul, speaking, no doubt, under immediate inspiration, expressly says, that when *the end shall come, that God shall have subdued all things to his Son* (in which he observes, that *he must be excepted who did subdue all things unto him) he must deliver up the kingdom to God, even the* FATHER, *and be himself subject to him who hath put all things under him, that God may be all in all.* 1 Cor. xv. 24, &c. Nay he himself says expressly that he had not the disposal of the highest offices of his kingdom, Mat. xx. 23. *To sit on my right hand and on my left is not mine to give; but it shall be given to them for whom it is prepared of my Father.*

So clear, my brethren, so full, and so express, is the uniform testimony of the scriptures to the great doctrine of the proper *unity of God,* and of the subordination of Christ, and all other beings to him, that the prevalence of so impious a doctrine, as the contrary must be, can be ascribed to nothing but to that *mystery of iniquity,* which though it *began to work* in the times of the apostles themselves, was not then risen to so enormous a height as to attack the supremacy of the *one living and true God,* and *give his peculiar glory to another.* This, my brethren, among other shocking corruptions of genuine christianity, grew up with the system of Popery; and to shew that nothing is impossible to the superstition and credulity of men, when they were *become vain in their imaginations,* after exalting a man into a god, a creature into a creator, they made a piece of bread into one also, and then bowed down to, and worshipped the work of their own hands.

But though it seemed fit to the unsearchable wisdom of God, that all the errors and abuses of Popery should not be reformed at once; and though this great error was left untouched by the first reformers, blessed be God the bible is as open to us as it was to them; and by the exertion of the same judgment and spirit, we

may

may free christianity from the corruptions which they left adhering to it; and then, among other excellencies of our religion, *Our God will be one and his name one.* Zech. xiv. 9.

If you ask *who*, then, is Jesus Christ, if he be not God; I answer, in the words of St. Peter, addressed to the Jews, after his resurrection and ascension, that *Jesus of Nazareth was a man approved of God, by miracles and wonders and signs, which God did by him,* Acts ii. 22. If you ask what is meant by *man*, in this place; I answer, that *man*, if the word be used with any kind of propriety, must mean the same kind of being with yourselves. I say, moreover, with the author of the epistle to the Hebrews, that *it became him, by whom are all things, and to whom are all things, to make this great captain of our salvation in all respects, like unto us his brethren, that he might be made perfect through sufferings,* Heb. ii. 10. 17, *and that he might have a perfect feeling of all our infirmities,* iv. 15. For this reason it was that our Saviour and Deliverer was not made of the nature of an *angel*, or like any superangelic being, but was of *the seed of Abraham,* ii. 16, that is (exclusive of the divinity of the Father, which resided in him, and acted by him) a mere *man*, as other Jews, and as we ourselves also are.

Christ being made by the immediate hand of God, and not born in the usual course of generation, is no reason for his not being considered as a man. For then Adam must not have been a man. But in the ideas of St. Paul, both *the first and second Adam* (as Christ, on this account, is sometimes called) were equally men; *By man came death, by man came also the resurrection from the dead,* 1 Cor. xv. 21. And, certainly, in the the resurrection of a *man*, that is, of a person in all respects like ourselves, we have a more *lively hope* of our own resurrection; that of Christ being both a *proof* and a *pattern* of ours. We can, therefore, more firmly believe that *because he lives, we* who are the same that he was, and who shall undergo the same change by death that he did, *shall live also.* John. xiv. 19.

Till

of Christianity.

Till this great corruption of christianity be removed, it will be in vain to preach the gospel to Jews, or Mahometans, or, indeed, to any people who retain the use of the reason and understanding that God has given them. For how is it possible that *three* persons, *Father, Son and Holy Ghost*, should be separately, each of them, possessed of all divine perfections, so as to be *true, very,* and *eternal* God, and yet that there should be but *one God*; a truth which is so clearly and fully revealed, that it is not possible for men to refuse their assent to it; or else it would, no doubt, have been long ago expunged from our creed, as utterly irreconcileable with the more favourite doctrine of a *Trinity,* a term which is not to be found in the scriptures. Things *above* our reason may, for any thing that we know to the contrary, be true; but things expressly *contrary* to our reason, as that *three* should be *one*, and *one three*, can never appear to us to be so.

With the Jews, the doctrine of the Divine Unity is, and indeed justly, considered as the most fundamental principle of all religion. *Hear, O Israel, the Lord our God is one Lord.* Deut. vi. 4. Mark xii. 29. To preach the doctrine of the Trinity to the Jews, can appear to them in no other light, than an attempt to seduce them into *idolatry*, a thing which they dare not entertain the most distant thought of.

The great creed of the Mahometans is, that *There is one God, and Mahomet is his prophet*. Now that Mahomet is not the prophet of God, it is to be hoped they may, in time, be brought to believe; but we must not expect that they will so easily give up their faith in the unity of God. To make the gospel what it was originally, *glad tidings of great joy*; and as at last it certainly will be to all the nations of the world, we must free it from this most absurd and impious doctrine, and also from many other corruptions which have been introduced into it. It can no otherwise appear worthy of God, and favourable to the virtue and happiness of mankind.

VI. *Of* ATONEMENT *for sin by the death of Christ.*

YOU have been taught by divines, that if Christ be not God, he could not have made an *infinite satisfaction* for the sins of mankind. But, my brethren, where do you learn that the pardon of sin, in a finite creature, requires an infinite satisfaction; or, indeed, any satisfaction at all, besides repentance and reformation, on the part of a sinner? We read in the scriptures that we are *justified freely by the grace of God.* Rom. iii. 34; but what free grace, or mercy, does there appear to have been in God, if Christ gave a full price for our justification, and bore the infinite weight of divine wrath on our account. We are commanded to *forgive others, as we ourselves hope to be forgiven.* Matt. vii. 14. and to be *merciful, as our Father, who is in heaven, is merciful.* But surely we are not thereby authorized to insist upon any atonement, or satisfaction, before we give up our resentment towards an offending and penitent brother. Indeed, how could it deserve the name of *forgiveness* if we did? If he only *repent*, we are commanded to *forgive* him. Luke xvii. 4.

You read in the scriptures that Christ died *a sacrifice for our sins.* Heb. ix. 26. So he did, and a sacrifice it was, of a *sweet smelling savour to God.* To die, as Christ did, in the glorious cause of truth and virtue; to die, as he did, in order to shew us an example of patiently suffering death for our religion, and the good of mankind, and in a firm hope of a resurrection to a future and eternal life; to die, as he did, in express attestation of his own divine mission, by his manifest resurrection from the dead, and as the fullest proof of that doctrine, by means of which sinners are continually reconciled unto God, was a noble sacrifice indeed. We also are commanded to *yield our bodies living sacrifices.* Rom. xii. 1. And we are required to offer the *sacrifices of praise continually.* Psal. cxvi. 17. But it is plain that all these are only figurative expressions, and used by way of comparison. Neither our *bodies*, nor our

of Christianity.

our *prayers*, can be considered as *real* sacrifices; nor are we, therefore, obliged to suppose that Christ was a real sacrifice. And though we, like him, should be called actually to *lay down our lives for our brethren*, 1 John iii. 16, which, in imitation of him, we are enjoined to be ready to do, we should be sacrifices only in the figurative sense of the word.

It is true, that no man who is a sinner (and all men have sinned) can be *justified by his works*. We all stand in need of, and must have recourse to *free grace* and *mercy*; but it is a great dishonour to God to suppose that this mercy and grace takes its rise from any thing but his own essential goodness; and that he is not *of himself*, and independent of all foreign considerations whatever, what he solemnly declared himself to Moses, at the time of the giving of the law, to be, namely, *a God merciful and gracious, long suffering, abundant in goodness and in truth*, Exod. xxxiv. 6; or that he requires any other sacrifices, but *the sacrifice of a broken spirit, and a contrite heart, which he will never despise*. Psalm li. 17.

Can we wish for a more distinct, and perfect representation of the manner in which God forgives the sins of his offspring of mankind, than our saviour has exhibited to us in that most excellent parable of the *prodigal son*; in which the good father no sooner sees his child, who had abandoned him, and wasted his substance in riotous living, returning to him and to his duty; but, without waiting for any atonement or propitiation, even *while he was yet a great way off, he ran to him, fell upon his neck, and kissed him*. Luke xv. 20. The same representation we see in the parable of the creditor, who freely forgave his servant, because he humbly *desired* him. Let us not then, my brethren, deprive the ever blessed God of the most glorious and honourable of all his attributes, and leave him nothing but *justice*, or rather *vengeance*, which is expressly said to be *his strange work*. Isaiah xxviii. 21.

These, my brethren, are the principal heads on which I proposed to expostulate with you, in the plain and free manner in which I have done. Do you yourselves, *search the scriptures, and see whether these things be* be *so*. Pray to the God of truth, to lead you into all truth, and may he give you understanding in all things.

VII. *Practical consequences of the above doctrines*

THE sound knowledge of christianity is not of importance as a matter of *speculation* merely; though abstract truths, especially truths that relate to God, and the maxims of his moral government, are not without their utility and obligation; but the truths that I here contend for nearly affect the sentiments of our hearts, and our conduct in life; as, indeed, has been shown in many respects, already. Considering God as possessed of the character in which some divines represent him, it is impossible, while human nature is what it is, that he should appear in an amiable or respectable light. Such a God may, indeed, be the object of *dread* and *terror* to his creatures, but by no means of their *love* or *reverence*. And what is obedience without love. It cannot be that of the *heart*, which, however, is the only thing that is of any real value in religion. Also how can a man love his fellow-creatures in general, when he considers the greatest part of them as the objects of the divine abhorrence, and doomed by him to an everlasting destruction, in which he believes that he himself must for ever rejoice? And what can remain of virtue, when these two great sources of it, the *love of God and of mankind*, are thus grosly corrupted? Lastly, how must the genuine spirit of *mercy* and *forgiveness*, which so eminently distinguishes the gospel of Christ, be debased, when God himself (whose conduct in this very respect is particularly proposed to our imitation) is considered as never forgiving sin without some previous atonement, satisfaction, or intercession.

On the other hand, loving God, as the compassionate Father of all his offspring, as *willing that all men should be saved, and come to the knowledge of his truth*; and also loving all mankind as our brethren, as, together with ourselves, the children of the same gracious Father, we cannot want the most generous

and

and powerful motives *to do, the will of God*, and *to provoke one another to love and to good works*; being in no fear of counteracting the secret designs of the Almighty, which we believe are aimed, not at the destruction, but the happiness of all his creatures.

Think not however, that I am so uncharitable as to suppose that all those who profess to maintain the doctrines I have been arguing against, are universally destitute of the genuine love of God, or of their fellow-creatures. I am sensible, and truly thankful, that it is not always the consequence; but it is because the hearts of such persons are really influenced by better principles than those which they avow. They by no means habitually regard the Divine Being in the light in which their principles represent him, but as the *true Father* of all the creatures that he has made, and, as such, are sincerely desirous to promote their best interests.

Also, notwithstanding, if they be asked, they will not hesitate to say, that Christ is God, the supremacy of the Father, even with respect to the Son, is, at the same time, the real sentiment of their minds; and when they lift up their hearts to God, it is only *God the Father* that is the proper object of their adoration. The constant tenor of the scriptures is so contrary to their professed creed, that though they dare not call it in question, it is not able to counteract the plainer, more consistent, and better principles which will force themselves upon their minds from conversing with the bible.

Besides, it requires more subtilty and refinement to enter into the principles above-mentioned, than the common people are masters of. They cannot conceive how one man should sin, and another person, six thousand years after, be guilty of that sin, and punishable for it; how one person's righteousness should be considered as the righteousness of another; or that three distinct persons should each of them be God, and yet that there should be no more gods than one.

Men of plain understandings, in fact, never do believe any such thing; nor can it be supposed that the gospel, which was intended to be the solid foundation

of

of the faith, hope, and joy of common people, should require so much acuteness, as is necessary to give even a plausible colour to these strange assertions. The attempt to explain them (and, till they be explained, they can no more be believed than a proposition in an unknown tongue) can lead to nothing but endless and unprofitable controversy. It is happy, therefore, that so many persons make a better use of the gospel than their tenets would lead them to do; and that they consider it chiefly as a *rule of life*; and the *foundation of hope after death*. But, as far as the principles I have been arguing against are believed, they cannot but do harm to those who entertain them, as well as bring disgrace upon the christian name; both which every *lover of the gospel* should endeavour to prevent.

A practical exhortation, and conclusion.

PROFESSING the purity of the christian faith, let us be careful, my brethren, to adorn it by a blameless and exemplary life. More especially let us beware that we do not wear *the form of godliness*, when our hearts are destitute of the *power* of it; and that we indulge no secret hope, that by any peculiar strictness and austerity of life, by frequent or long prayers, or by attending on much preaching, and using other *means* of religion, we shall atone for a neglect of *the weightier matters of the law, righteousness, mercy and truth*. Let the integrity of our hearts appear in the chearfulness of our countenances, and let us show that *we love God whom we have not seen*, by loving our *brethren whom we do see*, and by being always ready to do them every kind office in our power.

To judge of our love to God, or of our love to Christ, directly, by what we *feel* when we think of them, especially when we are excluded from the world, as is the custom with many, is to expose ourselves to the grossest and most dangerous delusions. We find in the scriptures a much plainer, and safer method of judging in both these cases. *This*, says the apostle John, *is the love of God, that we keep his commandments. If ye love me,* says our Lord, *keep my commandments. Ye*

are

are my friends, if ye do whatsoever I command you; and *this is my commandment, that ye love one another. By this shall all men know that ye are my disciples, if ye have love one for another*

Remember that true Christian charity is humble, modest, and diffident; and that he is pronouced to be happy, who *feareth always*, so as to be circumspect in thought, word, and deed; and that, for this purpose, we are to *put on the whole armour of God*, that we may withstand the temptations of the world.

Rather than indulge a Pharisaical pride, in recounting your *experiences*, boasting how vile you have once been, or thought yourselves to be, in order to make others believe how holy and sanctified you are now, content yourselves with the language and practice of the humble publican, who, speaking to God and his own heart only, cried, *God be merciful to me a sinner*.

Rejoice in all the real good you see done by others, whatever may be their ill will, or opposition to you; and be especially upon your guard, lest your just aversion to what is corrupt in the principles or practices of others, lead you to dislike what is good in them. Let not the *Pharisaical rigour* of some throw you into the opposite extreme of *levity*; and let not their laying an undue stress upon praying, preaching, and other means of religion, make you neglect them, as we are too apt to do, with respect to any thing that has been much abused.

Having enough to do with our own hearts, let us be particularly upon our guard against that spirit of *censoriousness*, which many professing Christians indulge with too little restraint. Let us remember that the true Christian *beareth all things, and hopeth all things*; and let us never forget the aweful warning of our Lord, *Judge not, that ye be not judged: for with what judgment ye judge, ye shall be judged; and with what measure ye mete, it shall be measured to you again*.

Be not moved, my brethren, by the rash censures and reproaches of others. *Persecution*, of some kind, is what *all who will live godly in Christ Jesus must expect to suffer in this world*. To their *wrath, anger, clamour, evil speaking, and malice*, answer with *the wisdom that is from above; which is pure, peaceable, gentle, and easy to be be intreated; full of mercy and good fruits, without partiality, and without hypocrisy.* Let us even rejoice that we are *counted worthy to suffer shame,* and insult, *for the sake of Christ,* though our sufferings come not from the professed enemies of Christ, but from *false brethren*; and let us not be concerned at being counted *deceivers,* if we be conscious to ourselves that we truly love the gospel, and that we labour to promote and adorn it.

You will be called *Arminians* and *Socinians* by your adversaries, or something else that shall express more of their hatred and dislike. But let not this offend you. If there be any proper meaning in those epithets, it can only be that you hold certain opinions, which they deem to be false, but which you cherish, as the only genuine doctrines of the gospel. If nothing more is meant by those terms, besides mere *reproach* and *abuse,* think yourselves happy, as being *reproached for the name of Christ.* 1 Peter iv. 14. With many the appellation of *Lutheran* or *Calvinist* is reproachful, and with many also, that of *Christian* is much more so. Besides, both Arminius and Socinus were men who loved the gospel, and who suffered more for their adherence to it, than most others of the reformers, especially Socinus.

If we be Christians indeed, we shall consider ourselves as *not of this world,* but as *citizens of heaven. The friendship of this world,* therefore, together with popularity, and success in it, ought not to be considered as any object for us. If we *abide in Christ,* and *walk even as he also walked,* not *being conformed to this world, but being transformed by the renewing of our minds,* we are *heirs of a far* nobler inheritance, *an inheritance incorruptible, undefiled, and that fadeth not away, reserved in heaven for us;* and *when Christ, who is our life, and for whom we suffer reproach, shall appear, we also shall appear with him in glory,*

FAMILIAR ILLUSTRATION

OF CERTAIN

PASSAGES OF SCRIPTURE

RELATING TO

The Power of Man to do the Will of God,
Original Sin,
Election and Reprobation,
The Divinity of Chrift, and
Atonement for Sin by the Death of Chrift.

By a LOVER of the Gofpel.

Search the Scriptures. JOHN, V. 39.

LONDON:
Printed for J. JOHNSON, No. 72, St. *Paul's Church-Yard.*
1772.
PRICE Four Pence; or, Three Shillings and Six Pence *per* Dozen.

Published by the Author of this Treatise,
Price One Penny each,

I. An APPEAL

TO

The serious and candid Professors of Christianity,

On the following SUBJECTS, viz.

1. The Use of Reason in Matters of Religion,
2. The Power of Man to do the Will of God,
3. Original Sin,
4. Election and Reprobation.
5. The Divinity of Christ, and
6. Atonement for Sin by the Death of Christ.

II. The Triumph of Truth;

BEING AN ACCOUNT OF THE

Trial of Mr. E. ELWALL,

FOR

HERESY and BLASPHEMY,

At STAFFORD ASSIZES,

Before JUDGE DENTON.

To which are added,

Extracts from some other Pieces of Mr. ELWALL's, concerning the UNITY of GOD.

AND

A few ADDITIONAL ILLUSTRATIONS.

THE

PREFACE

My Christian Brethren,

IN all theological controversies our appeal lies to the *Bible*, which contains the writings of the inspired prophets, and of the apostles and evangelists, who have recorded the precepts and doctrines of Christ. To those who lived in the times in which these books were published, they were, no doubt, very intelligible; the language in which they are written, and the customs to which they allude, being perfectly known to them. But what was easy to them, a long course of time has rendered extremely difficult to us, who use a very different language, and whose manners and customs are so exceedingly unlike those of the Jews. On this account, it may puzzle the greatest scholar of the present age to make out the sense of a passage of scripture, which could not but have been perfectly understood by the most illiterate person in that age. In this state of things, the *ignorant* and *unlearned* are very liable to *wrest the scriptures*, as the apostle Peter says they ever have done, while good sense and sound learning often maintain a very unequal contest.

It is another unfavourable circumstance with respect to the right understanding of the scriptures in this country, that the English translation of them was made at a time when the christian world was but just emerged from the darkness of popery, and while the belief of all those opinions which are combated in the APPEAL was almost universally retained. Our transA 2 lators,

The PREFACE.

lators, therefore, having been educated in the belief of, and in a reverence for those particular opinions, and not having had their minds sufficiently enlightened to call them in question, it is no wonder that, without any ill design, they should, in many places of their version, have expressed their own sentiments, and not those of the apostles. In all these cases a just translation is all that is necessary to remove the errors into which a wrong translation has led us; but with respect to them, you, my brethren, who are not acquainted with the languages in which the scriptures were originally written, must necessarily depend upon other persons for the interpretation of them; but you may be able, in a great measure, to judge for yourselves concerning different translations, by considering, if you will take pains to reflect upon the subject, which rendering of a doubtful passage is most agreeable to the general strain of the scriptures, and to common sense. Do not, however, immediately conclude that an interpretation of a passage of scripture is *unnatural*, because, when it is first proposed to you, it may seem to be so; because this may arise from nothing but your having been long accustomed to understand it in a different sense, and from having imagined, though without sufficient grounds, that the tenor of scripture favoured a contrary sense. The Roman catholicks, I doubt not, think it very unnatural to interpret the words of our Saviour, *This is my body*, in any other than in the most literal manner; and they think that our Lord's saying upon another occasion, *Unless ye eat the flesh of the son of man, and drink his blood, ye have no life in you*, abundantly confirms their interpretation.

Now, in this little treatise, I desire no greater indulgence in the interpretation of scripture than all Protestants think themselves justified in taking, when they assert, that the meaning of these figurative expressions is, not that the *flesh and blood*, but that the *doctrine* of Christ is to be received and digested, that is, to be improved and practised by us, in order to our final salvation. Since the very strongest figures of speech are manifestly used in almost all the books of scripture, it must be very unreasonable to expect

that

The PREFACE.

that the moſt literal interpretation ſhould always be the beſt.

I muſt farther apprize you, my brethren, that the paſſages which I have attempted to explain, being, for the moſt part, highly figurative, are, on that account, peculiarly difficult to underſtand; ſo that though I may not have hit upon the preciſe ſenſe of the writers, there may be no doubt, from other conſiderations, that the ſenſe which I am combating is not the true one, which is quite ſufficient for my purpoſe. It by no means follows that becauſe I am wrong, my adverſaries are right. In theſe caſes there is the greateſt room for criticiſm, and diverſity of opinion. I have given what at preſent appears to me to be the real ſenſe of every text of ſcripture which I have taken into conſideration, but I ſhall gladly avail myſelf of the new lights, which may be thrown upon any of them in future editions of this pamphlet.

In the mean time, with great diffidence of my own judgment, I recommend what I have now written to your moſt ſerious and candid conſideration; deſiring that you would read it with your bibles at hand, turning to every paſſage to which I refer, and reading what goes before and after it; becauſe I have no doubt but that, in this manner, you will ſee much more reaſon, if not to approve of my interpretations, yet to reject thoſe of my adverſaries, than I have ſuggeſted in this treatiſe, in which I have made a point of being as conciſe as I poſſibly could, conſiſtently with perſpicuity.

The rapid ſale of the *Appeal* (5000 of them having been ſold in the ſpace of a few months) makes me hope that, inconſiderable as the performance is, it has been the inſtrument of ſome good, in the hands of that being who works by ſmall things as well as by great ones.

This publication, if the reader chuſe to have it ſo, may be conſidered as a reply to all the anſwers that I have yet ſeen to the Appeal; and I think I have already ſeen, or heard of, no leſs than ſeven, beſides the notice that has been taken of it in other publications, as thoſe of Mr. Madan and Dr. Halifax. The former of thefe gentlemen I refpect, becaufe he feems to be *in earneft*; but the latter, though he may be fo, he has not the appearance of it. His ftyle is too affected and declamatory. I know what it is to write from *the fulnefs of the heart*, and I likewife remember in what manner I wrote when I was a *fchool boy*.

As a fpecimen of the mereft *cavilling* that I have yet met with, I fhall juft obferve, that Dr. Halifax, and others, affect to fuppofe, that I was fo *weak* as to affert that the word *impious*, as well as *robbery*, was contained in the original of Phil. ii, 6. But if it be a robbery at all to affume the rights of divinity, let them fay whether it muft not be an *impious robbery*. Muft they not acknowledge then that I gave a *juft paraphrafe* of the paffage, though in a parenthefis, I inadvertently called it a *tranflation?*

May fuch remarks as thefe be peculiar to the enemies of truth. They can never have weight with thofe who are *ferious*, and who will take pains to *read*, and *think*; and if the object of my adverfaries be to gain reputation with *the reft of mankind*, they may *have their reward* unenvied by me.

I. Of the power of Man to do the will of God.

THAT the sacred writers consider all mankind as naturally possessed of sufficient power to do what God requires of them, is evident from their earnest remonstrances and expostulations, with persons of all ranks and conditions, and their severe censure of them when they refuse to comply with their exhortations. Nor was this the case with the *Jews* and *Christians* only, who were favoured with divine revelation. The apostle Paul evidently considers the *Gentiles* also in the same light; though much not being given to them, much was not required of them.

In the first chapter of the epistle to the Romans this apostle represents the Gentile world, in general, as having grossly corrupted themselves; yet, in that very representation, he not only says, v. 18, 19. that they had subjected themselves to the *wrath of God, revealed from heaven against all ungodliness and unrighteousness of men, who hold the truth in unrighteousness; because that which may be known of God is manifest, for God hath shewed it unto them*; but also, v. 32. that *knowing the judgment of God (that they which commit such things are worthy of death) not only do the same, but have pleasure in them that do them.* So that the degeneracy and depravity into which they were sunk were owing, not to want of *ability*, but to *wilfulness*, and a determined opposition to the powers of conscience with which their maker had endowed them, and which continued unceasing remonstrances within them. Reasoning with the Jews, in the 2d chapter, he gives the following representation of some of the Gentiles, v. 14, 15. *For when the Gentiles, which have not the law, do by nature the things contained in the law, these, having not the law, are a law to themselves. Which shew the work of the law written in their hearts, their conscience also bearing witness, and their thoughts, the mean while, accusing or else excusing one another:* and he adds, in the 26, 27, verses. *Therefore, if the uncircumcision,* i. e.

Passages of Scripture

the uncircumcised Gentiles, *keep the righteousness of the law, shall not his uncircumcision be counted for circumcision?* i. e. shall he not be equally accepted by God as a righteous Jew? *and shall not uncircumcision, which is by nature, if it fulfil the law, judge thee, who by the letter and circumcision, dost transgress the law?* I presume no one will think so meanly of St. Paul's reasoning as to suppose, that he here puts a case which neither ever was true in *fact*, or possible in *nature*; but if this case either ever was true in fact, or *possible*, those uncircumcised Gentiles, who should answer this description, must certainly have received from their maker capacities and powers to do the will of God acceptably. And if others did not act in like manner, it was not owing to their not having received like natural powers, but to their not making a like improvement of them.

But let us attend to some passages which have been produced in proof that man is not, by nature, able to do the will of God, or that his maker has not given him capacity, and ability to know and do his will acceptably, without the superadded operations of special grace to remedy his natural inability.

1 Cor. ii. 14. *But the natural man receiveth not the things of the spirit of God: for they are foolishness unto him; neither can he know them, because they are spiritually discerned.*

Upon this text I would observe first; That the word, which is here translated *natural*, properly signifies *animal* or *sensual*. Thus 1 Cor. xv. 44, 46. the apostle uses the same word three times for that body which dies, and is buried, to distinguish it from that *spiritual* body which shall rise again; where the word *animal* much better expresses the apostle's meaning than *natural*. Again James uses it, Ch. iii. 15. where our translators have rendered it *sensual*. *This wisdom descendeth not from above, but is earthly, sensual, devilish.* It is also used v. 19. of Jude's epistle, and rendered *sensual. These, are they who separate themselves,* sensual, *having not the spirit.* These are all the passages of the New Testament where I find this word used. And it appears, that where it

denotes

denotes the character of persons, or moral quality of things, our translators have rendered it *sensual*. Consequently, in consistency with themselves, they should have rendered the text under consideration, *But the sensual man* (who has no higher aims than the gratification of his animal senses) *receiveth not the things of the spirit of God*, &c. This would have been readily understood and acknowledged by all, and is perfectly consonant to what he says to the Romans. viii. 7. *The carnal mind is enmity against God; for it is not subject to the law of God, neither indeed can be.*

Secondly; In this chapter the apostle assures the Corinthians, that the doctrine which he had preached to them did not take its rise from worldly wisdom, or Philosophy, but was *that* only which had been revealed to the apostles by the spirit of God, v. 10. That he had preached this doctrine in those terms only which the same spirit dictated, comparing the several particulars of it one with another, and with those things which the same spirit had revealed to the Patriarchs and prophets of old: That none of the wise or powerful men of this world had, or could possibly have discovered these counsels of God revealed by the spirit of God in the gospel, which spirit the apostles have received, that they might know, and instruct others in the things that are freely given us of God. *But the sensual man receiveth not the things of the spirit of God*, revealed by it to the apostles, and preached by them to the world, *for they are foolishness to him*, contradicting all his former sentiments and principles, to which he still adheres, *neither can he know them, because they are spiritually discerned* i. e. by the sole instructions of the spirit, to which he neither attends nor submits. *But the spiritual man discerneth or judgeth all things.* i. e. all the forementioned things of God revealed by his spirit; all gospel truths; *but he himself is discerned or judged of no man.* i. e. he is not subjected in these respects to the judicature of the powers of this world, to the principles of human science, or the rules of human oratory.

Hence I would observe, first, that the *deep things of God*, or the things of the spirit of God, which the apostle

apoſtle ſpeaks of in this chapter, are *the doctrines of the goſpel Revelation*. Now it is readily allowed, that men were not endowed with any natural powers whereby they could diſcover theſe: they could not know them before they were revealed. But then, they were not under obligation to know or comply with them, till they were revealed. Secondly, that they who did not receive and comply with them, when revealed, are not repreſented as *incapable* through want of natural abilities and powers, but only as *diſqualified*, or under a *moral impotence* through ſenſual diſpoſitions which they indulged, and habits which they had contracted.

By the *ſpiritual man* ſeems to be primarily meant here, the *apoſtles*, to whom the ſpirit of God revealed the truths of the goſpel; but they alſo may be comprehended under the denomination, who receive the goſpel truths, believing in the varacity, and ſubmitting to the authority of the ſpirit which revealed them.

John xv. 5. *Without me ye can do nothing.* This ſingle clauſe of a long ſentence, being ſeparated from its connexion with what goes before it, is produced as a proof that man is not able to do the will of God acceptably, without the immediate aſſiſtances of or operation of ſpecial grace upon him through Chriſt. But, if we look into our Lord's diſcourſe, we find him exhorting his diſciples to adhere ſteadfaſtly to him and his doctrine, *that they might bring forth much fruit*. He reminds them, that they had already gained much ſpiritual improvement by his inſtructions, v. 3. *Now ye are clean through the word which I have ſpoken unto you.* He intimates that, if they abandoned him and his doctrine, they would deprive themſelves of the means of fruitfulneſs. He is not ſpeaking then of the natural powers of man, but of the importance of the doctrines he taught to render men fruitful in good works; but this ſeems neceſſarily to ſuppoſe a *capacity* in man to underſtand and improve his doctrines to theſe purpoſes.

It ſeems to be treating Chriſt and his words with great irreverence, to apply them to other purpoſes than thoſe for which he uſed them. We all readily agree that (in our Lord's ſenſe of the expreſſion) *without him*

him we can do nothing. i. e. If we abandon him and the gospel, we cannot be fruitful in holiness or good works; and are very thankful for the provision he hath made, and the assistances, he hath afforded us by his word, *that we may bring forth much fruit.*

Philip. ii. 13. *For it is God which worketh in you both to will and do of his good pleasure.*

In this passage the apostle exhorts the Philippians to *work out their own salvation with fear and trembling,* from a grateful sense of the goodness of God in granting them, for that purpose, the instructions and motives of the gospel, by which such convictions had already been awakened in them, as had excited them both to choose and perform what God required. The *energy,* or operation of God here spoken of, seems to be the energy of *instruction* and *persuasion.* No doubt it is a very reasonable and powerful motive to us all to work out our salvation, that God, in unspeakable love and good-will, is continually working in us, by the truths and motives of the gospel, to choose and perform what he hath required of us.

I am far, however, from having any objection to the doctrine of *divine influence* upon certain occasions (even similar to that which was promised to the apostles, when our Lord told them, that *it should be given them,* when they should be called before magistrates, *what they should speak*) provided we take it for granted, that it depends upon previous dispositions and habits of mind, that is, upon men themselves, whether they be the proper subjects of such extraordinary assistance.

1 Cor. xv. 10. *But by the grace of God I am what I am.*

Let any one carefully attend to the whole case of Paul's conversion, from being a persecutor to become a preacher and apostle of Jesus Christ, and then say whether it be reasonable to draw general conclusions respecting all men from such a case. However, we will all readily adopt his words, and say *through the grace of God,* and his favours bestowed freely upon us by the gospel, *we are what we are.*

Eph. ii. 8. *For by grace are ye saved through faith; and that not of yourselves: it is the gift of God.*

Passages of Scripture

The word *that* doth not refer to faith: as is evident from the original, but to the preceding clause of the sentence. *That ye are saved by grace through faith, this is not of yourselves: it is the gift of God.* He is the sole author of this method of salvation.

Ezekiel xxxvi. 25, 26, 27.° *Then will I sprinkle clean water upon you, and ye shall be clean: from all your filthiness, and from all your idols I will cleanse you. A new heart also will I give you, and a new spirit will I put within you: and I will take away the stony heart out of your flesh, and I will give you an heart of flesh. And I will put my spirit within you, and cause you to walk in my statutes, and ye shall keep my judgments and do them.*

Look into the prophet himself, and I think it will appear, that this is a prediction of the Restoration of the people of the Jews to their own country at the end of the Babylonish captivity, and that afterwards they should no more return to the practice of *idolatry*, to which their fathers had been so prone. Now, the history of that people informs us that this prediction was verified in fact. When God promises to give them a new heart, and to put a new spirit within them, it relates to the particular subject spoken of, viz. idolatry: and, in reality, there was a wonderful change wrought in the dispositions and practice of that people in this respect. This was effected by the deep impressions made upon them by the righteous judgment of God for the idolatries of their forefathers and themselves. But the *new heart and new spirit* must not be understood of an universal, or general change from evil to good, because the whole subsequent history of the Jews, and particularly in the gospel times, contradicts it. It may, however, refer to some greater change to be produced in the moral character of the Jewish nation, on their return from their present dispersion, produced by the consideration of the hand of God in it, as the just punishment of their former vices. But it seems a strange perversion, to make this particular prediction to the returning captives, a general promise to mankind, at least to Christians, of producing in them a thorough change

change of heart and life by the immediate operation of the fpirit of God. This may be called, *accommodating* fcripture paffages, but it feems taking very bold liberties, of making what we pleafe out of them, very inconfiftent with a fincere belief in them, as containing the word of God.

Pfalm li. 10. *Create in me a clean heart, O God, and renew a right fpirit within me.*

We ought not to interpret the figurative expreffions of Hebrew poetry too literally, or to expect in it the rigid accuracy of expreffion of our cold weftern profe. The Pfalmift feems to mean no more by *create*, than to produce, or caufe; which does not exclude the inftrumentality of ordinary means, any more than the word *renew*. Nay, the Pfalmift feems to expect that the clean heart muft be *created*, and the right fpirit *renewed*, not by an immediate operation of fovereign and almighty grace, but by the inftrumentality of thofe ordinary and ufual *means* of grace he had long enjoyed, and experienced the good effects of; and therefore he adds in the following words, v. 11. *Caft me not away from thy prefence*, i. e. deprive me not of the ordinances of thy worfhip in the tabernacle, when thou manifefteft thy prefence in a glorious manner, *and take not thy holy fpirit from me*, i. e. that holy fpirit with the illuminations of which he had, as a prophet, been fo often favoured, and from which he had reaped great fpiritual improvement.

Luke xxiii. 43. *To day fhalt thou be with me in Paradife.*

Altho' certain writers and teachers of religion profefs not to mention the cafe of the penitent thief to encourage prefumption and careleffnefs in any one, yet they mention it fo often, and infift on it fo much, as an inftance of a great and fudden change taking place at the laft hour of a poor finner's life, at the fame time infinuating that the fame change may take place in others *(for the Lord's hand is not fhortened, that it cannot fave, neither his ear heavy that it cannot hear)* that I fear they do, in fact, unhappily encourage prefumption and careleffnefs in many. Let us therefore confider this cafe with a little attention.

The

The abovementioned writers, &c. take for granted, what is by no means certain, that the penitent thief's knowledge of Chrift, and repentance of his own fins, commenced only at the time of his crucifixion along with Jefus. But is it not poffible, that the crime for which he fuffered might have been committed a long time before, though he had been apprehended for it only very lately; when, whatever change might in the mean time have been wrought in his character and converfation, the law muft take its courfe, and he muft fuffer the punifhment due to his mifdeeds, though he had repented of them very fincerely, and become a new man. The Evangelift has faid nothing that precludes this fuppofition, and therefore we are at liberty to make it, efpecially if it will contribute to render the circumftances of the narrative more confiftent and accountable. Let us fee then what thofe circumftances are.

Firft, obferve that this penitent, in the reproof which he gave to his fellow criminal, makes a candid and ingenuous confeffion of his crimes, and the juftice of his punifhment, and *that* grounded upon a juft and proper principle, *the fear of God. Doft not thou fear God, feeing that thou alfo art in the fame condemnation. And we indeed juftly, for we receive the due reward of our deeds.* This feems much more like the language of one who had long reflected upon, been ferioufly affected with, and formed mature conclufions from the fad fubject, than of one who was but juft now ftruck with a conviction of his fins, and a fenfe of his miferable ftate.

Secondly, obferve alfo the clear and confident declaration which he makes concerning Jefus. *This man hath done nothing amifs.* Can we fuppofe this declaration made by a man who had not known any thing of the perfon to whom he bears this teftimony before this unhappy occafion? Doth it not feem rather the atteftation of one who had had confiderable knowledge of the rectitude of his character and the unblameablenefs of his conduct?

Thirdly, Obferve further the petition which he made to Jefus. *'Lord, remember me when thou comeft into thy*

thy kingdom. Is it conceivable that a man who had had no knowledge of Jesus, or his doctrines and pretensions, before this hour, should make such a request to his dying fellow sufferer, unless it were by inspiration, of which the Evangelist gives not the least hint? Upon what ordinary principle of human reason could a person, going into eternity, request of another, going likewise into eternity, to remember him when he should come into his kingdom? It seems much more rational to conclude that this man must some time have heard Jesus discourse upon the subject of his kingdom, and that he had not only believed in the *truth*, but entertained more just and proper ideas of the *nature* of that kingdom than the twelve disciples themselves. What hinders us from supposing that, if the theft for which he now suffered was committed in the city or jurisdiction of Jerusalem, he might have fled to escape punishment into Galilee, which was under Herod's jurisdiction, and that there he might have been one of the multitude who heard and were astonished at the doctrines delivered in the sermon on the mount: towards the close of which our Lord made the following declaration concerning the rule by which he will reject some, and receive others into the kingdom of heaven? Matthew vii. 21. &c. *Not every one that saith unto me, Lord, Lord, shall enter into the kingdom of heaven; but he that doth the will of my father which is in heaven. Many will say unto me, in that day, Lord, Lord, have we not prophesied in thy name,* &c.—*And then will I profess unto them, I never knew you; depart from me, ye that work iniquity.* Convinced and deeply affected by the truths he had already heard, in the former part of the discourse, how must he have been struck with this declaration, so alarming to one conscious of so great and heinous crimes. Would it not be likely that, from that moment, he would change his sentiments, character, and conduct, and take every opportunity to attend the instructions of such a teacher? Nay, it seems not at all improbable, that out of affection and zeal for him, he might even venture to quit his retreat in Galilee and follow Jesus to Jerusalem,

lem, which expofed him to be apprehended for his former crimes, and brought him to die with him.

This fuppofition feems to furnifh us with a reafonable account both of the candour of his confeffion, the confidence of his teftimony to Jefus, and the extraordinary petition he made to him; and alfo renders our Lord's favourable anfwer to him perfectly correfpondent to the ftated and declared meafures of God's moral government. But then, the doctrine of a probability of repentance at the article of death proving acceptable will no longer have countenance from the cafe of the penitent thief.

John vi. 44. 65. *No man can come to me except it were given him of my Father. Every man therefore that hath heard, and learned of the Father cometh unto me.* ——*No man can come to me, except the Father who hath fent me draw him.* Now how is it that God is elfewhere faid to *draw* men, but by the force of motives and inftructions, which fuppofes that men have a power of attending to them and improving by them. It is alfo to be obferved that, in the whole of the difcourfe, in which the words quoted above are introduced, Jefus is blaming the Jews for their infidelity; and it would be very extraordinary, indeed, if for this purpofe he fhould make ufe of an argument, which would intirely exculpate them, intimating that it was not in their power to do otherwife.

Our Lord fufficiently gives us to underftand in what fenfe he ufes the word *drawing* in the paffage quoted above. He explains himfelf v. 45. *It is written in the prophets.* Ifaiah liv. 13. *And they fhall be all taught of God. Every man therefore that hath heard and learned of the father, cometh unto me.* This was the way in which God the father drew fome of the Jews to Chrift at that time; viz. fuch of them as, influenced by reverence, love and duty to him, heard attentively, and learned the truths which he had already taught them by Mofes and the prophets; but they who were of a different fpirit and conduct, with refpect to the divine truths already revealed, could not come to Chrift, who conftantly referred them to the teftimonies of Mofes and the prophets in proof of his divine miffion.

To

illuſtrated. 11

To them *it was not given to know the myſteries of the kingdom of heaven,* Mat. xiii. 11. Agreeably hereto he ſays on another occaſion, *If any man will do his will, he ſhall know of the doctrine, whether it be of God, or whether I ſpeak of myſelf,* John vii. 17. And he thus remonſtrates againſt the unbelieving Jews, Ch. v. 39, &c. *Search the ſcriptures, for in them ye think ye have eternal life: and they are they which teſtify of me. —But I know you, that ye have not the love of God in you—How can ye believe, which receive honour one of another, and ſeek not the honour that cometh from God only.* This appears plainly to be the language of one who conſidered the cauſe of the unbelief of theſe Jews as ariſing, not from natural inability, or the withholding of the grace of God, but from contracted evil principles and habits, to which they determinedly adhered; as he ſpeaks v. 40. *Ye will not come unto me that ye might have life.*

II. *Of Original Sin.*

THAT mankind are conſiderable *ſufferers* in conſequence of the fall of Adam is not denied; but all the evils which Moſes ſpecifies as affecting his poſterity on that account, are of a corporeal and temporal nature, viz. *labour, ſorrow,* and *death.* It is poſſible, indeed, that the body being more ſubject to diſeaſe, the mind may be more feeble, and therefore more prone to comply with ſome temptations; but then it ſhould alſo be conſidered, that a ſickly conſtitution is favourable to many virtues, and we ſee that a ſtate of confirmed health is often highly dangerous in a moral reſpect; ſo that upon the whole it is probable that our condition is more favourable to virtue than that of Adam. That the ſacred writers did not conſider it as, upon the whole, worſe than his, is evident from their never giving the leaſt hint, that any allowance will be made to men for that natural diſadvantage. Nay many of the ſinful poſterity of Adam are blamed more ſeverely than he was for his ſin; and if we conſider his ſituation and the circumſtances of his fall, we cannot ſuppoſe that he had greater

ſtrength

strength of mind to resist temptation than we are now possessed of. Since, however, some particular texts are alledged, to prove that the nature of man is totally depraved by the fall, insomuch that all mankind, without exception, are now altogether incapable of any good thought, word, or action; and, moreover, that we are all subject to the everlasting wrath of God on account of the sin of Adam, I shall give a brief explication of the principal of those texts.

Gen. vi. 5. *And God saw that the wickedness of man was great in the earth; and that every imagination of the thoughts of his heart was only evil continually.* If we understand this passage literally, it will be contradicted by the character which is immediately afterwards given of Noah, of whom it is said v. 9. *that he was a just man, and perfect in his generation, and that he walked with God.* But it is plain that this wickedness of mankind was not owing to any *natural depravity*, which their derivation from Adam rendered necessary, but that it was a *voluntary corruption*, and had its rise from themselves only; for it is said, v. 12. that *God looked upon the earth, and behold it was corrupt; for all flesh had corrupted his way upon the earth.* Besides, this state of the world is alledged as a justification of the divine proceedings against them, whereas, if they had been corrupt by the *necessity of nature*, it must have operated as a plea in their favour, with that being who considers our frame, and remembers that we are but dust. If he makes suitable allowance for the infirmities of our *bodies*, much more would he consider the natural and necessary disorders of our *minds*.

Job xiv. 4. *Who can bring a clean thing out of an unclean? not one.* This is a proverbial expression, signifying that nothing can be more perfect than its original; but Job is not speaking in this place of the guilt and pollution of man, but of his sorrows and mortality.

Psalm li. 5. *Behold, I was shapen in iniquity, and in sin did my mother conceive me.* This also has very much the air of a proverbial expression, signifying great depravity of heart, and very early habits of vice. That it was not intended to express a natural and invincible propensity to vice, is plain, because

that

illuſtrated. 13

that would be inconſiſtent with the tenor of the whole pſalm, in which the humble author ſeems diſpoſed to aggravate, rather than to extenuate his offences, to which this laſt mentioned conſideration would have greatly contributed.

Rom. v. 12. 13. 14. *Wherefore, as by one man ſin entered into the world, and death by ſin; and ſo death paſſed upon all men, for that all have ſinned,* &c.

I think a careful and impartial reader will obſerve, that the Apoſtle ſpeaks not here of the death of children, whom he does not once mention, or refer to, through the whole argument. But he ſpeaks of thoſe who were not only *capable* of ſinning but had *actually* ſinned, and refers us to the Moſaic hiſtory of mankind in the ages between the fall of Adam and the giving of the law by Moſes. Sin and death entered into the world by Adam, and death hath paſſed upon all men, for that all have ſinned, conſequently muſt have transgreſſed ſome law, v. 14. *For, before the* giving of the *law* by Moſes, *Sin was in the world, but ſin is not imputed where there is no law:* and the law of Moſes they could not ſin againſt before it was given. *Nevertheleſs, death reigned from Adam to Moſes, even over them that had not ſinned after the ſimilitude of Adam's tranſgreſſion.* i. e. by eating the forbidden fruit, or violating any poſitive law of life given to them. What law then had they ſinned againſt? Moſt evidently, the law of righteouſneſs which God had written on their hearts; the ſanctions of which they were alſo well apprized of (as the Apoſtle ſpeaks of the Gentiles in general, Ch. i. 32. of this Epiſtle) *Who knowing the judgment of God (that they which commit ſuch things are worthy of death) not only do the ſame, but have pleaſure in them that do them.* Hence it appears that the Apoſtle does not ſpeak of the ſin of Adam being imputed to make men ſinners, and ſubject them to death; but of actual and perſonal ſins, and of death as the recompence of them. Now look into the Moſaic hiſtory of this period, and we find before the flood *that the wickedneſs of man was great in the earth*—Gen. vi. 5. *The earth alſo was corrupt before God, and the earth was filled with violence. For all fleſh had corrupted his way upon the earth,*

v. 11,

v. 11, 12. And after the flood, excepting the faith and obedience of Abraham, Isaac, and Jacob, we have little else recorded besides transgressions of the law of righteousness: sins which men committed, though *not after the similitude of Adam's transgression.* As to the death of infants; God, the great giver of life, hath, undoubtedly, a perfect right to resume it, whenever it seemeth meet to his infinite wisdom. But I do not recollect that the sacred writers do any where represent it as a *punishment* either for Adam's sin, or their own. In a few cases they speak of it as a punishment of the sin of their immediate parents, but then, as a punishment to the parents, who had sinned, not to the children, who had not sinned.

Rom. v. 6, 8. *For when we were yet without strength, in due time, Christ died for the ungodly. But God commendeth his love towards us, in that while we were yet sinners, Christ died for us.*

Let the intelligent reader judge for himself, whether the apostle doth not speak here of the state of mankind (particularly of himself and the persons he writes to) before Christ's death, and the consequent publication of the gospel to the world, and intimate that the case is very different since that happy event? Doth he not plainly make the distinction in both verses, that we might not mistake his meaning, *When we were yet without strength,* and *while we were yet sinners.* But doth the case continue the same, since Christ died, with those to whom the blessings of the gospel are imparted? then hath Christ died, and the gospel been published in vain. Yet some writers represent the state of those for whom Christ died, and who have received the gospel, as just the same, as to *strength,* with them who had not received it, and lived before it was published. Surely, any of us would be displeased to have our words wrested to purposes so different from our intentions; especially, when we had endeavoured to guard them from such abuse. God our maker hath given us intelligent capacities, suited to those discoveries which he hath made of his will, whether by the light of nature, or revelation;

he

he hath given us also freedom of choice and action for the conduct of ourselves; he hath granted us the light and motives of the gospel for our fuller instruction and persuasion; he is ever present with us and ready to assist our sincere endeavours to know and do his will: surely then, it is *unjust* and *ungrateful* to him to say that we are still *without strength*: and if we be sinners, it is wholly our own fault. As for the gentiles, even the worst of them, the apostle no where ascribes their want of strength, to their not having received from their maker sufficient abilities to know and do his will acceptably, but to their having voluntarily corrupted themselves and one another, and thereby lost the abilities which God had given them, and become *dead in trespasses and sins*.

Rom. vii. 7, 8. *Because the carnal mind is enmity against God; for it is not subject to the law of God, neither indeed can be. So then, they that are in the flesh cannot please God.*

It appears to me, that the apostle speaks here only of personal character and conduct, and the effects of them in producing governing habits; but not at all of any corruption or depravity of the *nature* of man effected by Adam's sin, whereby he is become *incapable* of doing that which is good, or of pleasing God. Adam, or his sin, is not mentioned by the apostle in treating of this subject. It is readily acknowledged, that a person who attaches himself to the gratification of his *carnal* or sensual appetites and passions cannot perform the will of God, but must daily become more and more alienated from *him*, and from his duty: but this is saying no more than that a wicked man cannot be a good man, or please God so long as he continues wicked. But it by no means follows that this man is unable to hear, understand, and receive salutary convictions from the truths of God, revealed by his Son Jesus Christ, and thereby become changed in his sentiments, dispositions, and conduct, and from *carnally minded* become *spiritually minded*. The various forms of speech which the apostle uses in the preceding and following verses seem only to express one and the same thing, viz. the change produced in the dispositions

positions and conduct of men by the preaching of the gospel to them, and their attention to it, and sincere reception of it, together with the happy effects and consequences of it.

Ephesians. ii 3. *And were by nature children of wrath even as others.*

If we compare the passages in which the apostle uses the word *nature*, we shall find that he did not mean by it that internal frame, constitution, or condition of being wherewith God our maker hath formed us; but that external condition, or those outward circumstances (especially with relation to God and religious concerns) in which divine providence hath caused us to be born and live. Human nature, in our sense of the phrase, is the same in all mankind; but different persons may be brought forth into life, and spend it under very different natural circumstances, in the apostle's sense of the word *nature*. Thus Rom. ii. 14. He says, *when the Gentiles, which have not the law, do* by nature *the things contained in the law*. and v. 27. *Shall not uncircumcision, which is* by nature, *if it fulfill the law, judge thee, &c.* He here plainly speaks not of an internal frame, constitution, or powers, or what we call a nature, which the Gentiles had, different from that of the Jews; but of their external, moral, and religious state and circumstances, as destitute of the instructions and assistances of the law of Moses, by which they were much below the Jews. Again, in the remonstrance which he tells us he made to Peter, we find these words, Gal. ii. 15. *We who are Jews by nature, and not sinners of the Gentiles;* when certainly he doth not mean to intimate that the Jews had a different sort of nature, or internal constitution, whereby they were Jews; but only we who are natural born Jews, and have all along enjoyed the privileges of that people. So likewise in the text under consideration, having spoken of the Ephesians as formerly *dead in trespasses and sins, wherein, in time past, ye walked, according to the course of this world, according to the prince of the power of the air, the spirit that now worketh in the children of disobedience;* he adds v. 3. *among whom also we all had our conversation illustrated.*

sation in times past, in the lust of our flesh, fulfilling the desires of the flesh and of the mind. Observe, hitherto he speaks of external condition and circumstances, and of personal character and actual vices, and not at all of internal constitution, or a nature corrupted by the effects of Adam's sin. He adds: *and were by nature children of wrath, even as others.* i. e. (conformable to his use of the word nature in other places) in consequence of our birth and situation among children of disobedience, where we were kept ignorant of the truth, deceived by false principles, and misled by bad examples, we ourselves were *children of wrath*, as others about us were, and many still continue. By *children of wrath* I apprehend the apostle does not mean here *objects of the wrath and displeasure of God*, but only describes further the personal character of those whom he so denominates. As in the close of the former verse he had mentioned *children, or sons of disobedience.* i. e. disobedient children, (and St. Pet. 1. Ep. i. 14. speaks of *obedient children*, in the original it is *children of obedience*) so here he mentions *children of wrath*, i. e. wrathful, furious, malignant, and mischievous persons. In a striking and beautiful figure, he represents disobedience and wrath under the persons of two fruitful mothers, whose offspring they had been. Accordingly, when the apostle comes in the beginning of the fourth chapter to exhort the Ephesian christians to a conversation conformable to *the vocation wherewith they were called*, and quite the reverse of the description he gives in this verse of their former character and conduct, he begins with describing it thus v. 2, 3. *With all lowliness and meekness, with long suffering, forbearing one another in love. Endeavouring to keep the unity of the spirit in the bond of peace.* He also concludes the chapter thus. *Let all bitterness, and wrath, and anger, and clamour, and evil speaking, be put away from you with all malice. And be ye kind one to another, tender hearted, forgiving one another, even as God for Christ's sake hath forgiven you.* Do we not see a greater propriety and force in these exhortations, when we consider them as addressed to persons who had formerly been *children of wrath?*

III. *Of*

III. *Of Election and Reprobation.*

Rom. ix. 11, &c. *For the children being not yet born, neither having done any good or evil, that the purpose of God according to election might stand, not of works, but of him that calleth, it was said unto her, The elder shall serve the younger; as it is written, Jacob have I loved, but Esau have I hated. What shall we say then, is there unrighteousness with God? God forbid; for he saith to Moses, I will have mercy on whom I will have mercy, and I will have compassion on whom I will have compassion. So then it is not of him that willeth, nor of him that runneth, but of God that sheweth mercy, &c.*

These verses, and the whole of this chapter, relate not to the election of particular persons to eternal life, but to the calling of the Gentiles, and the rejection of the Jews from the privileges of the gospel; and it is manifest that the apostle is not speaking in this place of the *final state*, or, indeed of the *persons* of Esau and Jacob, but of their posterity, and that only with a view to temporal privileges and prerogatives.

The whole body of christians, consisting of Jews and Gentiles, are frequently stiled the *chosen*, and *elect of God*, on account of their external privileges, as the whole Jewish nation had been so named before, on the same account. This is an easy and plain sense of *election*, reflects not at all on the perfections of God, is consistent with the offers and exhortations of scripture, and preserves a harmony between the language of the old and new testament.

It must be acknowledged, however, that in order to vindicate the divine conduct in the calling of the Gentiles, the apostle alleges some facts, in which not whole nations, but *particular persons* are spoken of, and which seem to imply, that their minds were under supernatural influence in forming *bad* as well as *good* resolutions; and there are other passages of scripture, which at first sight seem to look the same way.

The hardness of Pharaoh's heart, Exod. ix. 16. Rom. ix. 17. the obstinacy of Sihon king of Heshbon,

bon, Deut. ii. 30. and the unbelief of many of the Jews, If. vi. 10. Mat. xiii. 14. Mark. iv. 12. Luke. viii. 10. John. xii. 40. Acts. xxviii. 26. Rom. xi. 8. are all afcribed to the purpofe, act, or decree of God, who had important defigns to anfwer by means of thefe blameable determinations of men. On the other hand, when perfons believe and obey the gofpel, it is afcribed to the divine influence upon their minds. Mat. xi. 25. *I thank thee, O Father, Lord of heaven and earth, becaufe thou haft hid thefe things from the wife and prudent, and haft revealed them unto babes. Even fo, Father, for fo it feemed good in thy fight.* John. vi. 27. *All that the Father giveth me fhall come to me.* See alfo John. 17. Acts. xvi. 14. *And the Lord opened the heart of Lydia, that fhe attended to the things that were fpoken of Paul.* Moreover, every thing of this nature is exprefsly referred to the arbitrary difpofition of God, in Rom. ix. 18,—23. *Therefore hath he mercy on whom he will have mercy, and whom he will he hardeneth. Thou wilt fay, then, unto me, Why doth he yet find fault, for who hath refifted his will? Nay but, O man, who art thou, that thou repliest againft God? Shall the thing formed fay to him that formed it, why haft thou made me thus? Hath not the potter power over the clay, of the fame lump, to make one veffel unto honour, and another unto difhonour? What if God, willing to fhew his wrath, and to make his power known, endured with much long fuffering the veffels of wrath fitted to deftruction; and that he might make known the riches of his glory on the veffels of mercy, which he had afore prepared unto glory.*

To underftand fuch paffages as thefe, we fhould confider that in the language of the fcriptures, God is faid to *do* thofe things, which come to pafs according to the natural courfe of things, as well as to perform things of a miraculous nature; becaufe they take place in confequence of the laws which he has originally eftablifhed. And, certainly, if God had not made men liable to be feduced by temptation, they would not have finned, any more than they could embrace truth without the means of becoming acquainted with it; and it muft depend upon the good pleafure of

God whether he will afford men more, or fewer advantages for attaining to knowledge, virtue, and happiness. But, notwithstanding this, if the means have been such as would have been effectual, provided there had been no criminal prejudice to frustrate them, men are blamed, and God is just and wise in punishing them, as well as in rewarding those whose minds are so disposed, as to receive advantage from the means of virtue and knowledge which are afforded them.

Now that, in this sense the sacred writers considered God as just to all mankind, is evident from the many earnest exhortations and expostulations addressed to sinners in the books of scripture, and from the blame and reproach which men are represented as incurring, when they continue in vice and ignorance. It is not possible that any persons could be so inconsistent with themselves, as to exhort sinners to repent, and to blame and reproach them for not repenting, if they did not consider them as having a natural power to comply with the exhortation. Nay, in this very passage of the apostle Paul, which is, perhaps, the most favourable to the doctrine of *absolute decrees* of any thing in all the books of scripture, God is represented as *enduring, with much long suffering, the vessels of wrath fitted to destruction*, which evidently implies that they had sufficient power and time to repent, and prevent their impending destruction; and therefore proves that their destruction was not *decreed*, but in case of their impenitence.

How much soever, therefore, the sacred writers refer to God, upon particular occasions, and whatever use they may suppose that his infinite wisdom will make of the errors and vices of some individuals of mankind, in order to promote the interests of truth and virtue more at large, we cannot but conclude, that they considered every man's own determination as final with respect to his future state; and it is to be observed, that neither the obstinacy of Pharaoh, nor even the infidelity of the Jews, had any necessary connection with their state after death. The former might be hard-hearted with respect to the Hebrews, and either rewarded for other virtues, or punished for other vices,

in

in a future state; and if the unbelieving Jews were in other respects such men as Paul, who had a zeal for God, though not acording to knowledge, they may find mercy in the day of judgement. There is not a single passage in the scriptures which represents the future misery of any individual of mankind as determined by an arbitrary decree of God; but a thousand passages in which it is expressly said, that the future state of all mankind depends entirely upon their own voluntary actions.

After these observations, short remarks on an other passage may suffice for the purpose of this section.

Rom. viii. 28. *And we know that all things work together for good to them that love God, who are the called according to his purpose. For whom he did fore know, he did also predestinate, to be conformed to the image of his son, that he might be the first-born among many brethren. Moreover, whom he did predestinate, them he also called; and whom he called, them he also justified; and whom he justified, them he also glorified.*

All that we can fairly infer from this passage is, that the end of the christian dispensation, or of the calling of mankind to the faith of the gospel, is their sanctification and future glory; for it is manifest that *all* who are *called* are not *justified*. If this term *called* be restricted in its meaning, let it be restricted by St. Paul himself, viz. to those *who love God*; which is sufficiently represented as depending upon men themselves, by being the subject of precept and exhortation. *Thou shalt love the Lord thy God, with all thy heart*, &c.

IV. *Of the Divinity of Christ.*

Nothing can be more evident, from the whole tenor of the New Testament, than that the person who is distinguished by the name of the *Father* is the only true God, exclusive of the *Son*, or any other being whatever. Nevertheless, there are some single and unconnected passages, especially in our tranflation of the bible, which seem to favour the contrary opinion, namely, that of the divinity of Christ. The intimate union which subsisted between God and Christ, the powers communicated to him by God, especially after his resurrection and ascension, and the distinguished honours conferred upon him, easily lead us to the genuine sense of the most considerable of these expressions, and make it evident that nothing was meant by them in the least derogatory from the sole proper divinity, and absolute supremacy of the father.

I. Christ being appointed the *king* and *judge* of men, has powers given him adapted to those offices, especially the knowledge of the human heart, and the prerogative of declaring the forgiveness of sin, which always accompanies regal authority; but being assisted by divine wisdom and discernment, as well as by divine power in the exercise of this high office, it is, in effect, the same thing as the judgment and mercy of God displayed by the instrumentality of Jesus Christ. We ought not, therefore, to be surprized at such expressions as these. Mat. ix. 4. *And Jesus knowing their thoughts.* John ii. 35. *He knew what was in man.* Mat. ix. 2. *Thy sins be forgiven thee.* The multitude, who saw Christ exerting a miraculous power upon this occasion, and heard him express himself in this manner, had no idea of his claiming any extraordinary power, as *naturally inherent in himself*; for it is said v. 8. *that when the multitude saw it, they marvelled, and glorified God, who had given such power unto men.* The scribes and pharisees, indeed, said within themselves, upon this occasion, v. 3. *This man blasphemeth.* But the Jews called it *blasphemy* to pretend to be the Christ; for when the high priest solemnly adjured our Lord by the living God, Mat. xxvi. 63. that he would tell him *whether he was the Christ, the son of God,* and our Lord expresly replies that he was the Christ, we read, v. 65. *then the high priest rent his cloathes, saying, he hath spoken blasphemy.*

Col. ii. 9. *In him dwelleth all the fullness of the Godhead bodily.* This is a very proper expression, being strictly and literally true, though Christ himself was a mere man, since the wisdom and power of the one true God, the

the Father, were manifest in, and acted by him, agreeable to his own declarations, that *the words which he spake were not his own, but the father's who sent him, and that the father within him did the works.* Nay, this very expression, that the fullness of the Godhead dwelled or resided in him, seems to imply that it did not naturally belong to him. Besides, phrases similar to this are applied by way of figure to christians in general. They are said to be *partakers of the divine nature*, 2 Pet. i. 4. *to be filled with all the fullness of God*, Eph. iii. 19. and to *be the fullness of him, that filleth all in all*, Eph. i. 13.

These observations will easily help us to understand what is meant by Christ being called the *image of the invisible God*, 2 Cor. iv. 4. Col. i. 15. and *the express image of his person*, Heb. i. 3. and also his being *in the form of God*, Phil. ii. 6. for they all allude to the divine power and wisdom which were displayed in him when he was on earth, but more especially now that he is ascended into heaven; at the same time, Christ being called only the *image* of God, is a sufficient intimation that he is not *God himself*. Indeed, if this expression was to be allowed to be any proof of the divinity of Christ, it would follow that Adam was God; for it is said, Gen. i. 26. 27. *That God made man in his own image, and after his likeness.*

It is with as little appearance of reason that Christ is argued to be very and eternal God, because he is stiled the *Son of God*; for all christians have the same appellation, 1 John iii. 2. *Now are we the sons of God*. We are also called not only the *children*, but also the *heirs of God*, and *joint heirs with Christ*, Rom. viii. 17. Adam is more especially called the *son of God*, Luke iii. 18. and Ephraim is called *his dear son*, Jer. xxxi. 20.

John x. 30. *I and my Father are one.* xiv. 10. *I am in the Father, and the Father in me*, That is, we are one in design and interest. But whatever be the union between the Father and the Son; it is of such a kind, that his disciples are capable of it with respect to them both; for, in his prayer for his disciples, he says, John xvii. 20. *Neither pray I for these alone, but for them*

them also who shall believe on me through their word, that they all may be one, as thou Father art in me, and I in thee, that they also may be one in us.——and the glory which thou gavest me, I have given them, that they may be one, even as we are one. I in them, and thou in me, that they may be made perfect in one, and that the world may know that thou hast sent me, and hast loved them as thou hast loved me.

John v. 23. *That all men should honour the son, even as they honour the Father*; that is *as well as* the Father. The same word is used where it can have no other sense, in John xvii. 23. *And hast loved them as thou hast loved me*; that is, not in the same degree, but *likewise*. To explain the sense of the intire passage in which the words abovementioned occur, let it be observed, that the Jews had persecuted Jesus, because he had made a man whole on the sabbath day. By way of apology, he says v. 17. *My Father worketh hitherto*, that is, in the course of his providence on the sabbath, as well as on other days, and *I work*; that is, on the sabbath day also. Upon this the pharisees were more inraged, *because he called God his father, and because he made himself* (not *equal with God*, as we render it) but *like unto God*, assuming so much of his prerogative, as to claim the privilege of working on the sabbath day as well as God. However, to shew them that he meant nothing arrogant in what he had said, and that this privilege was given to him by God, he immediately replies, v. 19. *Verily verily I say unto you, the Son can do nothing of himself; but what he sees the Father do; for what things soever he doth, these also doth the son likewise.* He then proceeds to represent all his extraordinary power as the gift of his Father, v. 20. *For the Father loveth the son, and sheweth him all things that himself doth; and he will shew him greater things than these, that ye may marvel. For as the Father raiseth up the dead, and quickeneth them, even so the Son quickeneth whom he will. For the Father judgeth no man, but hath committed all judgment unto the Son, that all men should honour the Son, even as they honour the Father. He that honoureth not the Son, honoureth not the Father who hath sent him.* Indeed, this very last clause sufficiently shews

that

illustrated. 25

that the honour to which Christ is intitled is not on account of what he is, or has, *of himself*, but on account of what he derives from God, as his ambassador.

II. Very high titles are justly given to Christ as the founder of the christian religion, and especially as superintending the affairs of his church, and as controuling whatever can affect the interest of his church. Thus the author of the epistle to the Hebrews stiles him *the author and finisher of our faith.* Heb. xii. 2. He is also said to be the *head over all things to his church*, Eph. i. 2; and in Rev. i. 8. he says *I am Alpha and Omega, the beginning and the ending, which is, and which was, and which is to come, the almighty.* These high titles are attributed to Jesus with respect to the state of glory, and universal dominion, to which he is exalted by the Father. The word which we render *almighty*, signifies *ruler over all*, and is very properly applied to Christ, to whom *all power is given in heaven and in earth*, that is, all power which can respect his church, or be useful to him in the management of it.

The author of the epistle to the Hebrews makes use of a phrase of the same import with this of the apostle John, where he only means to express the unchangeableness of the doctrine of Christ, as the connection of it with what goes before and after, makes very evident. Heb. xiii. 7. *Remember them which have the rule over you, who have spoken unto you the word of God, whose faith follow, considering the end of their conversation, Jesus Christ, the same yesterday, to day, and for ever. Be not carried away with diverse and strange doctrines.* The whole is intended to inculcate a steadfast adherence to the genuine doctrine of Jesus Christ.

It is plain, from many passages in this book of Revelation, that the author of it considered Christ as a person subordinate to the Father, and the minister of his will, and therefore no single expression should be interpreted in such a manner as to make it imply the contrary. The very first words of the book sufficiently express this. *The Revelation of Jesus Christ, which*

B 4 *God*

Passages of Scripture

God gave unto him v. 6. *Who has made us kings and priests unto God; and*, or rather, *even his Father* ii. 26. *And he that overcometh and keepeth my works unto the end, to him will I give power over the nations—even as I received of my Father*, iii. 14. *Him that overcometh, will I make a pillar in the temple of my God, and he shall go no more out, and I will write upon him the name of my God, and the name of the city of my God, which is new Jerusalem, which cometh down out of heaven from my God*, v. 21. *To him that overcometh, will I grant to sit with me in my throne, even as I also overcame, and am set down with my Father in his throne.* Farther, this writer, evidently speaking of Christ in his highest capacity, uses the following expressions, v. 14. *These things saith the amen, the faithful and true witness, the beginning*, or the most excellent, *of the creation of God*; which plainly implies that, how excellent soever he may be, he is but a creature.

Mat. xxviii. 29. *And lo I am with you always, even to the end of the world.* Christ, who is constituted head over all things to his church, undoubtedly takes care of its interests, and attends to whatever concerns his disciples; and *being with* a person, and *taking care* of him are, in the language of scripture, equivalent expressions. See Gen. xxi. 20. 22. xxviii. 15. xxxix. 2. Besides, Christ having a near relation to this earth, may even be *personally present* with his disciples when they little think of it. But it is by no means necessary that he be personally present every where at the same time; since God may communicate to him a power of knowing distant events, of which he appeared to be possessed when Lazarus was sick. This is certainly no greater a power than God may communicate to any of his creatures.

Another passage which seems to suppose the omnipresence of Christ is, Mat. xviii. 20. *For where two or three are gathered together in my name, there am I in the midst of them*; but if we consider the whole of this passage, in which our Lord is speaking of the great power of which his apostles would be possessed, and especially of the efficacy of their prayers, we shall be satisfied that he could only mean, by this form of expression, expreffion, to reprefent their power with God, when they were affembled as his difciples, and prayed fo as became his difciples, to be the fame as his own power with God; and God heard him always. That our Lord could not intend to fpeak of himfelf as *the God who heareth prayer*, is evident from his fpeaking of the Father, in this very place as the perfon who was to grant their petitions, v. 19. *Again I fay unto you, that if two of you fhall agree on earth, as touching any thing that they fhall afk, it fhall be done for them, of my Father who is in heaven.*

III. Confidering the great power with which Chrift was invefted on earth, and more efpecially the authority to which he is exalted now that he is in heaven, it is certainly right that a very high degree of refpect fhould be paid to him; and from the manner in which this is expreffed, and efpecially becaufe the word *worfhip* is made ufe of on thofe occafions, in our Englifh tranflation, fome perfons have been confirmed in their opinion, that he is the proper object of fupreme or divine worfhip, and is therefore truly and properly God; but any perfon who will confider the real import of the following paffages, muft fee that they afford no foundation for fuch a conclufion.

Heb. i. 6. *When God bringeth in the firft begotten into the world, he faith, Let all the angels of God worfhip him.* Alfo the leper, Mat. viii. 2. the ruler, Mat. ix. 18. the woman of Canaan, Mat. xv. 25. the poor people in the fhip, Mat. xiv. 33. and his difciples, Mat. xxviii. 9, - - - - 17. are all faid to have *worfhipped* him. But the very circumftances in which this worfhip was paid to Chrift fufficiently prove that *divine worfhip* was not intended; becaufe it is well known that the Jews had no expectation of any other perfon than a man for their Meffiah; and when Nicodemus was convinced of the miraculous power of Jefus, he concluded, not that he was God, but that he muft have been *impowered by God*; for he fays, John iii. 2. *Rabbi, we know that thou art a teacher come from God; for no man can do thefe miracles that thou doeft, except God be with him.* Befides, it is well known that the Greek word, which, in the abovementioned paffages, is rendered *worship*, is frequently used to express a very high degree of respect; but such as may be lawfully paid to men of a proper character and rank, and indeed our word *worship*, though it is now appropriated to that worship which is due to God only, was formerly used with greater latitude, and even in our translation of the bible; as when a servant, in one of our Saviour's parables, is said to have fallen down and *worshipped* his master, saying, *Have patience with me, and I will pay thee all*; where certainly divine worship could not be meant. It is also an evidence of this use of the word, that in our marriage service, the man is directed to say to the woman, *With my body I thee worship*; and the terms *worship*, and *worshipful*, are still applied to several of our magistrates, and bodies of men.

Also, in the Greek translation of the Old Testament, the same word that we render worship in the New is frequently used where supreme worship could not be intended. Otherwise, Abraham must be supposed to have intended to pay supreme worship to the angels, when he took them to be men; and to the sons of Heth, when he was making a bargain with them for a piece of ground to bury his dead.

IV. Arguments have been brought to prove the divinity of Christ from the *names* and *titles*, which are given to him, as well as from the *powers* ascribed to him, and the *worship* that is paid him; but if we consider the proper meaning of other *scripture names*, and the occasions on which they were conferred, we must be satisfied, that very little stress is to be laid on such an argument as this.

Isaiah vii. 14. *Behold a virgin shall conceive, and bear a son, and shall call his name Emmanuel*, Mat. i. 23. *Behold a virgin shall be with child, and bear a son, and shall call his name Emmanuel, which is, being interpreted, God with us.* These texts have been thought to imply that Christ is a compound being, or that he is *God incarnate*; but if we consider other instances of names imposed by the divine direction in the scriptures, we shall find that they do not always express any thing characteristic of the person on whom they are

are impofed, but that they were intended to be a memorial of fome divine promife or affurance, refpecting things of a public and general concern. Thus the prophet Ifaiah, vii. 1, &c. was directed to call his fon *Shear Jafhub*, which fignifies *a remnant fhall return*, to exprefs to the Jews, that only a fmall number of their enemies fhould return from the invafion with which they then threatened them, or that a number of their own people who had been carried captive fhould return. Another child he was directed to call *Maherfhalalhafhbaz*, on a fimilar account; and of Jerufalem it is faid, *This is the name wherewith fhe fhall be called, the Lord our righteoufnefs*, to exprefs that God would appear in that character to his people. In like manner the divine being, by appointing Chrift to be called *Emmanuel*, engaged to manifeft his own prefence with his people, by protecting and bleffing them, and inflicting vengeance on their enemies and oppreffors. For this prediction was given upon the occafion of an invafion by the Ifraelites and Syrians.

Ifaiah ix. 6. *Unto us a child is born, unto us a fon is given, and the government fhall be upon his fhoulders; and his name fhall be called wonderful, counfellor, the mighty God, the everlafting father, the prince of peace.* In this, as in the former cafe, thefe titles may not exprefs what *Chrift is*, but what God will manifeft himfelf to be in him, and by him; fo that, in the difpenfation of the gofpel, God, the wife and benevolent author of it, will appear to be a wonderful counfellor, the everlafting father, and the prince of peace. If this name be fuppofed to characterize Chrift himfelf, it will by no means favour the common doctrine of the trinity; becaufe it will make him to be the *Father*, or the firft perfon, and not the *Son*, or the fecond perfon. Befides, whatever powers or dignities are to be poffeffed by Chrift, it is fufficiently intimated in this place, that he does not hold them *independent*, and *underived*; fince he himfelf, and all the bleffings that he beftows, are faid to be *given*, that is, by God; and at the conclufion of the prophefy, in the next verfe, it is faid, that *the zeal of the Lord of hofts will perform this*. I would alfo obferve that that part of the title on which the greatest stress has been laid may be rendered *the mighty God my father for ever*, or *the mighty God is my father for ever*, which is exactly agreeable to many declarations of the scripture concerning Christ, and his usual title of *the son of God*; and to this the angel, in his salutation of Mary, might probably allude, when he said Luke i. 32. *He shall be great, and shall be called the son of the highest*; and it is very observable, that what he adds corresponds most remarkably with the remainder of this very prophesy of Isaiah. The prophet says, v. 7. *Of the increase of his government, and peace, there shall be no end, upon the throne of David, and upon his kingdom, to order it, and to establish it, with judgment and with justice, from henceforth even for ever.* The angel says, *He shall be great, and shall be called the son of the highest, and the Lord God shall give unto him the throne of his father David, and he shall reign over the house of Jacob for ever, and of his kingdom there shall be no end.*

V. Many of the texts which are usually alleged in proof of the divinity of Christ, relate to God the Father only. One of the most remarkable of these is John. i. *In the beginning was the word, and the word was with God, and the word was God. The same was in the beginning with God. All things were made by him, and without him was not any thing made that was made. In him was life, and the life was the light of men; and the light shineth in darkness, and the darkness comprehended it not. There was a man sent from God, whose name was John. The same came for a witness, to bear witness of the light, that all men through him might believe. He was not that light, but was sent to bear witness of that light. That was the true light, which lighteth every man that cometh into the world. He was in the world, and the world was made by him, and the world knew him not. He came unto his own, and his own received him not. And the word was made flesh, and dwelt among us, and we beheld his glory, the glory as of the only begotten of the Father, full of grace and truth.*

These words, interpreted in the most literal manner, only imply that *the word*, or Christ, had a being
before

before the creation of the world; that he had the title of *God*, or a God, and was the instrument by whom the supreme God made all things; but they by no means imply that he was true and very God; for magistrates, and others are sometimes called *Gods*, on account of their power and dominion, in which they resemble God. Nay the derivation of Christ from the Father, and consequently his dependence upon him is sufficiently expressed by his being called, in the last of these verses, *the only begotten of the Father*.

To me, however, it appears, that the apostle does not speak of the preexistence of Christ in this place; • but only of the power and wisdom of God, which dwelled, or tabernacled in his flesh; and that he probably meant to condemn an opinion which is known to have prevailed in his time, namely, that the spirit which animated Christ having (in common with the souls of all other men) preexisted, was that being who formed this world. Christ being called *the word of God*, on account of his being in a more eminent manner commissioned to declare the will of God, they imagined that he was meant in many passages of the Old Testament, in which mention is made of the *word of God*, as in that of the psalmist, *by the word of the Lord were the heavens made*, &c. Now, in contradiction to all this, the apostle here asserts, that by the *word of God*, we are not to understand any being distinct from God; but only the *power*, or *energy of God*; which is so much *with God*, that it properly belongs to his nature, and is not at all distinct from God himself; and that the same power which produced all things was manifest to men in the person of Jesus Christ, who was sent to enlighten the world; that though this power made the world, it was not acknowledged by the world, when it was revealed in this manner, nor even by God's peculiar people, the Jews; and notwithstanding this power was manifested in a more sensible and constant manner than ever it had been before, dwelling in human flesh, and tabernacling, or abiding some considerable time among us; so that his glory was beheld, or made visible to mortal eyes, and was full of grace and truth.

Others

Others suppose that *the word*, in this introduction to the gospel of John, is the name of an *office*, or *character*, sustained first by God himself, and, after his ascension, by Jesus Christ, viz. the immediate source of supernatural communications, *the giver of light and life*. The reason why John calls Christ the *word of God*, was probably his seeing that name or title, written upon his thigh, in the Revelation, which is supposed to have been written before his gospel. Rev. xix. 13.

Rom. ix. 5. *Whose are the Fathers, and of whom, as concerning the flesh, Christ came, who is over all, God blessed for ever.* This may with equal propriety and truth be rendered, *God, who is over all, be blessed for ever*, the former sentence ending with the word *came*; and since no ancient manuscripts are pointed, all the pointings have been made and the different sentences have been distinguished as fallible men have thought the best sense required. It affords an argument favourable to my construction of these words, that it is usual with the apostle Paul to break out into a doxology, or form of thanksgiving to God, after mentioning any remarkable instance of his goodness. See Eph. iii. 21. 1 Tim. i. 17. vi. 16. See also 1 Pet. iv. 11. Indeed, it is very common in Jewish writings to add a doxology after barely mentioning the name of God.

1 John. v. 20. *And we know that the son of God is come, and hath given us an understanding, that we may know him that is true, and we are in him that is true, even in his Son Jesus Christ. This is the true God, and eternal life.* This last clause is manifestly explanatory of the title *him, that is true*, or *the true one*, in the preceding clauses, of whom the Son of God has given us an understanding, or with whom he has made us acquainted. As the word *even* is a mere addition of our translators, instead of *we are in him that is true, even in his Son Jesus Christ*, we may read, we are in him that is true, *in* or *by* his Son Jesus Christ; and this makes a far more consistent sense, and may be considered as an allusion to the words of Christ addressed to the Father, and recorded by this very apostle,

apoſtle, John. xvii. 3. *This is life eternal, that they might know thee, the only true God, and Jeſus Chriſt, whom thou haſt ſent.* Without this interpretation, theſe two texts would flatly contradict one another; for how can the Father be *the only true God*, if the Son be true God alſo.

1 Cor. i. 23, 24. *But we preach Chriſt crucified, unto the Jews a ſtumbling block, and unto the Greeks fooliſhneſs; but unto them that are called, both Jews and Greeks, Chriſt the power of God and the wiſdom of God.* The meaning of this plainly is, that the power and wiſdom of God were diſplayed in this very circumſtance of the crucifixion of Chriſt, which was ſuch a ſtumbling block, and appeared ſo fooliſh to men; agreeable to what he immediately adds, *for the fooliſhneſs of God is wiſer than men, and the weakneſs of God is ſtronger than men*. That which the Jews and Greeks had rejected, as fooliſh and weak, was, in reality, and appeared to thoſe who were *called*, and who were taught to underſtand it better, to ſurpaſs the wiſdom and power of man.

Tit. ii. 13. *Looking for that bleſſed hope, and the glorious appearing of the great God, and our Saviour Jeſus Chriſt.* In this place God and Chriſt are mentioned as diſtinct perſons, the judgment of the world being ſometimes aſcribed to the one, and ſometimes to the other; which is eaſily accounted for by conſidering that, in that great day, Chriſt acts by commiſſion from God, and will come in the glory of his Father, and of the holy angels, as well as in his own glory, upon that moſt ſolemn occaſion.

John. xx. 28. *Thomas anſwered, and ſaid unto him, my Lord, and my God.* This is an abrupt exclamation, and no connected ſentence at all, and ſeems to have proceeded from a conviction, ſuddenly produced in the apoſtle's mind, that he who ſtood before him was, indeed, his Lord and maſter raiſed to life by the power of God. The reſurrection of Chriſt and the power of God, had ſo near a connection, that a conviction of the one could not but be attended with an acknowledgement of the other; and therefore they are frequently mentioned together, the one as the

cauſe,

cause, and the other as the *effect*. Rom. i. 4. *Declared to be the son of God with power, by the resurrection from the dead.* Rom. vi. 4. *Raised from the dead by the glory of the Father.* x. 9. *If thou shalt confess with thy mouth the Lord Jesus, and shalt believe with thine heart, that God has raised him from the dead, thou shalt be saved.* Here we plainly see, that he only who raised Christ from the dead is stiled God, and not Christ, who was raised by his power.

1 Tim. vi. 13, &c. *I give thee charge in the sight of God, who quickeneth all things, and before Jesus Christ, who before Pontius Pilate witnessed a good confession, that thou keep this commandment without spot unrebukable, till the appearing of our Lord Jesus Christ, which, in his times, he shall shew, who is the blessed and only potentate, the king of kings, and Lord of Lords; who only hath immortality, dwelling in the light which no man can approach unto, whom no man hath seen, nor can see; to whom be honour and power everlasting, amen.* The meaning of this passage, as the construction of the words in the original incontestably proves, is as follows; *which appearing,* or second coming of Christ to judge the world, he who is the blessed and only potentate, that is the only true God, the Father, shall shew, or declare. And this exactly agrees with what our Lord himself says, that the day and hour of this his appearing was not known either to the angels of God, or to himself, but to the Father only; and consequently he only could shew, or declare it. Besides, the very verses I quoted above sufficiently demonstrate, that the writer of them considered God and Christ as distinct persons. *I charge thee in the sight of God and before Jesus Christ*; and how could he with truth say of Christ, that *no man had seen him, or could see him.*

Heb. i. 10. *And thou, Lord, in the beginning hast laid the foundation of the earth, &c.* As there are several expressions in the first part of this chapter, which are not easy to be understood, I shall give a brief explanation of them all, in their order. The great objection which the Jews made to christianity being the meanness of Christ's appearance, and the ignominious death that he suffered; to obviate this, the

the author of this epistle begins with representing the great dignity to which, for the suffering of death, Christ is now exalted at the right hand of God. Having said that, *God, in these last days, had spoken to us by his Son,* he immediately adds, v. 2. *whom he hath appointed heir,* or Lord, *of all things; by whom also he made* or appointed, not the material *worlds*, but *the ages;* that is, the present dispensation of God's government over mankind, which is established by the gospel, the administration of which is committed to the Son. *Who being the brightness of his,* that is God's *glory, and the express image of his,* that is God's *person,* and *upholding all things by the word of his,* that is, God's *power,* &c. *sat down on the right hand of the majesty on high.* It is plain from this passage, that whatever Christ is, he is by divine appointment, whom he *appointed* heir of all things.

Afterwards this writer proceeds to prove that Christ is superior to angels, and at the close of this argument, he has these words, *but concerning the son he says, Thy throne, O God, is for ever and ever;* or, as it may be rendered, *God is thy throne for ever and ever;* that is, God will establish the authority of Christ till time shall be no more, *a scepter of righteousness is the scepter of thy kingdom. Thou hast loved righteousness and hated iniquity, therefore God, even thy God, has anointed thee with the oil of gladness above thy fellows.* From this passage nothing can be more plain, than that, whatever authority belongs to Christ, he has a Superior, from whom he derives it; *God, even thy God, has anointed thee.* This could never have been said of the one true God, whose being and power are underived.

In verses 10, 11, 12. the Apostle quotes an address to God, as the great Creator and everlasting Ruler of the universe, but without any hint of its being applied to Christ, from Psalm cii. 25, 27. *And thou, Lord, in the beginning hast laid the foundation of the earth, and the heavens are the works of thine hands. They shall perish, but thou remainest; and they all shall wax old as doth a garment, and as a vesture shalt thou fold them up, and they shall be changed: but thou art the same, and thy years shall*

shall not fail. This quotation was probably made with a view to expreſs the great honour conferred on Chriſt, on account of the dignity of the perſon who conferred it. For it immediately follows, ver. 13. *But to which of the angels ſaid he,* that is, the great Being to whom this deſcription belongs, *Sit thou on my right hand until I make thine enemies thy footſtool.* Or, ſince this quotation from the Pſalmiſt deſcribes a perpetuity of empire in God, it may be intended to intimate a perpetuity of empire in Chriſt, who holds his authority from God, and who muſt hold it, unleſs God himſelf be unable to ſupport it.

Acts xx. 28. *Feed the church of God, which he has purchaſed with his own blood.* In the moſt ancient manuſcripts this text is, *Feed the church of the Lord;* which generally ſignifies Chriſt. Alſo in ſome copies it is, *which he purchaſed with blood;* that is, the blood of his Son. As the *blood of God* is a phraſe which occurs no where elſe in the ſcriptures, we ought to be exceedingly cautious how we admit ſuch an expreſſion. If Chriſt was God, his blood could not be his blood as God, but as man.

VI. I ſhall here introduce a few texts, which are not reduceable to any of the above-mentioned heads; being either interpolations, or mis-tranſlations of the ſcriptures, or having no relation to the ſubject, in favour of which they have been quoted.

Matt. xxviii. 19. *Go ye, therefore, and teach all nations, baptizing them in the Name of the Father, and of the Son, and of the Holy Ghoſt.* This form of baptiſm ſeems to be intended to remind Chriſtians of the different parts which God, and Chriſt, and the Holy Ghoſt, acted in the ſcheme of man's redemption; God ſending his Son on this gracious errand; the Son faithfully performing the work which God gave him to do, and being made head over all things to the church; and the Holy Ghoſt confirming the word of truth by miraculous gifts. But it is quite an arbitrary ſuppoſition, that, becauſe they are mentioned together upon this occaſion, they muſt be equal in all other reſpects, partaking of Divinity alike, ſo as to be equal in power and glory. The Apoſtle Paul ſays, 1 Cor. x. 2. that *the children of Iſrael were baptized unto Moſes;*
but

but he certainly did not mean that Moses was their God.

Col. iii. 10. *And have put on the new man, which is renewed in knowledge after the image of him that created him; where there is neither Greek nor Jew, circumcision nor uncircumcision; Barbarian, Scythian, bond, nor free, but Christ is all, and in all*; that is, there is no other distinction to be made now, but only whether a man be a real Christian.

1 Cor. i. 2. *With all that in all places call upon the Name of Jesus Christ, our Lord, both theirs and ours.* That adoration, such as is due to the one living and true God, was not meant by the Apostle in this place, is evident from the very next words; *Grace be unto you, and peace, from God our Father, and from the Lord Jesus Christ*; where Christ is evidently spoken of as distinct from God. It is probable, therefore, that the Apostle meant nothing more than such as call themselves by the Name of Christ, or who professed Christianity.

Acts vii. 59. *And they stoned Stephen, calling upon God, and saying, Lord Jesus, receive my spirit.* The word *God* is not in the original, as our translators have signified, by their directing it to be printed in the Italic character; so that this text by no means implies that Stephen acknowledged Christ to be God, but only informs us, that Stephen addressed himself to Christ, whom he had just seen in person, in a state of great exaltation and glory; as we read, ver. 55, 56. *He, being full of the Holy Ghost, looked stedfastly into heaven, and saw the glory of God, and Jesus standing on the right hand of God; and said, Behold, I see the heavens opened, and the Son of man standing on the right hand of God.* This very language clearly implies, that he considered the Son of man, and God, as distinct persons.

The word which is here, and in 1 Cor. i. 2. rendered to *call upon*, is far from being appropriated to *invocation*, as peculiar to the divine Being. It is the same word that is rendered to *appeal to*, as when Paul appeals to Cæsar; and is used when a person is said to be called by any particular name; as, Judas, *called* Iscariot, &c. There can be no doubt, therefore,

fore, but that it has the same meaning both in 1 Cor. i. 2. and also in Acts ix. 21. *Is not this he that destroyed them who called on this name in Jerusalem?* that is, all who called themselves *Christians*. It is so rendered, James i. 7. *Do they not blaspheme the worthy Name by which ye are called?* or, as it is more exactly rendered, *which is called*, or imposed, *upon you?* that is, by which ye are distinguished. Had it implied *adoration*, it would at least have been *which is called upon by you*.

1 John v. 7. *There are three that bear record in heaven, the Father, the Word, and the Holy Ghost; and these three are one.* Sir Isaac Newton, and others, have clearly proved that this verse was no part of John's original epistle, but was inserted in later ages. It is not to be found in any ancient manuscript, and has been omitted in many printed copies and translations of the New Testament, at a time when the doctrine which it is supposed to contain was in a manner universally received. I say *supposed to contain*, because, in fact it expresses no more than that these three agree in giving the same testimony, which is the only kind of union which the *spirit*, the *water*, and *the blood*, in the verse following can have.

1 Tim. iii. 16. *And, without controversy, great is the mystery of godliness. God was manifest in the flesh, justified in the spirit, seen of angels, preached unto the Gentiles, believed on in the world, received up into glory.* Sir Isaac Newton has fully demonstrated, that, in the original, this text was not, *God* was manifest in the flesh, but *who* was manifest in the flesh, and a very small alteration in the manner of writing Greek is sufficient for that purpose. The oldest manuscipt in the world, which I have examined myself, has been manifestly altered from the one to the other, as appears by the difference in the colour of the ink. Besides, it is even literally true, that God was manifest in the flesh of Christ; since he himself acknowledges, that *the very words which he spake were not his own, but the Father's who sent him*, and that *the Father, who was in him, did the works*. It was, therefore, with the greatest propriety that our Lord said, John viii. 19.

If

If ye had known me, ye would have known my Father also, the wifdom and power of God being confpicuous in him. They who will have this text to be a proof of the godhead of Chrift, muft fuppofe him to be the *Father,* or the firſt perfon in the trinity, and not the *Son,* or the fecond.

Zech. xiii. 7. *Awake, O ſword, againſt my ſhepherd, and againſt the man that is my fellow, faith the Lord of hoſts.* So fays our Engliſh verfion, but the word in the original fignifies a perfon that is *near,* or *joined in neighbourhood* to another, and, except this fingle text, it is every where rendered *neighbour* by our tranflators.

Philip ii. 5, &c. *Let this mind be in you which was also in Chriſt Jefus, who being in the form of God thought it not robbery to be equal with God, but made himfelf of no reputation;——Wherefore God alſo hath highly exalted him,——That every tongue ſhould confefs that Jefus Chriſt is Lord, to the glory of God the Father.* The proper rendering of this text is, *Who being in the form of God, did not think that being equal to God, or a ſtate of equality with God, was a thing to be fiezed* (i. e. by him) *but made himfelf of no reputation.* This makes the whole paſſage perfectly juſt and coherent, as a recommendation of humility; and alſo hints a fine contraſt between the conduct of Chriſt, whom St. Paul elſewhere calls *the ſecond Adam,* and the firſt, who is alſo ſaid to have been made *in the likenefs of God*; but afpiring to be *as God* fell, and was puniſhed; whereas Chriſt, who had more of the likenefs or *form of God,* on account of his extraordinary powers, not graſping at any thing higher, but humbling himſelf, was exalted. It is in this fenfe, or a fenfe fimilar to it, in which this very text is quoted by thoſe Fathers of the chriſtian church who wrote before the controverfy about the divinity of Chriſt was ſtarted. In this manner, even ſome who maintain the divinity of Chriſt, render the words. Thus, Father Simon, who contends that being in the form of God, is equivalent to being truly God, renders the latter part of the verſe, *did not imperiouſly aſſume to himſelf an equality with God.* Indeed the word *but,* which introduces the next verſe, evidently leads us to expect ſome contraſt between

what

what goes before and after it, which is very striking in the manner in which I translate this text; but is altogether lost in our common version. *For he made himself equal to God, but humbled himself,* is not even sense. Lastly, I would observe that the word which is here rendred *equal to,* is also used to express a very high degree of resemblance, which it is very certain that Christ was possessed of with respect to God; and Dr. Doddridge renders it, *to be as God.*

VII. Christ may be supposed to have *pre-existed,* or to have had a being before he was born of the virgin Mary, without supposing him to be the eternal God; but it appears to me that the apostles considered Christ as being, with respect to his *nature,* truly and properly *a man,* consisting of the same constituent parts, and of the same rank with ourselves, *in all things like unto his brethren*; and the texts which are thought to speak of him as having existed before he came into this world, appear to me to bear other interpretations very well. Some of them have been explained in a different sense already, and I shall now endeavour to explain the rest.

John viii. 56, &c. *Your father Abraham rejoiced to see my day, and he saw it, and was glad. Then said the Jews unto him, thou art not yet fifty years old, and hast thou seen Abraham? Jesus said unto them, Verily verily I say unto you, before Abraham was I am.* The meaning of this passage clearly is that Abraham *foresaw* the day of Christ, and that Christ was the subject of prophecy before the times of Abraham. This saying of our Lord is also illustrated by what the author of the epistle to the Hebrews says concerning all the ancient worthies, viz. that *they all died in faith, not having received the promises, but having seen them afar off.* In this manner, therefore, Abraham also *saw* the day of Christ. Agreeable to this it is easy to explain John xvii. 5. *Glorify me with the glory which I had with thee before the world was,* of the glory which was intended for him in the councils of God before all time. Nay this must necessarily be our Lord's meaning in this place; since in many other places the power and glory which was conferred upon Christ are expresly
said

said to be the reward of his obedience, and to be subsequent to his resurrection from the dead. It is with peculiar propriety, therefore, that this request of our Lord follows his declaration that he had done the work for which he was to receive the reward. v. 4. *I have glorified thee on the earth, I have finished the work which thou gavest me to do; and now O Father glorify thou me,* &c. As the connection of this prayer shews that whatever it was that our Lord requested, it depended upon the part which he had to act in the world, it is plain that it could not be any thing which he had enjoyed antecedent to his coming into it.

In the same manner we may explain the following prophecy of Micah concerning Christ. v. 2. *Thou Bethlehem Ephratah, though thou be little among the thousands of Judah, yet out of thee shall he come forth unto me that is to be a ruler in Israel, whose goings forth have been from of old, from everlasting.* For this may be understood concerning the promises of God, in which the coming of Christ was signified to mankind from the beginning of the world. The Chaldee paraphrase renders it, *whose name was foretold of old.*

As to those who think that our Lord meant to intimate that he was truly and properly God because he uses that expression *I am*, by which the true God announced himself to Moses, they will perhaps be sensible how little stress is to be laid upon it, when they are informed, that, though the same phrase occurs very often in the history of Christ, our translators themselves, in every place excepting this, render it by *I am he*, that is, I am the Christ. It is used in this sense in the 24th verse of this chapter. *If ye believe not that I am he, ye shall die in your sins.* And again in the 28th verse, *When ye shall lift up the Son of man, then shall ye know that I am he.* That the words *I am* in this place do not mean the eternal God, is manifest from the words which are immediately connected with these; *then shall ye know that I am he, and that I do nothing of myself, but as the Father hath taught me, I speak these things,*

John xvi. 28. *I came forth from the Father, and am come into the world; again, I leave the world, and go unto the Father.* In order to understand this text, it should be observed, that by *the world* is not always meant *the material world*, and least of all in the discourses of our Saviour; but the world considered as *a state of trial, exercise, and discipline,* and especially the unbelieving and ungodly part of the world. *The world shall hate you,* John xv. 10. *I pray not for the world,* xvii. 9, &c. Our Saviour also speaks of sending his Disciples into the world; though, considered as part of the material system, they had been in it long before. John xvii. 18. *As thou hast sent me into the world, even so also send I them into the world.* Since, therefore, the mission of Christ, and that of the Apostles, are spoken of in the very same words, and represented as commencing in the same manner, there can be no more reason to suppose that Christ had a being before he came into the world, than there is to suppose that the Apostles had pre-existed. Also when our Lord says, John xvii. 11. *Now I am no more in the world,* he could not mean the material world: for, after his resurrection, he was seen by many, and even after his ascension he was seen by Paul, if not by Stephen; and he is probably in this world at present, attending to the affairs of his church; and therefore may even be literally *with his disciples,* upon important occasions, *even to the end of the world;* and the notion of a *local heaven,* above the clouds, is altogether fanciful.

John v. 13. *No man hath ascended up to heaven, but he that came down from heaven, even the Son of man, who is in heaven.* This language is evidently figurative; but if Christ could be in heaven, at the same time that he was on earth, conversing with Nicodemus, it is plain that his being said to have come down from heaven, cannot necessarily imply that he had ever been any where but on the earth. In fact, the phrases *being in heaven, being with God,* or *in the bosom of God,* &c. express a state of very intimate communication with God, such as qualified Christ to speak of heavenly things, as he expresses himself to Nicodemus, and to make his Father known to us. John i. 8. *No man hath seen God at any time: the only-begotten Son, which is in the bosom of the Father, he hath declared him.*

The

illustrated.

The omnipresence, and consequently the proper divinity of Christ, could not be meant by his being said to be in heaven at the same time that he was visible on earth, because he is, on this occasion, called *the son of man*, which is always allowed to denote his *humanity*, and which certainly could not be present in two places at the same time.

John vi. 51. *I am the living bread, which came down from heaven; if any man eat of this bread, he shall live for ever, and the bread that I will give is my flesh, which I will give for the life of the world. Verily verily I say unto you, except ye eat the flesh of the son of man, and drink his blood, ye have no life in you.* By these and other expressions of a similar nature, our Lord staggered not only those who followed him for the sake of the *loaves* with which he had fed them, but even many of his other disciples; and perceiving this, he says unto them, v. 61. *Doth this offend you, what and if ye shall see the son of man ascend up where he was before. It is the spirit that quickeneth, the flesh profiteth nothing. The words that I speak unto you, they are spirit, and they are life.* In this our Lord seems to be reproving the stupidity of his disciples, in not understanding that by *himself*, and *his flesh and blood*, he meant his *doctrine*, which came down from heaven. For if it was his *body* that was to be of such benefit to mankind, what would they say if they should see it taken from them, ascending into heaven, from whence he had spoken of its descending to be the life of the world. They must then be satisfied that his *flesh* could profit them nothing, and therefore must conclude that his *doctrine* must have been the *spirit, and the life*, of which he spake. Or we may, perhaps, understand our Saviour, in this place, as referring to his ascension, which was an ocular proof of his having had that intimate communication with God, and having been sent of God, concerning which he had been speaking.

Coll. i. 15. *Who is the image of the invisible God, the first born of every creature. For by him were all things created, that are in heaven, and that are in earth, visible and invisible, whether they be thrones, or dominions, or principalities, or powers; all things were created by him, and for him, and he is before all things, and by him all things consist: and he is the head of the body, the church, who is the beginning, the first born from the dead; that in all things he might have the pre-eminence. For it pleased the Father, that in him should all fulness dwell.*

In this passage we have a view given us of the great dignity and dominion to which Christ is exalted by his Father, and of the great and happy change that was made in the world by his gospel; for by *creation* we are to understand *the new creation*, or *renovation*, in which sense, the same word is used by the apostle, when he says, *We are his workmanship created in Christ Jesus unto good works.* Eph. ii. 10. So great a change is produced in the world, in the tempers and conduct of men by the gospel, that both the terms *creation* and *regeneration* are made use of to express it. *Verily verily I say unto thee, except a man be born again he cannot see the kingdom of God,* John iii. 3; so that by *regeneration* or *new creation* we are to understand a *new modelling*, or *new constituting*. We shall see less harshness in this figure, when we consider, that what is called the *Mosaic creation* was probably similar to this; since for any thing we know, it was only the *re-making* or *re-constituting* of the world, out of a former chaos.

There are several passages in which the words which we generally render to *create* or *creation* signify only a *renewal* or *restoration*. Eph. ii. 10. *To make in himself, of twain, one new man, so making peace.* 2 Cor. v. 17. *If any man be in Christ he is a new creature.* In 1 Pet. ii. 13. the same word is rendered *ordinance*. *Be ye subject to every ordinance of man for the Lord's sake.* The places in which the influence of the gospel is termed a new creature, are illustrated by the following prophesy of Isaiah, in which it is described in the same language, Is. lxv. 17, &c. *Behold I create a new heaven and a new earth, and the former shall not be remembered, nor come to mind. But be ye glad, and rejoice for ever in that which I create; for behold, I create Jerusalem a rejoicing, and her people a joy.*

The word *all* must necessarily respect the subject concerning which the affirmation is made, and be limited by

illuſtrated. 45

by it. Thus when *all the world* is ſaid to be taxed, Luke ii. 1. it is plain that nothing but the *Roman empire* could be underſtood. In like manner, when *all things* are ſaid to be created by Chriſt, or for him, and alſo when *all things* are ſaid to be *ſubject to him*, or *put under his feet*, nothing can be meant, but ſuch things as can properly come under his government as the Meſſiah, and be ſubſervient to him in the conduct of it, including probably the *viſible* powers and kingdoms of this world, and the *inviſible* adminiſtration of angels; and therefore the apoſtle, with great propriety, concludes and ſums up the whole of Chriſt's authority, by ſaying that *he is the head of the body the church.*

Before often ſignifies before in point of *rank*, and *pre-eminence*, and not in point of *time*; ſo that when Chriſt is ſaid to be *before all things*, the meaning is, that he is the *chief*, or *moſt excellent* of all. And when it is ſaid that *in him all things conſiſt*, we are to underſtand that in him all things are *completed*, and compacted; ſince the Chriſtian diſpenſation is the laſt, and moſt perfect of all, completing one great and regular ſcheme of revelation, continually advancing from the the more imperfect to the more perfect.

We ſhall have a clearer underſtanding of this paſſage in the epiſtle to the Colloſſians, if we compare it with a parallel paſſage in the epiſtle of the ſame apoſtle to the Epheſians, i. 17. *That the God of our Lord Jeſus Chriſt, the Father of glory, may give you the ſpirit of wiſdom, that ye may know——the exceeding greatneſs of his power,——which he wrought in Chriſt Jeſus, when he raiſed him from the dead, and ſet him at his own right hand, in the heavenly places, far above all principality, and power, and might, and dominion, and every name than is named, not only in this world; but alſo in that which is to come; and hath put all things under his feet, and gave him to be the head over all things to the church, which is his body, the fulneſs of him who filleth all in all.* In this paſſage we ſee moſt clearly that all the power and authority to which Chriſt is advanced is ſubſequent to his reſurrection.

The origin and extent of the power of Chriſt are alſo moſt diſtinctly expreſſed, Phil. ii. 8. - - - - 11.

C 2 *He*

He humbled himself, and became obedient unto death, even the death of the cross; wherefore God also hath highly exalted him, and given him a name which is above every name, that at the name of Jesus every knee should bow, of things in heaven, and things in earth, and things under the earth; and that every tongue should confess that Jesus Christ is Lord, to the glory of God the Father.

To the same purpose also, 1 Pet. xx. 21. *Who (Christ) verily was foreordained before the foundation of the world, but was manifest in these last times, for you, who by him do believe in God, that raised him up from the dead, and gave him glory, that your faith and hope might be in God.* I should think it was hardly possible to read this single passage with attention, and not see that the writer of it considered Christ as a being distinct from God, and subordinate to him; that all his glory was subsequent to his resurrection; and also, that, though he was *foreordained before the foundation of the world*, he was not *manifested* or brought into being, till *these last times*, or those of the gospel.

There are some other passages in the New Testament, which are similar to those which I have quoted above, and may serve to illustrate them, John xvi. 15. *All things that the Father hath are mine,* xvii. 10. *All mine are thine, and thine are mine, and I am glorified in them,* 1 Cor. viii. 6. *To us there is but one God, the Father, of whom are all things, and we in him; and one Lord Jesus Christ, by whom are all things, and we by him.*

That there is nothing, in any of the passages which I have now quoted, that implies any proper divinity in Christ, is sufficiently evident, even without the addition of such expressions as directly assert the contrary; as when the apostle Paul says, that *to us there is one God, even the Father*; and our Saviour calls his Father *the only true God.* To signify that the authority of Christ is not underived, like that of God; and at the same time to inform us from whence it does proceed, the apostle says, that *it pleased the Father, that in him should all fulness dwell.* In the very same language our Saviour speaks of his disciples, *Fear not, little flock, it is the Father's good pleasure to give you the kingdom.*

V. Of

V. *Of the Doctrine of Atonement.*

THE death of Christ being an event of the greatest consequence to the end of his coming into the world, and being, at the same time, the great *stumbling block* both to the Jews and Gentiles, who could not easily reconcile themselves to the notion of a *suffering Saviour*, it is no wonder that the writers of the New Testament speak much of it, and represent it in a great variety of lights, and especially such as would appear the most favourable to the christian converts. In this case we naturally expect bold comparisons and allusions, especially considering how much more figurative is the style of the books of scripture, and indeed of all oriental writings, than ours. But in whatever lights the sacred writers represent the death of Christ, there is resemblance enough sufficiently to justify the representation, at the same time that this event being compared to *so many things*, and things of such *different natures*, proves that the resemblance in all of them is only in *certain respects*, and that they differ considerably in others.

For example, the death of Christ is compared to a *sacrifice* in general, because he gave up his life in the cause of virtue and of God, and more especially a *sacrifice for sin*, because his death and resurrection were necessary to the confirmation of that gospel, by which sinners are brought to repentance, and thereby reconciled to God. It is called a *curse*, because he died in a state of suspension, which was by the Jews appropriated to those persons who were considered as reprobated by God; and it is called a *passover*, because it may be considered as a sign of our deliverance from the power of sin, as the passover among the Jews was a sign of their deliverance from the Egyptian bondage. It is also called a *ransom*, because we are delivered by the gospel from sin and misery. On the same account, he is said by his death, *to bear, or take away our sins*, since his gospel delivers us from the power of sin, and consequently from the punishment due to it.

These are all bold, but significant figures of speech, the death of Christ really corresponding to them all to a certain degree; but they differ so very widely from one another, that no one thing can correspond to any of them throughout; for then it must exclude all, or at least most of the rest. The same thing for instance, could not be a curse, and a sacrifice; because every thing accursed was considered as an abomination in the sight of God, and could never be brought to the altar; and the killing of the paschal lamb was a thing essentially different from a sacrifice for sin.

These observations appear to me to be a sufficient guide to the interpretation of all the language of the New Testament respecting the death of Christ, without supposing that it had any proper influence upon God, so as to render him propitious to his offending creatures, or that it made it consistent with the divine justice to forgive the sins of mankind, which is contrary to a thousand plain and express declarations of scripture, which represent God as being essentially, and of himself, merciful and gracious, without the least reference to any other being or event whatever, and as forgiving sin *freely*, and gratuitously, upon our repentance and amendment, without any other atonement or satisfaction. I shall therefore content myself with reciting a few of the passages in which the death of Christ is represented in these several lights.

Eph. v. 2. *Christ also has loved us, and given himself for us, an offering and a sacrifice to God, of a sweet smelling savour.* Heb. vii. 27. *Who needed not daily to offer sacrifice, first for his own sins, and then for the people. For this he did once, when he offered up himself.* With the same idea he says, ix. 22. *And without shedding of blood there is no remission.* This view of the death of Christ occurs pretty frequently in this epistle to the Hebrews, but not more than about half a dozen times in all the other books of the New Testament; the principal of which is 1 John ii. 1. *And he is the propitiation for our sins.* But if the great object of the death of Christ was the establishment of that religion by which the world is reformed, in consequence of which the divine being is rendered propitious to them, how natural is it to represent his death as a *sacrifice* to God, for that great purpose. Besides, sacrifices for

sin

sin under the law of Moses, are never confidered as standing in the place of the sinner; but as the people were never to approach the divine presence, upon any occasion, without some *offering*, agreeable to the standing and universal custom of the East, with respect to all sovereigns and great men, so no person after being unclean (which not only moral guilt, but a number of things absolutely indifferent to morality were supposed to render a man) could be introduced to the tabernacle or temple service, without an offering proper to the occasion.

This idea may explain 2 Cor. v. 21. *He made him sin for us who knew no sin, that we might be made the righteousness of God in him*; because by *sin*, in this place, may perhaps be understood a *sin offering*. Or it may correspond to Rom. viii. 3. *What the law could not do, in that it was weak, through the flesh, God sending his own Son, in the likeness of sinful flesh, and for sin, (on account of sin, or on the business of sin.* i. e. to destroy and take it away) *condemned sin in the flesh*. In this case, the sense of the passage will be, that Christ was made, not *sin*, but *in the likeness of sinful flesh*, that is, he was made *a man* for our sakes.

Many persons are carried away by the sound of the word *redemption*, as if it necessarily implied that mankind, being in a state of bondage, a price must be paid for their freedom, and that the death of Christ was that price. But the word which we render *redemption* signifies only *deliverance*, in general, in whatever manner it be effected, and it is frequently so rendered by our translators. Belonging to this class of texts, are the following, Matt. xx. 28. Mark x. 45. *The Son of man came not to be ministered unto, but to minister, and to give his life a ransom for many.* 1 Tim. ii. 8. *Who gave himself a ransom for all.*

In order to judge of the meaning of this expression, let the preceding passages be compared with the following, in which the same Greek word is used, Luke xxiv. 21. *We trusted that it had been he who should have delivered*, or (as it might have been translated) *redeemed Israel*. In this case, the disciples certainly meant a deliverance, or redemption, from a state of sub-

subjection to the Romans, which they could not suppose was to be effected by *purchase*, but by the exertion of wisdom and power. Luke i. 68. *He has visited, and redeemed his people*; which is explained in v. 71. by *a deliverance from our enemies, and from the hands of all that hate us.* In Acts vii. 35. Stephen stiles Moses a *ruler and deliverer*, or *redeemer*, but what price did he pay for their redemption? In the Old Testament also God is frequently said to have *redeemed* Israel, from the hand of the Egyptians; but he certainly did not redeem them by paying any price for their redemption, and much less by becoming a bondman in their place, but, as it is often expressed, he redeemed, or delivered them, with *an high hand and an outstretched arm*. So also may Christ be said to redeem, or deliver from sin, viz. by his precepts, by his example, and by the precious promises of his gospel; by the consideration of which we are induced to forsake sin.

Stress has been laid upon the word *for* in the abovementioned passages, as if Christ dying a ransom *for* all, necessarily implied that he died *in the stead*, or *in the place*, of all; but the same word has other significations, as *because* of, and so it is rendered Luke i. 20. *Because thou hast not believed my word.* Heb. xii. 2. Who *for*, or *because of the joy that was set before him.* It also signifies *on the behalf*, or *on the account of*, as Mat. xvii. 27. *That take, and give them for thee and me*, that is *on the account of*, not *instead of* me and thee. So Christ died, and gave his life a ransom, not instead of many, but *on the behalf of many*, or *for their benefit*.

Much stress has also been laid on Christ being said to *bear the sins of mankind*; as if they had been ascribed or imputed to him, and he had taken them upon himself, and suffered the wrath of God for them. If. liii. 11. *He shall bear their iniquities.* 1 Pet. ii. 24. *Who his own self bare our sins in his own body, on the tree.* Heb. ix. 28. *So Christ once suffered, to bear the sins of many.*

These, I think, are all the places in which this particular view of th death of Christ occurs. But, beside the manifest injustice, and indeed absurdity, of an innocent

nocent perſon being puniſhed for one that is guilty, the word does not ſignify to bear *or take upon another*, but to *bear away*, or to *remove*, by whatever means; ſo that the texts abovementioned correſpond to, 1 John iii. 5, 6. *And ye know that he was manifeſt to take away ſin, and in him was no ſin.*

The phraſe *bearing ſin* is never applied in the Old Teſtament, but to the *ſcape goat*, which was not ſacrificed, but turned looſe into the wildernefs, to ſignify the removal of the ſins of the people, which God had freely forgiven, to a place where they ſhould never more be heard of. The goat itſelf, which was emblematically ſaid to *bear* their ſins, ſuffered nothing in conſequence of it; but, as its name imports, was ſuffered to *eſcape*, or was let looſe. Perhaps the ſending away of the ſcape-goat was intended for a monitory ſign to the people, that they ſhould ceaſe to commit thoſe ſins which had been ſo ſolemnly confeſſed over him, and which he was ſaid to *bear away into a land of ſeparation.* See Levit. xvi. 22. in the margin.

The evangeliſt Matthew had, moſt evidently, this idea of the meaning of the paſſage in Iſaiah, when he applied it upon the occaſion of Chriſt's healing the bodily diſeaſes of men, viii. 17. For he ſays, that he performed theſe cures, *that it might be fulfilled which was ſpoken by the prophet Iſaiah, Himſelf took our infirmities, and bare our ſickneſſes.* Now how did Chriſt *bear* the bodily diſeaſes which he cured? Not, ſurely, by taking them upon himſelf, and becoming diſeaſed, as the poor wretches themſelves had been; but by *removing* them by his miraculous power. In like manner, Chriſt *bears*, or *takes away* ſin, in general; not by ſuffering himſelf to be treated as a ſinner, but removing it, by the doctrines and motives of his Goſpel. Agreeably to this, when Peter had ſaid, *Who his own ſelf bare our ſins in his own body on the tree*, he explains his meaning in the words next following; *that we being dead to ſin, might live unto righteouſneſs.*

Chriſt is ſaid to die a *curſe* for us, in Gal. iii. 10. *Chriſt has redeemed us from the curſe of the law, being made a curſe for us; as it is written, Curſed is every one that hangeth on a tree.* Now it is proper enough to ſay, that

that Chrift died a curfe; becaufe the manner of his death was fimilar to that by which thofe who were deemed *curfed* under the law were put to death. But if by *accurfed* we mean lying under the difpleafure of God, this was fo far from being the cafe, with refpect to Chrift, and his death, that in this very circumftance he was the object of the divine approbation, and complacency in the higheft degree; as he himfelf fays, *For this reafon does my Father love me, becaufe I lay down my life*: and it is a general obfervation of the Scriptures, that *precious in the fight of God is the death of his faints.*

Chrift is called *a Paffover*, in 1 Cor. v. 7. *Chrift our Paffover is facrificed for us*: and this view is alfo alluded to when it is faid, *a bone of him was not to be broken*. The reafon of this view of the death of Chrift was fufficiently intimated before.

As a proof that Chrift took our fins upon him, and that we, on the other hand, are juftified by the *imputation of his righteoufnefs to us*, fome alledge. Jer. xxiii. 56. *And this is the name whereby he fhall be called,* THE LORD OUR RIGHTEOUSNESS. But, according to the method of interpreting fcripture names, explained above, all that we can infer from this text is, that God will be our Righteoufnefs, or receive us into his grace and favour by means of Chrift, or by the Gofpel of Chrift. That we muft underftand this text in fome fuch fenfe as this, is evident from the fame name being afterwards applied to Jerufalem. Jer. xxxiii. 16. *This is the name wherewith fhe fhall be called,* THE LORD OUR RIGHTEOUSNESS: for certainly it cannot be thought that the merits of Jerufalem are imputed to mankind.

Many divines, finding themfelves obliged to give up the notion of Chrift's fuffering *in our ftead*, and our being juftified by his righteoufnefs, as contrary to the genuine fenfe of the fcriptures, alledge, however, that God forgives the fins of mankind *on account of the merit of Chrift,* and *his interceffion for us*; and this opinion, like the former, is favoured by the literal fenfe of a few paffages of fcripture; but is contrary to the general and plain tenor of it, which reprefents all acts of mercy as proceeding from the effential placability and goodnefs of God the Father only.

only. Besides, there are many passages in the Old Testament in which God is represented as forgiving the Israelites, and receiving them into his favour, on the account of Abraham, Isaac, and Jacob; and their posterity plead the merit of these their religious ancestors in their prayers. God is also represented as ready to forgive the people of Sodom at the intercession of Abraham. Admitting, therefore, that God may grant favours to mankind at the intercession of Christ, this is not a privilege *peculiar* to Christ, but is common to him and other good men who went before him; so that the *general system*, of the forgiveness of sin, can by no means depend upon the merit and intercession of Christ only.

The following passages seem to represent the divine being as dispensing mercy to mankind on the account of Christ, 1 John ii. 12. *Because your sins are forgiven you for his name's sake*, Rom. viii. 34. *Who also maketh intercession for us*, 1 Cor. vi. 4. *But ye are justified in the name of the Lord Jesus*, Heb. vii. 25. *He ever liveth to make intercession for them*.

But let these passages be compared with the following from the Old Testament, Gen. xxvi. 24. *Fear not, I am with thee, and will bless thee, and multiply thy seed, for my servant Abraham's sake*. Moses, pleading in behalf of the Israelites, says, Exod. xxxii. 13. *Remember Abraham, and Isaac, and Israel, thy servants*, Deut. xix. 27. *Remember thy servants, Abraham and Isaac and Jacob. Look not to the stubbornness of this people, nor to their sin.* There are many other passages to the same purpose with these.

It must also be observed that *in the name of Christ* which occurs in some of the abovementioned passages, means *as Christ*, or *in the place of Christ*. Thus our Lord says, *Many shall come in my name*, that is, pretending to be what I am, the Messiah; and again, *the Comforter, whom the Father shall send in my name*, that is *in my place*, as it were, to succeed me in his kind offices to you. Praying, therefore, *in the name of Christ* may mean, in allusion to this sense of it, praying with the temper and disposition of Christ, or as becomes Christians, those who follow the directions of

Christ, both with respect to prayer, and every other duty of the Christian life. So also being *justified in the name of Christ*, may signify our being justified, or approved of God, in consequence of our being Christians, in deed and in truth, having the same mind that was also in Christ Jesus. Agreeably to this, the apostle Paul exhorts us *to put on Christ*, as if it were to appear like him, the very same person.

If the pardon of sin had universally depended upon the *advocateship* of Christ only, it can hardly be supposed that the Spirit would have had that name given to him, and especially by way of eminence, and distinction; for the word which we render *comforter* is the same that is rendered *advocate* in 1 John ii. 1. *We have an advocate with the Father, Jesus Christ the righteous.* The spirit is also said to intercede for us, Rom. viii. 26. *The spirit itself maketh intercession for us.*

Besides, the passages in which any regard is supposed to be had to the merit or intercession of Christ, in dispensing mercy to sinners, are exceedingly few, in comparison of those which represent this *free gift*, as proceeding from God only; and in some of them we are misled by our translation, as in Eph. iv. 32. *And be ye kind to one another, tender hearted, forgiving one another, even as God, for Christ's sake, has freely forgiven you.* It ought to have been rendered *as God in Christ*, that is, in the gospel of Christ, has forgiven you. Besides, the word which is here rendered *forgive* signifies *conferring favours* in general, and not the forgiveness of sin in particular; and the whole passage was intended to inculcate a benevolent disposition, in imitation of God, who has conferred the most valuable favours upon mankind, in the gospel of Christ.

Many passages in which we are said to be *justified by faith*, and not by *the works of the law*, were intended to oppose the doctrine of the Jews, who maintained that the observance of the law of Moses was absolutely necessary to salvation. Writing upon this subject, the apostle Paul expresses himself in the following manner, Rom. iii. 21, &c. *But now the righteousness of God, without*

without the law, is manifested, being witnessed by the law and the prophets; even the righteousness of God, which is by faith of Jesus Christ, unto all and upon all that believe, for there is no difference. For all have sinned, and come short of the glory of God, being justified freely by his grace, through the redemption that is in Christ Jesus; whom God has set forth to be a propitiation, through faith in his blood, to declare his righteousness, for the remission of sins that are past, through the forbearance of God; to declare, I say, at this time, his righteousness, that he might be just, and the justifier of him that believeth in Jesus. Where is boasting then? It is excluded. By what law? of works; nay, but by the law of faith. Therefore we conclude that a man is justified by faith, without the deeds of the law.

If we consider the whole of this passage, and the connection in which it stands, we shall be satisfied, that the apostle is here asserting that, in the gospel of Christ, which was confirmed by his death and resurrection, the divine being, as from a *a mercy seat* (which the word ought to be rendered, and not *propitiation*) declares his goodness and mercy to mankind; and since the patriarchs who believed and obeyed before the law, were justified without the works of the law, so God, acting still upon the same maxims, is just, and the Jews have no reason to complain of it, when he justifies sinners who believe and obey, *freely*, and *without the works of the law of Moses*, under the gospel.

N. B. I do not pretend that this pamphlet contains an illustration of *all* the texts that have been urged in favour of the doctrines which are controverted in the *Appeal*; for then I must have written a commentary upon the *whole bible*, as there is hardly a text in which some persons do not imagine that they see their own peculiar sentiments; but I think I have taken notice of all that can well be said to be of *much consequence*. If any considerable omission be pointed out to me, it shall be supplied in future editions.

A PRAYER,

A

PRAYER,

Respecting the *present State of Christianity*.*

ALMIGHTY God, the giver of all good, and especially the *Father of lights*, and the fountain of all wisdom and knowledge; we thank thee that *thou hast put a spirit in man, and that thine inspiration giveth us understanding*; that, being formed after thine own image, we find ourselves possessed of a nature superior to that of brute creatures; and being endowed with the faculty of reason, are capable of investigating important truths, and of governing our conduct, so as to attain to very distinguished degrees of excellence and happiness.

We thank thee that, in aid of this *light of nature*, thou hast superadded the gift of *revelation*; having, from time to time, communicated to mankind, by thy servants the prophets, the most useful information, concerning thy nature, perfections, and government, concerning our duty here, and our expectations hereafter. And we more especially rejoice that, upon every occasion of thy gracious intercourse with mankind, thou hast represented thyself to us as the proper object of our reverence, love, and confidence ; as a being of boundless goodness, and the greatest compassion to those frailties and infirmities, to which it has seemed good to thy infinite wisdom to subject us ; as one who expectest no more of us than thou hast enabled us to perform; and who, upon our sincere return to our duty, art ever ready to extend the freest mercy and forgiveness

---
* This Prayer was printed before, but only in a local and temporary publication.

towards

A PRAYER.

towards us, even after our moſt aggravated and repeated offences.

We thank thee, more eſpecially, for the laſt and moſt perfect revelation of thy will to mankind, in the goſpel of Jeſus Chriſt, in whom it has pleaſed thee, that *all fullneſs ſhould dwell*; who has eſtabliſhed, upon the fureſt foundations, the great and important doctrines of the proper *unity* and *mercifulneſs* of thy nature, and thy unrivalled *ſupremacy* with reſpect to himſelf, as well as to all other beings, and all other things; and who has likewiſe given us the moſt ſatisfactory aſſurance of a reſurrection from the dead, confirmed to us by his own death and reſurrection; whereby we are encouraged to expect, that, becauſe he lives, we ſhall live alſo.

It has ſeemed good to thy unſearchable wiſdom, (which permits the riſe and continuance of evil, in order, we doubt not, to bring about the greateſt good) that this moſt excellent religion, ſo honourable to thee, and ſo beneficial to mankind, ſhould, by means of the baſe *artifices* of ſome, and the general *ignorance*, which lately overſpread the world, become groſsly corrupted; whereby ſuch opinions have prevailed among the profeſſors of chriſtianity, as greatly diſhonour thy nature, imply the moſt unjuſt reflections on thy righteous moral government, and are highly injurious to the virtue and happineſs of men. How has the gold become dim, how is the moſt fine gold changed!

The great and important doctrine of thy divine *unity* has been generally abandoned, and objects of ſupreme worſhip multiplied. Thy meſſenger and ſervant, the meek and humble Jeſus, who, upon all occaſions, referred his wiſdom and mighty works to thee, his God and Father, ſpeaking and acting by him, has been advanced to a proper equality with thyſelf; and even his mother, the virgin Mary, and innumerable ſaints and angels, have likewiſe, been addreſſed, as if they were omnipreſent beings. Having thus divided thy being, robbed thee of thy eſſential attributes and perfections, and diſtributed them among a multiplicity of inferior beings, depraved and unworthy notions of thy moral character have conſequently prevailed, and many of the

evils

evils of *idolatry* have been introduced, among the professors of that religion, which acknowledges but *one living and true God*, even thee, our Father in heaven, and one mediator, the man Chrift Jefus.

Having divefted thee, in their imaginations, of the moft amiable of all thy attributes, even the effential *placability* of thy nature, they have reprefented thy free mercy to penitent finners as purchafed by the blood of thy innocent fon. Forgetting that thou art good to all, and that thy tender mercies are over all thy works, and alfo that thou, the righteous Lord, loveft righteoufnefs, they have afcribed to thee an arbitrary and unreafonable partiality, in favour of fome of the human race, and a moft cruel and unjuft feverity towards others, as condemning them to everlafting torments, for crimes of which they could not be guilty, and expecting of them that which thou hadft not enabled them to do. And, having loft the idea of the *purity* of thy nature and thy regard to moral righteoufnefs, as the only juft ground of acceptance and favour with thee, they have had recourfe to unmeaning and even bafe and mifchievous fuperftitions, as compenfations for their non-obfervance of thy holy commandments.

To confirm all thefe, and innumerable other corruptions of thy holy religion, fupreme authority has been openly ufurped by men, over that church, in which thou haft given all power to our only Lord and Mafter Jefus Chrift; and thofe of thy faithful fervants who have juftly refufed to fubmit to their ufurpations, have by them been fubjected to the greateft hardfhips, and even perfecuted unto death; fo that thefe temporal antichriftian powers are drunk with the blood of thy holy martyrs.

We deeply lament this almoft univerfal departure from the true faith of thy fon's gofpel, the ftop that has by this means, been fo long put to the propagation of chriftianity among Jews, Mahomedans, and Heathens; and the prevalence which it has occafioned of infidelity and profanenefs in chriftian countries.

But we thank thee, who, in thine own due time, wilt, we doubt not, bring light out of all darknefs, and order out of all confufion, that, in
several

several christian countries, many of these corruptions and abuses have been reformed, and that antichristian tyranny is every where giving place to the power of truth, and the just liberties of mankind, in thinking and acting for themselves in all matters of religion.

For these great and invaluable blessings we are, under thee, indebted to the strenuous labours of thy faithful servants, who have not accounted even their lives dear unto them ; but, for the love of thy truth, have renounced all worldly advantages, boldly asserting their christian liberty, and holding themselves accountable to none but thee, the sole and immediate lord of conscience, and to the great shepherd and bishop of souls, acting by commission from thee, Jesus Christ.

We adore the wisdom of thy providence in bringing about the restoration of useful *learning*, and making it subservient to the reformation of thy Church ; so that thy servants, having recovered the genuine, but long forgotten sense of the scriptures, were able to discover the false grounds of the reigning superstition, and of the ecclesiastical tyranny of their times. Grant that, by a continued and diligent study of the same word of thy truth, we may, in due time, be led to the full discovery of every remaining corruption of our holy religion, and be brought to receive the whole truth in the love thereof.

Hasten, we intreat thee, the approach of that glorious time when, according to the faithful and true writings of thy servants the prophets, our holy religion shall recover its primitive purity and efficacy ; when thy self alone, as the only true God, a being of perfect rectitude, spotless purity, and essential goodness and mercy, shalt be the object of supreme worship ; when thy creatures of mankind shall have recourse to no method of rendering themselves acceptable to thee, but unfeigned repentance for their transgressions of thy laws, and a sincere endeavour to conform to them for the future, in a course of upright intentions and worthy actions through the whole of their lives ; and when no apprehension of arbitrary decrees shall alarm the fears of the humble, or encourage the presumption of the confident,

Dispose

Difpofe all who profefs the chriftian name to ftudy the fcriptures of truth with unprejudiced minds; and infpire all thofe who attain to the truth with a juft zeal for the propagation of it, as far as thy providence fhall give them ability and opportunity to do it. May neither the love of popular applaufe, of filthy lucre, or any worldly advantage; may neither the fear of man, of reproach, or of death, be a fnare to them, and hinder them in this work of love; and may they daily rejoice in the teftimony of their confciences, and in the happy fruits of their pious and affiduous labours.

May all thofe powers of this world, which have ufurped any authority belonging to our only rightful lord and king in his church, become difpofed to relinquifh their unjuft claims; and may thofe kings and princes, who will not acknowledge the fovereignty of Jefus in his church, and efpecially thofe who obftinately oppofe the reformation of it, be utterly confounded, and, by his power, be broken in pieces like a potter's veffel. Take to thyfelf, O Lord God almighty, thy great power, and reign; and may the gofpel of Jefus Chrift go forth conquering and to conquer. May the everlafting gofpel, in its primitive purity, be preached to all that dwell on the earth, to every nation, and kindred, and tongue, and people. By the brightnefs of our Lord's appearance, may the man of fin be utterly confumed, that all the kingdoms of this world may become the kingdoms of our lord and of his Chrift, and he may reign for ever and ever.

In the mean time, may we thy faithful fervants, in the patient waiting for this coming of our lord Jefus Chrift, be fearlefs and unwearied in afferting thy truth, be ready to lay hold of every favourable opportunity to promote it, and, more efpecially, be careful to recommend it by a fuitable life and converfation. May we diftinguifh ourfelves by having the fame mind that was alfo in Chrift Jefus, by genuine humility, meeknefs, forbearance, brotherly love, heavenly-mindednefs, and habitual chearful devotion; that when our lord fhall return, and take account of his fervants, we may be found without fpot and blamelefs, and not be afhamed before him at his coming.

Now

Now to thee who alone art eternal, immortal, and invisible, the only wise, living, and true God, be glory, through Jesus Christ, for ever and ever, Amen.

The CONCLUSION.

THIS publication completes the scheme which was begun in the *Appeal*, and continued in the *Triumph of Truth*; being intended to be a plain and earnest address to the common people, and especially to those of them who have but little money to spare for the purchase of books, or time for the reading of them.

I am not so little acquainted with human nature, as to expect any *great success* in this attempt to overturn long established errors; and least of all can I hope to convince those who refuse to read, or to hear, (which is the case with too many) on whom even miracles could produce no effect; but the restoration of christianity to its primitive purity and efficacy, after so long and so radical a corruption (which was foreseen and lamented by the inspired writers of the New Testament) is so great and so worthy an object, that every man who has the interest of religion at heart, will rejoice in every opportunity that divine providence affords him for promoting it, with respect to ever so few, or even a single individual of his fellow-creatures.

A zeal for the truth, and even to *contend earnestly* for it, does, certainly well become a christian. Since, however, the inspiring of a *christian spirit*, is the great purpose to which purity of *christian faith* is subservient, I hope that, with respect to myself, I have been careful not to lose the *end*, while I have been contending for the *means*. Of this my reader may be a pretty good judge; since that zeal which arises from the love of truth, and of mankind, will easily be distinguished from that spirit which actuates those whom St. Paul calls the *disputers of this world*, a spirit which favours strongly of *pride*, *hatred*, and *malice*, and which often

induces

induces them to have recourse to unfair and unworthy *artifices* in order to gain a victory.

Some persons think that in these publications I have attacked *too many* long established errors, and that it would have been more prudent to have attempted one thing at once, and to have proceeded gradually and gently. But it should be considered, that there are in the world persons in every possible state of mind with respect to these things; so that what will stagger some, is calculated to make the strongest and best impression upon others. Since, therefore, every thing that is published from the press must be distributed *promiscuously*, we can only take care that what we write be calculated to do good in general, and since a nice calculation of this kind is exceedingly difficult; it appears to me to be the best, upon the whole, for every person to endeavour to establish what appears to himself to be *the whole truth*, and not to trouble himself about any consequences. The gospel sower must cast his seed promiscuously on all kinds of ground, hoping that in some it may yield a good increase, though he must lay his account with its being lost, and even worse than lost upon others.

I also think it an objection to the slow and cautious proceeding which some persons recommend, that the evidence of any truth is exhibited to the most advantage in connection with the *whole system* to which it belongs. Nor would I conclude that because the minds of many are staggered by bold and undisguised representations of truth, this mode of proceeding is, upon the whole, less effectual. In many cases it may be the only method of gaining a sufficient degree of *attention* to a subject; and when this only is done, a great point is gained. The horror with which an offensive sentiment is viewed at first, may wear off by degrees, and a cool examination succeed. What could give more offence even to good minds than the manner in which Luther, and other reformers, attacked the church of Rome? Any person would have imagined, *a priori*, that it could only offend and irritate. We must wait a considerable time before we can form

a judg-

The CONCLUSION.

a judgment of the number of converts that any perfon makes.

I do not even know whether, for the purpofe of gaining attention to a fubject, it might not be good policy (tho' I never did it knowingly) to make fome little overfight in a feries of arguments, and to give fome handle for cavilling; as the feeming weaknefs of fome parts might tempt fome perfons to examine and attack a whole performance, which, if it was juft in the main, could not but be a gainer in the iffue.

I cannot help expreffing my furprize that fo many perfons, and efpecially of the clergy of the eftablifhed church, fhould profefs themfelves *Arminians*, rejecting the Calviniftic doctrines of election and reprobation, and yet entertain fuch a horror of *Arianifm*, or *Socinianifm*, contending with the greateft earneftnefs for the divinity of Chrift, and atonement for fin by his death; when it appears to me, that the literal interpretation of the language of fcripture (which is almoft all that can be pleaded in favour of any of thofe opinions) is even more favourable to the former than to the latter, as, I fhould think, would appear to any perfon who would attend to thofe which I have quoted in this treatife. I know that I have found much more difficulty in my attempts to explain them. I confider it, however, as an undoubted fign of the progrefs of juft thinking in matters of religion, that the *ftandard of orthodoxy* is fo much lower at prefent than it has been in former times.

Time was, and though I am not old, I well remember the time, when Arminians would have been reckoned no better than Socinians by thofe by thofe who were reputed the *orthodox* of their day; and yet with what rage have fome of thefe *heterodox writers*, attacked a *brother heretic*. How would the manes of thofe old champions fmile to fee us *fall out by the way*, when they were confident that we muft all come to the fame place of torment at laft; and the furious zeal of thofe veterans was far more plaufible, and refpectable, than that of the modern pretenders to orthodoxy.

There

The CONCLUSION.

There is something *striking* and *consistent* in the genuine *Supralapsarian system*, of the eternally destined fall of man, an infinite penalty incurred by one, and, by the imputation of his sin, affecting all, and an infinite atonement adequate to it, made by an infinite being; by which means a small remnant of the human race are necessarily saved; while all the rest of mankind, including new born children, unbelieving Jews, Mahometans and Heathens, Arminians and Baxterians, Arians and Socinians, without distinction (as destitute either of faith, or the right faith) are consigned to everlasting torments with the Devil and his angels; from whence results *glory* to a God, who, in all this dreadful scheme, is supposed to have sought nothing else.

These are the *tremendous doctrines* which have overawed mankind for so many centuries; and, compared with this, all the modern *qualified, intermediate systems*, are crude, incoherent, and contemptible things. My antagonists may cavil at *election and reprobation*, or any other single article in the well compacted system; but every part is necessary to the whole; and if one stone be pushed out of its place, the whole building tumbles to the ground. And when, in consequence of their ill-judged attempts to alter, patch, and repair, they have brought things to this catastrophe, there will be nothing left but the simple belief, that the merciful parent of the universe, who never meant any thing but the happiness of his creatures, sent his well beloved son, *the man Christ Jesus*, to reclaim men from their wickedness, and to teach them the way of righteousness; assuring them, for their encouragement, of the free and unbought pardon of their sins, and promising a life of endless happiness to all that receive and obey the gospel, by repenting of their sins, and bringing forth fruits meet for repentance.

This is the essence of what is called *Socinianism*; and though this simple doctrine, may, on account of its excellence and simplicity, be a stumbling block to some, and foolishness to ethers, I believe it to be the sum and substance of the gospel of Jesus Christ, and the wisdom and power of God.

For--

The CONCLUSION.

Formidable as the greateſt adverſary of the truth, may be, I make no doubt but that, by the help of reaſon, and the *ſword of the ſpirit, which is the word of God*, it will be finally overcome. And whenever the *holy apoſtles and prophets ſhall rejoice* at the fall of this laſt part of *myſtical Babylon*, Rev. xviii. 20; happy will they be who may join the chorus, as having employed their efforts, however feeble, with thoſe who, in this geat cauſe, fight under *the banners of the lamb*, and *who are called, and choſen, and faithful*; Rev. xvii. 14.

N. B. Having now compleated this ſcheme of publication, my intention is to republiſh the whole in one treatiſe differently arranged, and with ſuch additions and corrections as I may ſee reaſon to make; and at the ſame time that the three pamphlets, for the convenience of purchaſing and diſtributing them, continue to be ſold ſeparately.

F I N I S.

Lately Publiſhed,

A Free Addreſs to Proteſtant Diſſenters, as ſuch. By a Diſſenter. A new Edition, enlarged and corrected, Price 1s. 6d.—An Allowance is made to thoſe who buy this Pamphlet to give away.

Alſo a ſerious and earneſt Addreſs to Proteſtant Diſſenters of all Denominations, repreſenting the many and important Privileges on which their Diſſent from the Eſtabliſhment is founded. Second Edition, Price 4d. or 3s. 6d, per dozen.

Written by Dr. PRIESTLEY, and published by J. JOHNSON, No. 72 St. Paul's Church-Yard.

1. A Catechism for Children and Young Persons, 6d.
2. A Scripture Catechism consisting of a Series of Questions, with References to the Scriptures instead of Answers, 3d.
3. A Serious Address to Masters of Families, with Forms of Family Prayer, 6d.
4. Institutes of Natural and Revealed Religion, Vol. I. Containing the Elements of Natural Religion; to which is prefixed an Essay on the best Method of communicating Religious Knowledge to the Members of Christian Society, 2s. 6d. sewed.
5. A Free Address to Protestant Dissenters, on the Subject of the Lord's Supper, the second Edition, 1s.
6. Additions to the Address to Protestant Dissenters, with some Corrections of it, and a Letter to the Author of the Protestant Dissenter's Answer to it, 1s.
7. Considerations on Differences of Opinion among Christians: with a Letter to the Rev. Mr. Venn, in Answer to his Examination of the Address to Protestant Dissenters, 1s.
8. A Free Address to Protestant Dissenters, on the Subject of Church Discipline; with a Preliminary Discourse, concerning the Spirit of Christianity, and the Corruption of it by false Notions of Religion, 2s. 6d.
9. A View of the Principles and Conduct of the Protestant Dissenters, with respect to the Civil and Ecclesiastical Constitution of England, the second Edition, 1s. 6d.
10. An Essay on the First Principles of Government, and on the Nature of Political, Civil, and Religious Liberty, including Remarks on Dr. Browne's Code of Education, and Dr. Balguy's Sermon on Church Authority. Second Edition much enlarged, 4s. sewed.

Also published in Numbers, under the Direction of Dr. Priestley, The Theological Repository; consisting of original Essays, Hints, Queries, &c. calculated to promote religious Knowledge.

N. B. Two Volumes of this Work are completed, Price 6s. each, in Boards.

Triumph of Truth;

BEING AN ACCOUNT OF THE

Trial of Mr. E. ELWALL,

FOR

HERESY and BLASPHEMY,

At STAFFORD ASSIZES,

Before JUDGE DENTON.

To which are added,

Extracts from WILLIAM PENN's
SANDY FOUNDATION SHAKEN.

AND

A few ADDITIONAL ILLUSTRATIONS.

By the AUTHOR of
An APPEAL *to the ferious and candid Profeffors of Chriftianity. &c.*

The SECOND EDITION.

He, being dead, yet fpeaketh. Heb. xi. 4.

✝✝✝✝✝✝✝✝✝✝✝✝✝✝✝✝✝✝✝✝✝✝✝✝✝✝✝✝✝✝✝✝

LONDON:

Printed for J. JOHNSON, No. 72, St. Paul's
Church-Yard. [Price ONE PENNY.]

Published by the Compiler of this pamphlet,

Price One Penny,

I. An APPEAL
TO
The serious and candid Professors of Christianity,

On the following SUBJECTS, viz.

1. The Use of Reason in Matters of Religion.
2. The Power of Man to do the Will of God.
3. Original Sin.
4. Election and Reprobation.
5. The Divinity of Christ, and
6. Atonement of Sin by the Death of Christ.

II. A Familiar Illustration
OF CERTAIN
PASSAGES OF SCRIPTURE,
Relating to the same SUBJECTS.

PRICE Four-pence; or Three Shillings and Six-pence *per* Dozen.

ADVERTISEMENT.

THE dedication of the treatise, on account of which Mr. Elwall was prosecuted, is dated *the eighth day of the second month,* 1724; he speaks of his trial in a treatise intitled, *A declaration against all kings and temporal powers under heaven,* printed in 1732; and Judge Denton, before whom he was tried, went the Oxford circuit in 1726 and 1728. From these circumstances it may be concluded, that the former of these years is the date of this remarkable trial, especially as in some part of the same year 1726, Mr. Elwall published another defence of the unitarian system, in a treatise which he intitled *Dagon fallen before the Ark of God,* which would probably have been mentioned in the course of the trial, if it had been published at that time.

THE PREFACE.

THIS trial is printed from the author's second edition, even without altering fuch phrafes as are peculiar to that denomination of chriftians with whom he generally affociated, and whofe ftyle he adopted; and certainly the Quakers ought to think themfelves honoured even by this kind of relation to Mr. Elwall. Such firmnefs in the caufe of truth, and fuch prefence of mind in afferting and vindicating it, as appear in this trial, are truly apoftolical, and have had but few examples fince the firft promulgation of chriftianity. It is impoffible for an unprejudiced perfon to read this account of it (which is written with fo much true fimplicity, perfpicuity, and ftrength of evidence) without feeling the greateft veneration for the writer, the fulleft conviction and love of the truth, and a proportionable zeal in maintaining it. I fhould even think it impoffible for the moft prejudiced perfon to read it attentively, but, if he ufe no violence with his own mind, he will receive fome favourable impreffions both of the author, and of that caufe, which he fupports with fuch becoming dignity, and with a temper and difpofition of mind, in every refpect worthy of a true chriftian.

So great was the force of truth on this memorable occafion, that a reputable and honeft jury, directed by a good-natured and fenfible judge, acquitted the criminal contrary to the exprefs laws of this country, according to which this glorious man ought to have been fentenced to a fevere punifhment, as a convicted and avowed *blafphemer*. What muft a lover of *truth*, and of *free inquiry*, as fubfervient to truth, think of fuch laws, and of the ecclefiaftical conftitution of the countries in which they are in force!

It is to be wifhed that fuch a monument of the TRIUMPH OF TRUTH might be conftantly held out to the view of all mankind, and particularly in this country where it was exhibited. To render it a little more confpicuous, and to make it more generally ufeful, efpecially to the lower clafs of people, who have but

little

THE PREFACE.

little money to spare for the purchase of books; but who have as good natural understandings, and are as capable of judging concerning important truths as the most *opulent*, and even the most *learned* of their neighbours, a second very large and cheap impression of this pamphlet is now printed.

Instead of the extracts from the other writings of Mr. Elwall, which were given in the former edition of this pamphlet, I shall in this insert a few passages from a treatise of Mr. Penn, the celebrated Quaker, bearing the following title, which, because it is something remarkable, I shall give at full length: *The Sandy Foundation Shaken* : or, Those so generally believed or applauded Doctrines,

Of
{
One God, subsisting in three distinct and separate persons,
The impossibility of God's pardoning sinners, without a plenary satisfaction,
The justification of impure persons, by an imputative righteousness.
} Refuted.

From the authority of scripture testimonies, and right reason; By William Penn, jun. A builder on that foundation which cannot be moved. *But to us there is but one God the Father, of whom are all things*, 1 Cor. viii. 6. *Who is a God like unto thee, that pardoneth iniquity? He retaineth not his anger for ever, because he delighteth in mercy*, Micah vii. 18. *For I will not justify the wicked*, Exod. xxiii. 7.

For writing this piece Mr. Penn was, at the instigation of the Bishops, imprisoned in the Tower, in 1668, and in this imprisonment, which continued about seven months, he wrote his famous treatise *No cross No crown*. I am sorry to add that at length, he wrote a letter to Lord Arlington, principal secretary of state, and also published a short piece, entitled *Innocence with her open face*, in which, without pretending to retract any thing that he had advanced before, he endeavoured to soften things, by asserting that he did not deny the eternal deity of Christ. But when he explains himself, he only appears to have meant that the deity of the Father resided in the Man Christ Jesus, which is what every Socinian acknowledges. He asserts *the unity of God and of Christ*, " because," says he, " though nominally
nally

" nally diftinguifhed, yet they are effentially the fame
" divine light;" p. 267. And again, having fpoken
of the Father, p. 269. as, " one holy, juft, merciful,
" almighty, and eternal God," he says that " Chrift
" is the fame one, holy, juft, merciful, almighty, and
" eternal God, who, in the fulnefs of time, took and
" was manifeft in flefh."

That this truly great man, who behaved with fuch heroic conftancy upon other occafions, fhould have recourfe to this unworthy prevarication, is truly lamentable. To have perfifted in afferting the unity of God, though he had died in prifon in confequence of it, would have been infinitely more to his honour than being the founder of Pennfylvania. In the latter treatife, however, he gives an honourable teftimony to Socinus, and perfifts in difclaiming the doctrines of infinite fatisfaction, and imputed righteoufnefs.

The TRIAL of Mr. ELWALL, &c.

BECAUSE fo many perfons have earneftly defired to read this trial, I have here publifhed a fecond edition of it, in order to encourage all honeft men, who have the eternal law of God on their fide, not to fear the faces of priefts, who are generally the grand adverfaries of liberty and truth; and the baftions and bulwarks of all ceremonies, fopperies, and abfurd doctrines that are in the world.

I do this for the glory of the Moft High God, and for the honour of his facred law, and for the good of all my fellow-creatures; that they may obey God, and not man; Chrift, and not the pope; the prophets and apoftles, and not prelates and priefts; and God knoweth this is my fincere defire, that all religion and fpiritual things may be perfectly free, neither forced nor hindered; this being the true liberty of the gofpel of *Jefus Chrift*, who faid, *The kings of the Gentiles excercife authority, but it fhall not be fo with you.*

About fourteen years ago, I wrote a book entitled,
" A True Teftimony for God and his facred Law;
" being a plain, honeft defence of the firft command-
" ment of God, againft all the Trinitarians under
" heaven, *Thou fhall have no other Gods but me.*" I
lived

lived then at *Wolverhampton*, in *Staffordshire*, where my ancestors have lived above eleven hundred years, ever since the *Saxons* conquered the *Britons*.

When this book was published, the priests in the country began to rage, especially the priests of *Wolverhampton*; who had a great hand in the several troubles I underwent. In short, they never ceased till they had procured a large indictment against me at *Stafford* assizes; where I felt the power of God, enabling me to speak before a very great number of people; being accused of heresy, &c. But I truly answered as my beloved brother *Paul* did in his day, *viz. In that way which some call heresy, so chuse I to serve the God of my fathers, believing all that is written in the law and the prophets.*

After the long indictment was read, I was asked if I pleaded guilty, or not guilty. I said I was not guilty of any evil, that I knew of, in writing that book; but if they meant whether I wrote the book or not (for they had quoted many pages of the book in that indictment) I owned I did write it; and that if I might have liberty to speak, I believed I should make it manifest to be the plain truth of God.

Then the Judge stood up, and said, " Mr. *Elwall,* " I suppose you have had a copy of your indictment?" I told him I had not had any copy of it. Upon which he turned towards the priests, and told them that I ought to have had a copy of it. But they not answering, he turned to me, and said, That if I would give bail, and be bound to appear at the next assizes, he would defer my trial till then. But I told him, I would not give bail, neither should any man be bound for me; that if the Prince of *Wales* himself would, he should not; for, said I, I have an innocent breast, and I have injured no man; and therefore I desire no other favour, but that I may have liberty to plead to the indictment myself.

Upon which he said, very courteously, You may. The Judge having given me liberty of pleading to the indictment, I began my speech with the sacred first commandment of God, viz. *Thou shalt have no other Gods but Me.* I insisted upon the word *Me* being a singular; and that it was plain and certain, that God spake of himself, as one single person or being, and

not

not three diſtinct perſons. And that it was manifeſt, that all the church of God, which then heard thoſe words, underſtood it in the ſame plain obvious ſenſe as I do; as is moſt evident from the words of the prophet *Moſes*; who ſaid to Iſrael thus, *Unto thee it was ſhewed, that thou mighteſt know, that the Lord he is God, there is none elſe beſides him*; *out of heaven he made thee hear his voice*, &c. I told them, that from the words *he*, and *him*, and *his*, it was certain God was but one ſingle perſon, one ſingle *he*, or *him*, or *his*. I told them that all the patriarchs from the beginning of the world, did always addreſs themſelves to God, as one ſingle being. *O thou Moſt High God, poſſeſſor of heaven and earth*; and *Abraham* ſaid to the king of *Sodom, I have lift up my hand unto the Lord, the Moſt High God, the poſſeſſor of heaven and earth,* &c. they knew nothing of a Trinity, nor of God's being a plurality of perſons; that monſtrous doctrine was not then born, nor of two thouſand years' after, till the Apoſtacy and Popery began to put up its filthy head.

Then I told them, that all the prophets witneſſed to the truth of the ſame pure uncorrupted Unitarian doctrine *of one God, and no other but he*: *Have we not all one Father, hath not one God created us?* Then I told them the words of God to *Abraham, I am God Almighty, walk before me, and be thou perfect*; and by the prophet *Iſaiah, To whom will ye liken me, or ſhall I be equal, faith the holy One,* not the holy Three. I told them that the words *Me* and *One* did utterly exclude any other perſon's being God, but that *One* ſingle *Me*; and that God himſelf often teſtifies the ſame truth, by ſaying, *Is there any God beſides Me?* And then tells us plainly, *There is no God, I know not any*: *I am the Lord, and there is none elſe; there is no God beſides me.* Iſaiah xlv. 5.

Now, ſaid I, let God be true, but every man a liar, that is, every man that contradicteth him; for he is the God of truth; he ſays, *I lift up my hand to heaven, I ſay, I live for ever.*

After I had pleaded many texts in the Old Teſtament, I began to enter the New; and told them, that our Lord Jeſus Chriſt, the prophet, like unto *Moſes*, held forth the ſame doctrine that *Moſes* had done; for when a certain ruler came to aſk him which was the firſt

The Trial of Mr. Elwall.

first and great commandment (or how he expounded it) he told him the same words that *Moses* had said. *Hear, O Israel, the Lord thy God is one Lord,* not three, *and thou shalt love the Lord thy God with all thy heart,* &c. And the scribe said, *Thou hast answered right, for there is but one God, and there is no other but he,* &c. Then I mentioned the words of Christ, in the xviith of *John* and ver. 3, as very remarkable and worthy of all their observation: *This is life eternal, to know thee the only true God, and Jesus Christ whom thou hast sent.* And then I turned my face directly to the priests (my prosecutors, who all stood on the right side of the judge.) Now said I, since the lips of the blessed Jesus, which always spoke the truth, says, his father is the only true God; who is he, and who are they that dare set up another, in contradiction to my blessed Lord, who says, his father is *the only true God?*

And I stopped here, to see if any of them would answer; but the power of God came over them, so that all their mouths were shut up, and not one of them spake a word. So that I turned about over my left shoulder, and warned the people in the fear of God, not to take their religious sentiments from men, but from God; not from the Pope, but from Christ; not from Prelates nor Priests, but from the Prophets and Apostles.

And then I turned towards the judge, and told him, that I was the more convinced of the truth of what I had said, from the words of my blessed Lord; who said, *Call no man Father here upon earth; for one is your Father, even God. And call no man Master, for one is your Master, even Christ.* From hence, said I, I deduce this natural inference, That in all things that are of a spiritual nature, we ought to take our religion from God and his prophets, from Christ and his apostles. It will be too long to mention all the texts and proofs that I made use of; I will only add one or two, as that of *Paul,* 1 Cor. viii. 4, 5, 6, where the apostle tells us, *there is no other God but one; for though there be that are called gods (as there be gods many, and lords many) both in heaven and earth; but to us there is but one God, the Father, of whom are all things:* So that I told them, here was a plain demonstration; for he says, *there is but one god*; and tells us who that One God is, that

is,

The Trial of Mr. Elwall.

is, *the Father*. And therefore no other person could be God but the Father only; and what I had wrote in my book was the plain truth, and founded on God's own words, *Thou shalt have no other Gods but me.*

In short, I could plainly perceive there was a general convincement through the court. The judge and justices of the peace did not like the prosecution; but saw plainly, that *out of envy the Priests had done it.* I then began to set before them the odious nature of that hell-born principle of persecution, and that it was hatched in Hell; that it never came from Jesus Christ; that he and his followers were often persecuted themselves, but they never persecuted any; that we had now a very flagrant instance of it by the Papists at *Thorn*; where they first took away the schools where our brethren the Protestants educated their children; then they took away the places of their religious worship; then they put them in prisons; then confiscated their estates, and, last of all, took away their lives.

Now we can cry out loud enough against this, and shew the inhumanity, cruelty, and barbarity of it; but said I, if we, who call ourselves Protestants, shall be found acting in the same spirit, against others, the crime will be greater in us than in them; because we have attained to greater degrees of light than they.

However, I told them, that I had put my house in order, and made up my accounts with all men as near as I could: And that as I owed no man here any thing, so I would not pay a penny towards this prosecution. And that I was sure of it, that whatever fine they laid on me, or whatever hole or prison, said I, ye thrust me into, I shall find God's living presence with me, as I feel it this day: And so ended my speech.

Upon this a Justice of the peace, one *Rupert Humpatch*, got up, went to the Judge, laid his hand upon the Judge's shoulder, and said, My Lord, I know this man to be an honest man; and what I say, I speak not by hear-say, but experience; for I was his next door neighbour three years. Also, another Justice spoke to the same effect. Then the Judge spoke to me; Mr. *Elwall*, I perceive you have studied very deeply into this controversy; but have you ever consulted any of our reverend clergy and bishops of the church of *England*. I answered, Yes, I have; and

The Trial of Mr. Elwall.

among others, the Archbishop of *Canterbury* himself, with whom I have exchanged ten letters, viz. four I have had from him, and six he has had from me. (At which words, all the priests stared very earnestly.) Well, says the Judge, and was not the Archbishop able to give you some satisfaction in these points, Mr. *Elwall?* I said, No; but rather quite the reverse; for that in all the letters I sent to the Archbishop, I grounded my arguments upon the words of God and his prophets, Christ and his apostles; but in his answers to me, he referred me to acts of parliament, and declarations of state, &c. whereas I told the Bishop, in one of my letters, that I wondered a man of his natural and acquired abilities, should be so weak as to turn me over to human authorities, in things of a divine nature; for though in all things that are of a temporal nature, and concern the civil society, *I will be subject to every ordinance of man, for the Lord's sake;* even from the king upon the throne, down to the meanest officer in the land; but in things that are of a spiritual nature, and concern my faith, my worship of God, and future state, I would *call no man father here upon earth,* nor regard either popes or councils, prelates or priests of any denomination, nor convocations, nor assemblies of divines; but obey God and his prophets, Christ and his apostles. Upon which the Judge answered, Well, if his Grace of *Canterbury* was not able to give you satisfaction, Mr. *Elwall,* I believe I shall not; and so set down and rested him; for I think he had stood up for near an hour and a quarter.

Then he stood up again, and turning to the priests, talked softly to them. I did not hear what he said, or what they said to him; but I guessed from what the Judge said next; for, says he, Mr. *Elwall,* you cannot but be sensible that what you have writ, being contrary to the commonly received doctrines of the church, it has given offence to some of your neighbours, and particularly to the clergy; are you willing to promise, before the face of the country here, that you will not write any more on this head? I answered, God forbid I should make thee any such promise; for when I wrote this book, I did it in the fear of God; and I did not write it to please the church of *Rome,* nor the church of *England,* nor the church of *Scotland;*

The Trial of Mr. Elwall.

land; but to pleafe that God who gave me my breath; and therefore, if at any time I find myfelf drawn forth to write in defence of this facred firſt commandment, or any other of the ten, I hope I ſhall do it in the fame fpirit of fincerity as I have done this. And I perceived the Judge was not in any wife difpleafed at my honeſt, plain, bold anſwer; but rather his heart feemed to be knit in love to me; and he foon declared me acquitted: And then the clerk of the arraigns, or aſſizes, ſtood up, and faid, Mr. *Elwall* you are acquitted; you may go out of court when you pleafe.

So I went away through a very great croud of people (for it was thought there was a thoufand people at the trial) and having fpoken long I was a-thirſt, fo went to a well and drank. Then went out of town by a river-fide, and looking about and feeing no one near, I kneeled down on the bank of the river, and fent up my thank offering to that good God who had delivered me out of their hands.

By the time that I returned to the town, the court was up and gone to dinner; a juſtice of peace and another perfon met me, and would have me to eat and drink with them, which I did; and afterwards, as I was walking along the ſtreet, fome perfons hove up a great faſh-window and invited me up to them; and when I entred the room, I found ten or a dozen perfons, moſt of them juſtices of the peace; and amongſt them a Prieſt, whom they called Doctor. One of the juſtices took me by the hand, and faid, Mr. *Elwall*, I am heartily glad to fee you, and I was glad to hear you bear your teſtimony fo boldly as you did. Yea, fays another juſtice, and I was glad to fee Mr. *Elwall* come off with flying colours as he did: Upon which the Prieſt faid (in a very bitter manner) *He ought to have been hanged*. I turned unto him, and faid, Friend, I perceive *thou doſt not know what fpirit thou art of*; *for the fon of man came not to deſtroy, but to fave*: But thou wouldeſt have me deſtroyed. Upon which one of the juſtices faid, How, now Doctor, did not you hear one of the juſtices fay, that he was an honeſt man, and that what he faid, was not by hear-fay, but by experience, and would you have honeſt men hanged, Doctor? Is this good doctrine? So that the Prieſt faid but little more for fome time: So I took leave of the juſtices, and took horfe for *Wolverhampton*.

The Trial of Mr. Elwall.

verhampton, for I knew there would be great joy in my family, for the common people all expected to hear of my being fined and imprisoned. But a farmer that lived near, who had been upon the jury at *Stafford*, got to town before me, and the people went all up and asked him, What have they done with Mr. *Elwall* ? Have they put him in prison ? He answered " No, he " preached there an hour together, and our parsons could " say never a word. What must they put him in prison " for ? I told our foreman of the jury, Mr. *Elwall* " was an honest man, and his father was an honest man," " I knew him very well;" so they were all damped. But there was great joy in my family, and amongst all my friends : Praises, living praises be attributed to that good God who delivered me out of their hands !

Christ never told us of that scandalous Popish invention, of his human nature praying to his divine nature ; but, like a true obedient Son of God, submitted to death, even that cruel death which the hatred and envy of persecuting wicked priests inflicted on him, because he had so plainly and truly told them all of their blindness, covetousness, pride, and hypocrisy. And therefore God *raised him from the dead* ; and for his faithfulness, *God has exalted him to be a prince and a saviour* to all those that obey that pure doctrine which God gave him to teach ; *that denying ungodliness and sinful lusts, we should live soberly and righteously in this world. Then are we his disciples indeed, when we do those things that he hath commanded.* Then shall we be saved, not by the merits of *Christ*, that is another Popish invention ; for he never did any thing but what was his duty to do ; and therefore could not merit any thing for others ; but he taught us the true way to find acceptance with God, and that was by *doing the will of his Father which is in heaven* ; and therein *he is the way, the truth, and the life,* because *no one cometh unto the Father, but by that way.* -

Neither did he make satisfaction to God for us. It

The Trial of Mr. Elwall.

gospel or good tidings of *Jesus Christ, Repent ye, for the kingdom of heaven is at hand.* He tells us, *I am not come to call the righteous, but sinners to repentance*; and by that beautiful excellent parable of the prodigal son, he illustrates the tender mercy of his God, and our God, of his Father and our Father, without any satisfaction. The compassionate Father required none at all, but humble confession and submission, with sincere repentance, and reformation, and then comes *the best robe, the ring, the shoes, and the fatted calf*, to demonstrate the paternal acceptance without satisfaction or sacrifice, *but a broken and a contrite heart, which he will never refuse*; for he can as soon cease to be God, as cease to be merciful.

And as to the Trinitarians, nothing is more plain, than that they feed upon ashes; *a deceived heart hath turned them aside*, because they will not make use of those rational faculties which God hath given them; nor say, *Is there not a lye in my right hand?* otherwise they would never flatter the humble *Jesus*, nor make the most high God to be a plurality of persons.

For as to the Holy Ghost (their third God) it is evidently no distinct person from God, any more than a man's spirit is a distinct person from the man; so that the Spirit of God is God's spirit; as is manifest from scripture and reason, Gen. vi 3. *My spirit shall not always strive with man*: *And the spirit of God moved upon the face of the waters*: *And God said, Let there be light and there was light. And God said, Let there be a firmament in the midst of the waters. And God made all things by the word of his power.* So that the word of God, and the spirit of God, are not distinct persons from God, but the power of God, and the energy of God. So the word of a man, and the spirit of a man, are not distinct persons from the man, but the man himself; if his word be false, or his spirit be wicked, the man is false and wicked.

The same degree of stupidity that leads Trinitarians to call the word of God, and the spirit of God, distinct persons, would lead them to call the wisdom of God, the goodness of God, the love of God, the peace of God, the power of God, and the mercy of God, distinct persons; and make God to be a Trinity of Trinities; for it is certain, God is expresly called by all those names. But

But whosoever goes about to father this absurd and horrid doctrine of Trinity upon *Jesus Christ*, do egregiously abuse him; who told us plainly, *his Father was greater than he; and that he could do nothing of himself*, which is a demonstration that he is not God: For we are sure God is omnipotent, and can do all things of himself; being self-existent and independent, the supreme creator of the universe; and in this it is, that the Unitarians triumph as unanswerable, believing in *Jesus Christ*, who told us his Father was *the only true God*, John xvii. 3.

P. S. By these last words of *Christ*, I myself was convinced many years ago.

Extracts from Penn's Sandy Foundation Shaken.

HAVING recited several texts in proof of the proper unity of God, he adds "The before cited scriptures undeniably prove that one is God, and God only is that holy one; therefore he cannot be divided into, or subsist in an holy three, or three distinct and separate holy ones. Neither can this receive the least prejudice from that frequent but impertinent distinction, that he is one in substance, but three in persons or subsistences; since God was not declared or believed incompleatly, or without his subsistence: Nor did he require homage from his creatures, as an incompleat or abstracted being, but as God the holy one: For so he should be manifested and worshipped without that which was absolutely necessary to himself: So that either the testimonies of the aforementioned scriptures are to be believed concerning God, that he is intirely and compleatly, not abstractly and distinctly, the holy one, or else their authority to be denied by these Trinitarians: And on the contrary, if they pretend to credit those holy testimonies, they must necessarily conclude their kind of trinity a fiction.

If there be three distinct and separate persons, then three distinct and separate substances, because every person is inseparable from its own substance; and as there is no person that's not a substance in common acceptation among men, so do the scriptures plentifully agree herein: And since the Father is God, the Son is God

Sandy Foundation Shaken. 15

God, and the spirit is God (which their opinion necessitates them to confess) then unless the Father, Son, and Spirit, are three distinct nothings, they must be three distinct substances, and consequently three distinct Gods.

Before I shall conclude this head, it's requisite I should inform thee, Reader, concerning its original: Thou mayest assure thyself, it is not from the scriptures, nor reason, since so expresly repugnant; although all broachers of their own inventions strongly endeavour to reconcile them with that holy record. Know then, my friend, 'twas born above three hundred years after the ancient gospel was declared; and that through the nice distinctions, and too daring curiosity of the Bishop of *Alexandria*, who being as hotly opposed by *Arius*, their zeal so reciprocally blew the fire of contention, animosity, and persecution, till at last they sacrificed each other to their mutual revenge.

Thus it was conceived in ignorance, brought forth and maintained by cruelty; for though he that was strongest, imposed his opinion, persecuting the contrary, yet the scale turning on the trinitarian side, it has there continued through all the Romish generations.

Be therefore cautioned, Reader, not to embrace the determination of prejudiced councils, for evangelical doctrine; which the scriptures bear no certain testimony to; neither was believed by the primitive saints, or thus stated by any I have read of in the first, second, or third centuries; particularly *Ireneus, Justin Martyr, Tertullian, Origen*, with many others who appear wholly foreign to the matter to controversy.

The vulgar doctrine of satisfaction, *being dependent on the second person of the Trinity, refuted from scripture.*

AND *the Lord passed by before him* (Moses) *and proclaimed, The Lord, the Lord God, merciful and gracious, keeping mercy for thousands, forgiving iniquity, transgression and sin.* From whence I shall draw this position, that since God has proclaimed himself a gracious, merciful, and forgiving God, it is not inconsistent with his nature to remit, without any other consideration than his own love.

For

For if ye turn again to the Lord, the Lord your God is gracious and merciful, and will not turn his face away from you. Where how natural is it to observe that God's remission is grounded on their repentance; and not that it is impossible for God to pardon, without plenary satisfaction, since the possibility, nay, certainty of the contrary, viz. His grace and mercy, is the great motive or reason, of that loving invitation to return.

Let the wicked forsake his way, and the unrighteous man his thoughts, and let him return unto the Lord, and he will have mercy upon him, and to our God, for he will abundantly pardon. Come, let the unprejudiced judge, if this scripture doctrine, is not very remote from saying his nature cannot forgive sin, therefore let Christ pay him full satisfaction, or he will certainly be avenged; which is the substance of that strange opinion.

And forgive us our debts, as we forgive our debtors. Where nothing can be more obvious, than that which is forgiven, is not paid: And if it is our duty to forgive our debtors, without a satisfaction received, and that God is to forgive us, as we forgive them, then is a satisfaction totally excluded: How most unworthy therefore is it of God, and blasphemous, may I justly term it, for any to dare to assert that forgiveness is impossible to God, which is not only possible, but enjoined to men.

So that I can by no means conclude, but openly declare, that the scriptures of truth, are not only silent in reference to this doctrine of *rigid satisfaction*, but that its altogether inconsistent with the dignity of God, and very repugnant to the conditions, nature, and tendency of that second covenant, concerning which their testimony is so clear.

This Doctrine refuted from right Reason.

1. Since God is to be satisfied, and that Christ is God, he consequently is to be satisfied; and who shall satisfy his infinite justice?

But if Christ has satisfied God the Father, Christ being also God, 'twill follow then that he has satisfied himself, which cannot be.

But

Sandy Foundation Shaken. 17

But since God the Father was once to be satisfied, and that it is impossible he should do it himself, nor yet the Son or Spirit, because the same God; it naturally follows, that the debt remains unpaid, and these satisfactionists thus far are still at a loss.

Consequences irreligious and irrational.

It does not only dis-acknowledge the true virtue and real intent of Christ's life and death, but intirely deprives God of that praise which is owing to his greatest love and goodness.

It represents the Son more kind and compassionate than the Father; whereas if both be the same God, then either the Father is as loving as the Son, or the Son as angry as the Father.

It no way renders man beholding, or in the least obliged to God, since by their doctrine he would no have abated us, nor did he Christ the last farthing, so that the acknowledgments are peculiarly the Son's; which destroys the whole current of scripture-testimony, for his good will towards men. O the infamous portrature this doctrine draws, of the infinite goodness: Is this your retribution, *O injurious Satisfactionists?* But many more are the gross absurdities and blasphemies that are the genuine fruits of this so confidently believed *doctrine of satisfaction.*

Consequences irreligious and irrational from the doctrine of imputative righteousness.

It makes God guilty of what the scriptures says is an abomination, to wit, that he justifies the wicked.

It flatters men, whilst subject to the world's lusts, with a state of justification, and thereby invalidates the very end of Christ's appearance, which was to destroy the works of the devil, and take away the sins of the world; a quite contrary purpose than what the *Satisfactionists,* and *Imputarians* of our times have imagined, viz. to satisfy for their sins, and by his imputed righteousness, to represent them holy in him, whilst unholy in themselves.

Con-

Conclusion, by Way of Caution.

THUS *Reader*, have I led thee through those three so generally applauded doctrines, whose confutation I hope, though thou haft run, thou haft read; and now I call the righteous God of heaven to bear me record, that I have herein fought nothing below the defence of his *unity, mercy*, and *purity*, againft the rude and impetuous aflaults of tradition, prefs and pulpit, from whence I daily hear, what rationally induces me to believe, a confpiracy is held by counterplots, to obftruct the *Exaltation of truth*, and to betray evangelical doctrines, to idle traditions: But God will rebuke the winds, and deftruction fhall attend the enemies of his anointed. Miftake me not, we never have difowned a Father, Word, and Spirit, which are one, but men's inventions: For, 1. Their *Trinity* has not fo much as a foundation in the fcriptures. 2. Its original was three hundred years after chriftianity was in the world. [3. It having coft much blood. In the council of *Sirmium*, Anno 355, it was decreed, *That thenceforth the controverfy fhould not be remembered, becaufe the fcriptures of God made no mention thereof.* Why then fhould it be mentioned now with a *Maranatha*, on all that will not bow to this abftrufe opinion. 4. And it doubtlefs has occafioned idolatry, witnefs the Popifh images of *Father, Son*, and *Holy Ghoft*. 5. It fcandalizes *Turks, Jews*, and *Infidels*, and palpably obftructs their reception of the chriftian doctrine.

Extracts from *Innocency with her open Face.*

As for my being a *Socinian*, I muft confefs I have read of one *Socinus*, of (that they call) a noble family in *Sene* in *Italy*, who about the year 1574, *being a young man*, voluntarily did abandon the glories, pleafures, and honours of the *great Duke* of Tufcany's *Court at* Florence (that noted place for all worldly delicacies) and became a *perpetual exile* for his *confcience*, whofe parts, wifdom, gravity, and juft behaviour made him the moft famous with the *Polonian* and *Tranfilvanian* churches; *but I was never baptized into his name*, and therefore deny that reproachful epithet; and if in any thing

thing I acknowledge the verity of his doctrine, *it is for the truth's sake*, of which, in many things, he had a clearer prospect than most of his contemporaries; but not therefore a *Socinian*, any more than a son of the *English-Church*, whilst esteemed a *Quaker*, because I justify many of her principles, since the reformation, against the *Roman* church.

N. B. All these extracts are made from the folio edition of Mr. Penn's works, Vol. I, printed London 1726.

Farther observations concerning the Divinity of Christ.

LEST some common objections should hinder the reception of the great truths contended for in this trial and extracts. I shall briefly consider and reply to the principal of them. It is often said that Christ speaks of his *humanity* only, whenever he represents himself as inferior to the Father, and dependent upon him. But the scriptures themselves are far from furnishing the least hint of any such method of interpretation, though, according to the Trinitarians, it is absolutely necessary to the true understanding of them.

Besides, when it is applied to the passages in question, it is far from making them either true in themselves, or agreeable to the obvious purport and design of the places in which they are introduced. I shall just mention a few. Could our Lord say with truth, and without an unworthy prevarication that *the Father is the only true God*, if any other person, not implied in the term *Father*, was as much the true God as himself? Now the term *Father* being appropriated to what is called the *first* person in the godhead, cannot comprehend the *Son*, who is called the *second*. This key, therefore, is of no service in this case, and our Lord, by expressing himself as he has done, could not but lead his hearers into what is called a dangerous mistake.

When our Lord said that *his Father was greater than he*, did he make any reserve, and secretly mean, not *his whole self*, but only *part*, and the inferior part of himself, the other part being equal in power and glory with the Father? How mean the prevarication, and how unworthy of our Lord!

When

20   *Obfervations concerning*

When our Lord said that *the time of the day of judgment was not known to himfelf, the Son, but to the Father only*, could he mean that his *humanity* only did not know it, but that his *divinity* (which is fuppofed to be intimately united with his humanity) was as well acquainted with it as the Father himfelf? If the human nature of Chrift had been incapable of having that knowledge communicated to it, the declaration would have been needlefs; but as that was not the cafe, his hearers muft neceffarily underftand him as fpeaking of himfelf in his higheft capacity; as he certainly muft do, if at all, when he fpeaks of himfelf as the *Son*, correfponding to the *Father*.

If Chrift had not fatisfied the Jews that he did not mean to make himfelf equal with God, would they not have produced it againft him at his trial, when he was condemned as a blafphemer, becaufe he confeffed that he was the Chrift only: and yet no Jew expected any thing more than a man for their Meffiah, and our Saviour no where intimates that they were miftaken in that expectation. It is plain that Martha confidered our Lord as a different perfon from God, and dependent upon God, when fhe faid to him, John xi. 22. *I know that even now, whatfoever thou wilt afk of God, God will give it thee.*

Farther obfervations concerning the doctrine of Atonement.

WITH refpect to the doctrine of the *fatisfaction of Chrift*, of which Mr. Elwall and Mr. Penn fpeak with fuch great and juft indignation, I would obferve, that it is impoffible to reconcile it with the doctrine of *free grace*, which, according to the uniform tenor of the fcriptures, is fo fully difplayed in the pardon of fin, and the juftification of finners. When, therefore, the apoftle Paul fays, Rom. iii. 24. *That we are juftified freely by the grace of God, through the redemption that is in Chrift Jefus*, the meaning of the latter claufe muft be interpreted in fuch a manner as to make it confiftent with the former; and it is far from requiring any force or ftraining of the text to do it. For it is only neceffary to fuppofe that our *redemption* (or, as the word properly fignifies, and is indeed frequently rendered by our tranflators, our *deliverance)* from the power *the doctrine of Atonement.* 21

power of sin, *i. e.* our repentance and reformation, without which there is no promise of pardon, is effected by the gospel of Jesus Christ, who came *to call sinners to repentance*; but still God is to be considered as the *giver*, and not the *receiver* with respect to our redemption; for we read that *he spared not his own son, but gave him up for us all.* Rom. viii. 32.

To say that God the Father provided an atonement for his own offended justice is, in fact, to give up the doctrine. If a person owe me a sum of money, and I chuse to have the debt discharged, is it not the same thing, whether I remit the debt at once, or supply another person with money wherewith to pay me in the debtor's name? If satisfaction be made to any purpose, it must be, in some manner, in which the offender may be a sufferer, and the offended person a gainer; but it can never be reconciled to equity, or answer any good purpose whatever, to make the innocent suffer the punishment of the guilty. If, as Abraham says, it be *far from God to slay the righteous with the wicked, and that the righteous should be as the wicked*, Gen. xviii. 25, much farther must it be from him to slay the righteous *instead* of the wicked.

If it had been inconsistent with the divine justice to pardon sin upon repentance only, without some farther satisfaction, we might have expected to have found it *expressly said to be so* in the scriptures; but no such declaration can be produced either from the Old or the New Testament. All that can be pretended is, that it may be *inferred* from it. Though good works are recommended to us in the strongest manner, it is never with any salvo or caution, as if they were not *of themselves* acceptable to God. The declarations of the divine mercy to the penitent are all absolute, without the most distant hint of their having a reference to any *consideration* on which they are made. *Thou, Lord, art good, and ready to forgive,* Psalm lxxxiv 5. *To the Lord our God belong mercies and forgivenesses, though we have rebelled against him* Dan. ix. 3. When David and other penitents confess their sins, and intreat for pardon, they refer themselves to the divine mercy only, without seeming to have the least idea of any thing farther. *Remember not the sins of my youth, nor my transgressions; according to thy mercy remember thou me for thy goodness sake, O Lord.* Psalm xxv. 6. It

It is particularly remarkable, that when sacrifices under the law are expresly said not to be sufficient for the pardon of sin, we are never referred to any *more availing sacrifice*; but to good works only. *Thou desirest not sacrifice, else would I give it; thou delightest not in burnt offering. The sacrifices of the Lord are a broken spirit. A broken and a contrite heart, O God, thou wilt not despise.* Psalm li. 16, 17. If any of the Jews had had the least notion of the necessity of any atonement for the sins of mankind, they could not but have expected a *suffering Messiah*; and yet it is plain that the very best of them had no such idea. And though our Saviour frequently explains the reason of his coming, and the necessity of his suffering, it is never on any such account. If he had done it any where, it might have been expected in those discourses by which he endeavoured to reconcile his disciples to his death, in his solemn prayer before his sufferings, at the time of his agony in the garden, or when he was upon the cross; yet nothing of this kind drops from him on any of these occasions.

When our Lord describes the proceedings of the day of judgment, he doth not represent the righteous as referring themselves to the sufferings or merit of their judge for their justification; and the judge himself expresly grounds it on their good works only. Though St. Peter, in his discourse to the Jews on the day of Pentecost, speaks of their sin in murdering Christ as of a heinous nature, he says not a word of the necessity of any atonement, or that an ample satisfaction had just been made, by means of their very wickedness. How would a modern divine have harangued upon the occasion, and what advantage might he have taken of the cry of the Jews, *His blood be upon us, and upon our children*. But St. Peter only exhorts to repentance, and speaks of the death of Christ, as an event that took place according to the foreknowledge of God.

All the discourses of St. Paul upon various occasions, in the book of Acts, are intirely moral. In his celebrated speech at Athens, he only urges his hearers to repentance, from the consideration of a future judgment. He says not a word of what is now called the true gospel of Jesus Christ. In short, it is only from the literal interpretation of a few figurative expressions in the scrip-

the doctrine of Atonement.

tures that this doctrine of *atonement*, as well as that of *tranfubftantiation*, has been derived; and it is certainly a doctrine highly injurious to God; and if we, who are commanded to imitate God, should act upon the maxims of it, it would be fubverfive of the moft amiable part of virtue in men. We fhould be implacable and unmerciful, infifting upon the uttermoft farthing.

CONCLUSION.

MY Chriftian Brethren, if the reading of thefe tracts give rife to any *doubts* or *fcruples* in your minds, with refpect to fome doctrines which you have been ufed to confider as true and *fundamental*, in the chriftian religion, inquire farther; and if you be *fatisfied* that you have hitherto been miftaken, dare to avow the truth, and act confiftently with it. Dread the confequence of joining, with an enlightened mind, in the *idolatrous worfhip of any creature*, though enjoined by any human authority; remembering the words of Chrift, *Thou fhalt worfhip the Lord thy God, and him only fhalt thou ferve*; Matt. iv. 10, and alfo that awful voice from heaven, refpecting all antichriftian corruptions of the gofpel, in myftical Babylon; *Come out of her, my people, that ye be not partakers of her fins, and that ye receive not of her plagues.* Rev. xviii. 4.

Think not to avail yourfelves of the wretched equivocation of many divines, who imagine that they may fafely afcribe all divine honours to Jefus Chrift, on account of his *union with the father*, when they believe no more of his *proper divinity* than profeffed Arians or Socinians. By this artifice they fecure the reputation and emoluments of orthodoxy; but let them confider the value of the purchafe, and the price they give for it. To mere worldly confiderations, to the *praife* of *men*, and *filthy lucre*, they facrifice that *integrity*, for the lofs of which worlds cannot compenfate.

The publifher of thefe tracts does not conceal his name through the fear of any thing that *men* can *fay of him*, or *do to him*, but merely to give what he has written a better chance of being read without prejudice. What he has done is out of a fincere good-will and compaffion to the multitude, who believe *they know not what*, or *why*, and what is of more confequence, who

know

Conclusion.

know not what spirit they are of; but instead of *speaking the truth in love*, mistake bitterness and rancour for a zeal for God and his truth, and also for the sake of a better sort of people, who are unhappily drawn into the same delusions.

Considering the deference which the common people always pay to the judgment of men of learning, there can be little doubt but that, if those persons who, having studied this subject, have been convinced that Christ is not God, and ought not to be worshipped as God, had openly avowed their opinion, and had had recourse to no mean subterfuge or equivocation, this fundamental article of true and rational christianity had long ago been the prevailing belief; and our religion appearing more worthy of its divine author, there would have been, at this time, fewer unbelievers in all christian countries, and many more converts made to it from other religions. And, compared with this glorious advantage, what has been gained by all the arts and sophistry of ministers, who have concealed their real meaning under ambiguous expressions, lest, as they pretend, they should too much shock the prejudices of their hearers?

That some regard should be paid to the prejudices of the *weak* is allowed; but let not this lead men to criminal dissimulation, or extend to things of so much importance as this, respecting the *unity of God*. In this case, let us keep at the greatest distance from every thing that is *disingenuous*; let the truth be spoken in the most explicit manner, and let the consequences be left to the *power of truth*, and the *God of truth*. Besides, it is impossible that while men retain depraved and unworthy notions of God, their devotion and obedience should be such as God requires; so that this pretended tenderness injures those who are the objects of it, as well as bears an unfavourable aspect on the interests of christianity more at large. Such are the effects of the *wisdom of this world*, when it is put in the place of *sincerity*, and a regard to the plain *truth of the gospel* of Jesus Christ!

F I N I S.

www.ingramcontent.com/pod-product-compliance
Lightning Source LLC
Chambersburg PA
CBHW032141010526
44111CB00035B/706